DIRSHUNI

Dirshuni

CONTEMPORARY WOMEN'S MIDRASH

Edited with Commentary by Tamar Biala

Introduction by Tamar Kadari

Brandeis University Press / Waltham, Massachusetts

Brandeis University Press
© 2022 by Tamar Biala
Introduction © 2022 by Tamar Kadari
All rights reserved
Manufactured in the United States of America
Designed and composed in Arno Pro by Mindy Basinger Hill

For permission to reproduce any of the material in this book,
contact Brandeis University Press, 415 South Street, Waltham MA 02453,
or visit brandeisuniversitypress.com

Library of Congress Cataloging-in-Publication Data

Names: Biala, Tamar, editor.
Title: Dirshuni : contemporary women's midrash / edited with
    commentary by Tamar Biala ; introduction by Tamar Kadari.
Description: First edition. | Waltham, Massachusetts : Brandeis
    University Press, [2022] | Series: HBI series on Jewish women |
    Includes bibliographical references and index. | Summary: "Dirshuni:
    Contemporary Women's Midrash, is the first-ever English edition of
    an historic collection of midrashim composed by Israeli women.
    The volume features a comprehensive introduction to Midrash for
    the uninitiated reader by the distinguished scholar Tamar Kadari
    and extensive annotation and commentary by Tamar Biala."
    — Provided by publisher.
Identifiers: LCCN 2021058296 | ISBN 9781684580958 (cloth) |
    ISBN 9781684580965 (ebook)
Subjects: LCSH: Midrash. | Bible. Old Testament—Feminist criticism. |
    Women in the Bible.
Classification: LCC BM514 .D5613 2022 | DDC 296.1/4—dc23/eng/20211223
LC record available at https://lccn.loc.gov/2021058296

5   4   3

For Lori Kagan and Jody (Eliana) Sampson-Nair

And for Rochelle Isserow, of Blessed Memory

You were there for me

CONTENTS

TAMAR KADARI

Introduction The Enchanted World of Midrash and Its Unexpected Return in Recent Generations

Midrash's Enchanted World

When I am asked, "What is midrash?" I say that it must be understood first and foremost as an exercise in creativity, with an element of play and pleasure in which sweep and imagination are conjoined. No artistic work springs ex nihilo, but rather depends on many years of tradition and culture. Midrash leans on an ancient and uniquely significant literary creation, the Bible, which has come to be known as the "Book of Books." The Bible's importance and centrality in the lives of the Jews of antiquity cannot be exaggerated. It was seen as the very embodiment of God's own words and His revelations to His prophets, and from this, it drew its undisputed status as a holy text. The tales of the people's patriarchs, of the people's origin in Egypt, and of the wanderings in the desert and entry into the Land of Israel were much more than history. They were myths, foundational stories, tracing a way of life, moral principles, faith, and hope. The biblical laws and statutes became the central infrastructure of Jews' legal world and ways of life for generations to come.

The sealing of the biblical canon was an essential step in its becoming a book with sacred standing. Like powerful shafts of light, the Bible stood at the center of life, while the other works written in the following years were relegated to the margins. Those works became known as the Apocrypha (in Greek: hidden, concealed) and *Ha-Sefarim Ha-Hitzonim* (in Hebrew: the books on the outside), an undifferentiated category, fixing their being "outside" the sacred canon.

Unlike those books, the Bible became a source of inspiration and focus of ceaseless attention. At communal gatherings on Sabbaths and festivals, public reading of verses from the Torah stood at the center. Ceremonial readings aside, biblical tales were told and retold, again and again, and passed from generation to generation. Central scenes were immortalized by wall paintings and floor mosaics in public buildings and synagogues. The tales and images of biblical heroes were incorporated into religious liturgy and popular song. The biblical laws were expanded on and interpreted in legal works. This widespread, multifaceted creativity didn't threaten the Bible's sacred status, but rather anchored its centrality and sacredness. There were even those who studied the Bible word for word and knew all its parts by heart. It is in light of all this that we can understand the flowering of the distinctive literary creation called midrash.

WHAT IS MIDRASH, AND WHAT IS IT TRYING TO DO?

The creators of midrash were several thousand sages who lived in the first centuries of the Common Era, in Babylonia and the Land of Israel. They are generally divided into two categories: the *Tannaim*, sages who lived from roughly 1 to 200 CE and were active in the Land of Israel, and the *Amoraim*, who lived from roughly 200 to 500 CE, and were active in the two geographic centers, the Land of Israel and Babylon. These sages studied the Bible deeply and intensely, and they dealt with biblical verses in creative ways. This is, in essence, the meaning of the word "midrash," literally, "searching out and exploring sacred scripture."[1]

What is the central purpose of that search in biblical verses? What did the sages seek to find in the sacred texts? Many think, mistakenly, that the rabbis' central purpose was to explain difficult texts or explicate passages that were not understandable. This, though, can explain only a small part of the midrashic corpus. In the places where the rabbis reflect on what they were doing, their motives were matters of faith and flowed from an educational philosophy. They wanted to forge a strong, lively connection between the Torah and their lives and make it meaningful and relevant to their contemporaries.

Here lies a paradox and wonder: the centrality and holiness of the Bible didn't lead the sages to a frozen understanding of the texts or rigidity in understanding their contents. To the contrary. They brought forth rich and diverse innovation of a multiplicity of meanings by way of imagination and creativity. Rather than lock up the Scriptures and guard them like frail crystals easily shattered, the sages took pains to use verses over and over every which way to give them a real place in their lives. They didn't want the Torah to become something empty and irrelevant, and they thought that the responsibility to make sure that didn't happen rested on their shoulders. In one of the lovely images, they command themselves to dig in the Torah like farmers plowing their fields, turning its clods and working its mounds of earth. They believed that all truths were to be found, and they would find them by searching and exploring well.[2] Midrash, the searching and exploration within the verses, yielded educational messages, concepts and ideas, and approaches to contemporary problems, and expressed intellectual and philosophical depth.

THE MIDRASHISTS' TOOL KIT

The preoccupation with and searching in biblical verses was done through midrashic tools that forge a connection between the verse and an abstract thought. The midrashic process exhibits three components: the biblical verse, the starting point of every reading; the theological idea or educational message that the midrashist seeks to convey to listeners; and the midrashic methods, which combine the other two components. The task of midrashic methods is to forge the connection between biblical verse and abstract thought.

The contents of the midrashic tool kit are many and varied. To the sages, the sanctity of Scripture renders it capable of interpretation in almost any way. Almost any path is fit and worthy to find meaning in the Torah, in which, the rabbis believed, all was contained and all could be found. We detail a few. Sometimes the sages detached the verses from their syntactical confines and so changed their meaning and contents. Sometimes they removed a verse from its context and so poured into it new meaning. Sometimes they broke words into pieces and constructed new ones without feeling constrained by Scripture's own word divisions. At times they even interpreted single letters as though they stood by themselves, then expounded on the letters' sounds, their order in the alphabet, or the meaning of their names. The sages thought the order of biblical passages doesn't necessarily reflect a historical continuum, and so they sought out connections between different passages that happened to appear near one another and tried to explain their placement. At times they read proper names as telling something about the person's life story and character, and they also identified biblical place names with locations known to them.

These examples are but a small taste of the different, creative means through which the sages interpreted the Torah. The paths of midrash are so many and so varied that they can't all be enumerated. Every attempt to boil down midrash to a set of rules and definitions is bound for failure, because there is always in it some feature that is boundary defying and surprising.

SO, HOW DOES IT WORK?

The sages played creatively with biblical language, eliciting new ideas and original interpretations. Textual difficulties, real and imagined, stimulated the rabbis' religious thinking. Getting at a midrash's content requires first understanding the verse's original meaning, then identifying the way the midrashist is using the verse to create new meaning and establish the moral he is trying to convey via this reading to his listeners.

Here's an example of a derashah, which changes a word's vocalization (bearing in mind that the Hebrew alphabet consists entirely of consonants and the biblical text itself and as written in Torah scrolls is unvocalized) to elicit an educational message as well as deal with a theological problem. In the Garden of Eden, after Adam and Eve eat from the Tree of Knowledge, they hear God's voice approaching through the garden and hide from it among the trees. God calls out: *And Lord God called out to Adam and asked, Where are you?* (Gen 3:9). This verse raises a theological problem: Does God really not know where Adam is hiding? The midrashist solved this problem by changing the familiar vocalization. Instead of *ayekah* (Where are you?), he vocalizes it, *eykhah* (How?).[3] God's question shifts from Adam's physical location (Where are you?) to his degraded moral state (How did this happen to you?). The point of the question is to express astonishment, and rebuke, for Adam's degradation, from listening to his creator to listening to the serpent, to falling from wholeness into sin. There is also here a note of mourning, a dirge, for this wondrous, traitorous creature, as "eykhah" is also the opening word of the Book of Lamentations, the biblical elegy for the destruction of the Temple and Jerusalem. The real-live, educational message of this derashah is to emphasize the immense potential of human beings,

God's own handiwork, to recall the great expectations that God invests in them, and at the same time warn of the great temptation of sin, which may perhaps bring momentary pleasure but has far-reaching consequences that lead to moral failure, remoteness from God, and exile from the Garden.

With the aid of midrashic tools, the sages could reverse the plain sense of the text. A good example of this appears in the Genesis story of the destruction of Sodom and Gomorrah. After God informs Abraham of His intention to destroy the cities of the valley, Abraham cries out, *Don't do it, sweep away the righteous with the wicked, that so the righteous should be as the wicked; don't do it; shall not the Judge of all the earth do justly?* (Gen 18:25). On its face, Abraham is asking God to take His place as a judge and render proper judgment and justice. He argues that the righteous should be judged by their deeds, not by those of the city as a whole. Thus, justice will be done. Rabbi Levi introduces a derashah that turns the meaning upside down.[4] He reads the verse not as a question but as stating a fact: the judge of the world should not do justice. Abraham asks God to not do justice and stay the hand of the full severity of the law, for the world cannot endure if God holds it to account to the last jot and tittle. In Rabbi Levi's view, the world's existence depends on *middat ha-hesed*, God's attribute of loving-kindness, that which enables the world to exist and endure. This derashah beautifully illustrates how one can, through midrashic tools, upend the meaning of the verse. By the plain sense, Abraham sought that God do justice, and by Rabbi Levi's derashah he asked precisely the opposite, that God not go by the letter of the law, and choose kindness instead. The idea behind this derashah is that loving-kindness, *hesed*, is woven into the very fabric of human society and enables its very existence.

The midrashim regularly deal with visual and physical aspects of the text. For instance, Rabbi Jonah asks why God chose to create the world and open the Torah with the letter *bet*, the first letter in the word *Bereshit* (and the second in the Hebrew alphabet).[5] The answer to this question relates to the letter's graphic form: ב

Rabbi Jonah thinks that the letter *bet* was chosen for its being closed on three sides and open only on one (pointing toward the next letters to follow, because Hebrew is read from right to left). The point is to teach that one shouldn't try to investigate what preceded Creation, or matters concerning divinity or the netherworld, but rather on the words of Torah to follow.

Rabbi Jonah is fixing interpretive boundaries regarding the midrashic enterprise in general, and he sees in the first letter a kind of key to the whole.

It is important to emphasize that the midrashim, at times reversing the meaning of Scripture and transposing verses as they do, are not meant to negate the meaning of Scripture or undermine its sanctity. Our sages saw in Scripture the living words of a living God, the verses holding a vast treasure trove of insight and guidance and, in their folds, the past, present, and future. Engagement with Scripture through midrashic work revivified the verses and made them relevant to the lives of the faithful. The derashah was a tool for the sages to grapple with the problems of the hour and, with its help, lay out for their students and listeners a complex world of beliefs, doctrines, and opinions.

WHERE CAN YOU FIND MIDRASHIM?

The many, many derashot, or midrashic creations, of the sages were gathered together in collections which came to be known as "midrashim. This process started at the beginning of the third century CE and proceeded to the beginning of the seventh century CE (some works underwent revision for a long time after). The materials were gathered around the specific biblical books to which they related. One central characteristic of these compositions is that they are not the work of any one sage but rather anthologies of teachings by different sages over centuries. The derashot in the midrashic collections are sometimes attributed to known sages and sometimes are anonymous. At times, we find in the midrashic collections matters unrelated to scriptural interpretation, such as tales of the sages' contemporaries, aphorisms, maxims, and more.

Though the sages seem to have dealt with the entirety of Scripture, we have edited collections only on some of the biblical books. From the tannaitic period, we have collections on four of the five books of the Pentateuch: Exodus, Leviticus, Numbers, and Deuteronomy. These compositions are known as *Midrashei Ha-Tannaim* or *Midrashei Halakhah*, because they also contain derashot on legal and halakhic matters, chiefly establishing clear rules regarding concrete practice and daily life. The midrashim of the amoraim encompass the following books of the Bible: Genesis, Leviticus, and the Five Scrolls (Lamentations, the Song of Songs,

Ruth, Ecclesiastes, and Esther). We also have amoraic midrashim built around the annual cycle rather than specific biblical books as such. These midrashim are also called *Midrashei Aggadah*, for they deal mainly with conceptual matters and the sages' theological ideas, and hardly touch on legal or halakhic questions.[6] In later periods other midrashic collections took shape around the books of the Pentateuch (Tanhuma), some of the Prophetic books (Samuel and Jonah), the Writings (Psalms and Proverbs), and other portions as well.

Despite midrash's seeming confinement to one specific genre of interpretation of one specific set of texts, namely Scripture, the midrashic enterprise encompasses a surprising range of forms: delicately close readings alongside wildly imaginative renderings; legends that ascend the most sublime heights of religious thought, alongside comic descriptions; and more. The sages used a variety of rhetorical and literary forms. Their desire to center their work around the books of Scripture yielded an astounding interpretive and conceptual world. Moreover, aggadic midrashim regularly appear in the halakhic discussions of the Babylonian and Jerusalem Talmud; and they attest to the centrality and significance the sages accorded the midrashic interpretation of scripture.

Midrash continued to work its charms on succeeding generations and became a canonical text in itself. The riches it held served biblical commentators and thinkers, and theologians drew ideas from it. Its widespread diffusion throughout the Jewish diaspora is seen already in the Middle Ages. The midrashic collections were among the first to roll off the newly invented printing presses of the sixteenth century and were reprinted again and again in numerous editions. With the advent of the Internet, midrashim have become accessible to all via digital means. Thus the midrashic corpus has become a source of inspiration to teachers, scholars, artists, and thinkers in our day.

Midrash's Unexpected Return

Recent generations have seen a renewed flourishing of midrashic writing, including among women. The phenomenon of women writing midrash began in the United States in the 1970s. At first at the margins, then with growing legitimacy in different circles, it gathered momentum and spread to different geographic locations. The first appearance of this trend in Israel can be seen with the publication in 2003 of the booklet of Rivkah Lubitch, *Va-Telekh li-Drosh: Midrash Nashi Yotzer* ("And She Went Searching: Creative Women's Midrash").[7] The fruits of women's midrashic writing in the subsequent years we see, among others, in the two volumes of *Dirshuni— Midrashei Nashim* and in this book.[8]

The sages who produced the midrashim in the early centuries CE were elite male scholars. Their midrashic creativity reflects their perspectives on the biblical sources. We can learn from it their characteristic forms of expression and creative skill and the educational and moral messages they sought to impart to their contemporaries. We have not a single midrash written by a woman in those centuries. Although the texts at times give voice to female heroines and describe their deeds and works, those were formulated and transmitted to us by the sages. The estimation of any given female character, for good or ill, the way in which her place and role are depicted, was shaped by their point of view. So the very existence of midrashim written by women is a tremendous innovation in the annals of literary creativity in general and of Hebrew literary and cultural creativity in particular and holds within its folds many other innovations.

This anthology contains midrashim written by Israeli women in recent decades, with distinguishing characteristics of its own when compared to the women's midrashim that preceded them. To get a sense of this, let's look at the three components of midrashic process: the use of biblical verses, the use of the midrashic tool kit, and the theological and moral ideas reflected in these midrashim.

WHAT IS DISTINCTIVE ABOUT WOMEN'S INTERPRETATIONS OF SCRIPTURE?

Writing midrash takes deep knowledge not only of the biblical narrative but of the words themselves and of biblical grammar and syntax. Scholars have noted that the 1960s and 1970s saw an appreciable rise in the number of American women studying Bible and biblical interpretation in established educational institutions, which gave women unmediated access to Scripture.

From the first tendrils of women's midrashic writing up to this book, the extent to which women are drawn to female biblical figures is obvious. They feel deeply tied to them and easily identify with them when discussing the search for a mate, the tensions of marital life, the longing to embrace a child, the pains of childbirth, the difficulty of separation from a married daughter, exposure to domestic violence, silencing, rape, and more.

In writing on female biblical figures, we see innovation in training focus on the women and in sounding their voices. The number of women mentioned in the Bible is dramatically smaller than that of men. Their roles in the plots are limited, and the names of many of them go unmentioned. The midrashim written by women focusing on female figures give them visage and name, add depictions and feelings, articulate hidden thoughts, and vocalize their stances in their encounters with other biblical personages. Women writing about women regularly seek to dispel misleading impressions, to explain differently the motives for their actions. The writers generally display empathy and faithfulness to biblical women; only a few write critically of them. This writing from a point of identification can explain the force of the emotions coming to expression in midrashim written by women.

Nonetheless, the depiction of biblical women in women's midrashim is by no means uniform and reflects the worldviews of the writers themselves, which vary greatly from one another. Jody Myers, an American scholar of modern Jewish history and religion, and one of the first to note and research women's midrashic writing, understands the different faces of women's midrashic writing in North America in its early decades in terms of writers' affiliations to one social or religious group or another. Women in more conservative circles seek to ground and strengthen traditional concepts of women's place in home and society. They emphasize the virtue of self-sacrifice, of acceptance and equanimity, and the magnitude of the assistance afforded by the woman behind the curtain. Women seeking to further feminist perspectives emphasize the daring, pioneering spirit and shattering of conventions. Interestingly, this dichotomy does not reflect the midrashim gathered in the volume of *Dirshuni*. As time goes on, women of similar backgrounds articulate a range of feminist views and sometimes opposing views, and at times the same writer offers different feminist perspectives in different midrashim.

Another current of recent change has been in the expanded range of the writers toward biblical themes and topics not connected to women. For instance, women write midrashim on such topics as sexual violence between males, on theological issues such as humanity's relation to God, and post-Holocaust theology. The women's voices afford a new and different angle on these issues. Another current of change is exploration through midrash of issues that aren't biblical at all, such as tales of sages (a subgenre of the classical midrashim and, now, developed in the writers' imaginations); prayer; the Haggadah; Kabbalistic texts; and more.

HOW DO WOMEN USE MIDRASHIC TOOLS?

Every midrash holds a structural tension between preservation and innovation. The midrashist proceeds from the centrality of Scripture, seeks not to undermine it but to add another layer of meaning through which to express new ideas and connect them to contemporary questions. One can discern among some of the women midrashists, especially early on, a concern not to diminish the sanctity of Scripture and to present their writing as not threatening the status of messages of the Book of Books. The desire to retain hierarchy comes to expression in the use of language and intertextual citations seeking to legitimize new ideas by reliance on earlier exegeses.

One can see how over time and with the development of women's midrashic writing, these distinctions steadily disappear. The women's midrashim in this book are not seeking legitimacy for plowing the text again and again, interpreting them as did the sages. They take in hand the language and style of the classic midrashim in a range of forms and articulations.

Intimacy with the Hebrew Language One striking characteristic of this book, differentiating it from the midrashim written in North America, is the writers' intimacy with the language of the Bible and rabbinic literature. The writers speak Hebrew every day, feel at home in it, and use it as raw material with great untrammeled freedom. The midrashim in the Hebrew volumes of *Dirshuni* evince a clear return to the rabbinic tool kit and the rabbis' regularly playful engagement with words and their meanings. The writing in rabbinic language places the women firmly in the interpretive continuum and echoes the deep connections the sages themselves felt to the Hebrew language.

A Multiplicity of Views   Rabbinic literature displays a polysemic multiplicity of views. The Talmuds and the midrashim offer a range of interpretations to every verse and idea. In this book, we can see that the women midrashists seek to retain this diversity of views in their own work. Some midrashim depict women's study in a beit midrash—house of study, referred to as *Beit Midrashah shel Beruriah*—Beruriah's House of Study. This concept was invented by the midrashist Rivkah Lubitch and has since won adherents among other women midrashists. This is an imaginary beit midrash of women, at whose head stands Beruriah, a well-known figure in rabbinic literature, daughter of the Tanna, Hanina ben Teradion, and the wife of Rabbi Meir (a leading sage of the Mishnah), who was known for her wisdom and learning. Other midrashim bring the diversity of views by presenting differing interpretations of one biblical text or another, each reflecting differing life experiences, states of mind, or moral and theological stances. At times the varying voices reflect the writer's own internal ambivalences or simply enable them to explore different potential interpretations.

This phenomenon of multiple voices, displaying the diversity of women's views, sends the message that women are not uniform in their views and must not be seen in essentialized terms as all sharing the same worldview and theology. The desire to sound voices silenced until now does not prevent other voices from being heard and encourages a stance of tolerance.

Talmudic Expressions   In the volumes of *Dirshuni*, the place of the Babylonian Talmud as a source of inspiration is unmistakable. This phenomenon was made possible by the opening of the gates of Talmud study to women in recent decades. Unlike the study of Bible and midrash, the Talmud has always been seen as a masculine stronghold. Until recently, women were not allowed to study Talmud and were systematically excluded from every legal discussion that yielded authoritative rulings on Jewish law. Israeli anthropologist Tamar El-Or has shown that in recent decades, Modern Orthodox society in Israel has undergone dramatic change with the entry of women into the worlds of Talmud and Halakhah (traditional Jewish law) in women's high schools and higher education.

Starting in the 1980s, pluralistic batei midrash began to appear in Israel, part of a broader movement of Jewish cultural renewal, and these enabled women from a broader range of Israeli society to deeply explore Talmud and other Jewish sources. Two of these new batei midrash in particular stand out: Niggun Nashim in Oranim College and Beit Midrash Elul in Jerusalem. Both encourage creative responses to the study of texts, and many of the midrashim in the volume of *Dirshuni* originated there.

One of the things that opened up the Talmud to broader ranks of society, and women in particular, was the monumental work of the late Rabbi Adin Steinsaltz. His massive translation of the Babylonian Talmud into modern Hebrew comes with running commentary, vocalization, explanations of Talmudic realia, and introductions. The first volumes appeared in 1967, and the many volumes that have followed have transformed the landscape of Talmudic study in Israel.

The midrashim in this book exhibit deep understanding of and engagement with Talmudic texts, reflected not least in the regular use of Hebrew and Aramaic Talmudic expressions taken from both legal and nonlegal rabbinic texts. Some midrashim are written entirely in the distinctive forms of Talmudic give-and-take. This writing in Talmudic style, hitherto the sole province of men, at times raises a protest against masculine perspectives from within and reverses power relations in bold and unexpected ways.

Legal Discussions in Women's Midrashim The opening of the gates of Talmudic study to women has resulted, among other things, in their entry into the world of Halakhah, traditional Jewish law, which in the past was the exclusive preserve of men. Changes like these came as a revolution from below, beginning in the margins, dismissed by the establishment but penetrating to its heart, in time. In increasing numbers, women began to enter the world of halakhic adjudication and rule-making as *yoatzot halakhah,* halakhic counselors, *to'anot rabbaniyot,* pleaders in rabbinic courts, and *poskot,* rendering halakhic judgments and writing learned articles and opinions.

Perusing the biographies of the women whose midrashim appear in this book reveals that many of them are indeed active in these halakhic areas too, so one distinctive feature of this book is the striking extent to which halakhic issues relating to women feature in the midrashim: *agunot* (grass widows), *aqarut hilkhatit* (conception made difficult by misalignment between halakhic rules and women's varying menstrual cycles), *mesuravot get* (women whose husbands refuse to grant them a divorce), *yibum* (levirate marriage), and *mamzerut* (illegitimate children).

These midrashim make use of the familiar terminology of Midrashei Halakhah and make use of citations reflecting deep knowledge of halakhic literature through the centuries, from the Talmud, through the Middle Ages, up to the writings of contemporary halakhic authorities.

Blessings and Prayers Rabbinic literature contains blessings and prayers composed for different and special occasions, seeking to infuse significant moments in life with religious meaning. In this book, you will find midrashim in which the writers complete or add to traditional prayers and blessings, as well as introduce new ones that they feel are missing from their religious worlds, giving expression to women's subjective experiences that the male halakhic world cannot provide.

The world of ritual includes liturgical texts conveying the individual's connection to the community and the participants' identification with what the ritual represents. In this light, one cannot but be struck by the absence of women from traditional liturgies, such as the Passover Haggadah, prayers for rain and dew, and many others. A number of midrashim in this book seek to fill that void. The writers employ the familiar forms of prayers or conventional liturgies but put women and their actions at the center. This assertion demands the community to recognize women's place in the history of the Jewish people and emphasizes the importance of identification with female figures as part of the religious experience of men and women alike.

WHAT IDEAS AND IDEOLOGIES ARE THESE MIDRASHIM TRYING TO CONVEY?

Up to now, we have been exploring innovations in the ways women's midrashim offer new ways of reading biblical narratives and the ways they use rabbinic literary methods, style, and language. It is time to take a look at a third angle: the distinctive messages these women seek to impart via the moral and ideological world emerging from these midrashim.

Patriarchal Perspectives as Mistaken Understandings of God's Will and His Torah One issue regularly arising in this book is contention with offensive patriarchal notions, inappropriate comments about women, and the absence of gender equality. A dominant message is that these stances reflect a mistaken understanding of God's ways. This is not what God truly wants. The writers show how to use the same idiom and rabbinic tools to create a different and better reality. In some of the midrashim, God is described as looking with sorrow on human mistakes, yet because of the interpretive freedom He has given humanity and the absence of prophecy after the destruction of the Temple, He is unable to intervene.

One especially fascinating character appearing in the women's midrashim is Tanot, a literary figure appearing in a midrash of Rivkah Lubitch about Jephthah's daughter (see page 89). Tanot becomes a motif in the midrashim of other writers as well. Tanot is the soul of Jephthah's daughter, offered up as a sacrifice by her father, functioning as a heavenly intermediary between humanity and God. Tanot, sitting at the feet of the Shekhinah—the female countenance of God in rabbinic tradition—and pleading before Her women's wounds at the hands of patriarchy.

In some of the midrashim, God is attentive to the women's cries over the injustices done to them and seeks to redress the injustices in His world. Some offer the hope that in the future, the truth will come to light, and there will be repair.

The Significance of a Feminine Point of View   Different midrashim in this book engage women in forming their own identities by their own lights, in discovering feminine sexuality or describing the ways in which men come to feminist consciousness, as they come to understand the independence and subjectivity of women, bearers of will and aspirations of their own. An idea that appears in several midrashim is that women experience reality differently owing to biology and their life experiences.

The message arising from these midrashim is that the feminine point of view is essential for the world's balanced existence. Women's voices can bring about change and avoid catastrophe, domestic and political. Their rebellion and protest are meaningful even when their views do not prevail, as they endure as a sign and symbol for the generations to come. Women's faith flows from a deep, unmediated connection to God, since they have been exposed at firsthand to His ways, partners as they are to bringing life into the world. And so in a number of the midrashim, God pays careful attention to what women say and honors what they think.

In Her Image Divinity in women's midrashim is at times depicted as female, or as a Being who has feminine dimensions. According to these writers, God's being depicted as male and Her being accorded conventionally masculine attributes is the result of patriarchal conceptions, reflecting a partial and mistaken understanding of God. In this book, divinity is at times portrayed as a compassionate mother, as a woman seeking a mate, or as a woman who has miscarried and is now hopeless and depressed. The moral and ideological message here is that the model of God derives from the model of what is human. This is a reversal of the idea that humanity is created in God's image. God is recreated in the image of male or female. God is depicted as lacking, in need of completion and support. The humanity that God has created reveals to Him/Her new sides in themselves. This theological reversal enlarges and fortifies the divine image, enabling the faithful to identify more easily with it.

Women's Erudition as Spiritual Experience Within women's midrashim, we find reflections on the writing itself and its consequences. The writers seek to raise consciousness and stimulate discussion of the process in which we find ourselves today in which women work to achieve lives of study and spiritual experience akin to those of men. They depict the steep prices paid by women who lived in conservative Jewish frameworks, which encouraged only men to develop spiritually and assume leadership. They search for spousal relationships that will enable both partners to develop spiritually and to actualize themselves.

The sages believed that the study of Scripture and the work of biblical interpretation are of religious value. The ability to discover new facets and understandings is a form of revelation and a reenactment of the giving of the Torah at Mount Sinai. The ideology arising from the pages of *Dirshuni* is that women's engagement in the study and interpretation of Scripture and the discovery of new meanings is a process of revelation too. Hence, the phenomenon of women forging midrash is a kind of historical repair and recreates the revelation at Sinai anew, this time with women's meaningful participation.

In some of the midrashim, midrash is conceived of as an expression of longing for nearness to God and the result of a long quest. Some of the women exhibit awareness of the personal and social costs that they are likely to pay for their innovation, audacity, and the messages they are trying to convey. At the same time there is a sense of mission: they see this work as creating a better, repaired, reality for themselves and their daughters.

Democratization of Religious Authority: Women's Involvement in the World of Halakhah Rabbinic literature is replete with discussions of legal issues affecting everyday life. The sages created midrashei aggadah and, alongside them, midrashei halakhah tying biblical verses to legal matters. Similarly, the women in this book deal with legal issues through scriptural interpretation and so seek to influence contemporary halakhic discourse.

Among the contributors to this book are women who in their professional lives are responsible for the welfare and well-being of different women. They are physicians, attorneys, therapists, and educators, as well as advocates who represent women in the rabbinic court system. Through their writings, they offer criticism of the halakhic system, which displays lack of understanding of women, their bodies, and their life cycles. In the midrashim, they express their frustration at the conservatism and calcification of the rabbinic courts with regard to *mesuravot get*, levirate marriage and illegitimacy. Some of the midrashim contend with rabbinic legal pronouncements dealing with women's roles in the home, in education and childrearing, and in their standing as legal persons.

The women in the images offer reasoned, grounded halakhic solutions to problems or point to openings that will facilitate change in the system of adjudication itself that falls on deaf ears. The injustice is depicted as the result of conservatism, or poor judgment, misinterpretation of the spirit of the law in a way contrary to God's true will. The message is a demand from contemporary halakhic decision-makers to follow in the path of the sages, to show boldness and creativity so that the Halakhah finds solutions to the painful problems of today rather than being something petrified.

In some midrashim, God wails and mourns for the absence of justice in His world and the reality in which He and His intentions are distorted. Other midrashim depict a utopian reality in which a feminine beit midrash explores an halakhic issue that causes severe social distress and after a well-reasoned discussion establishes a precedential decision achieving the right result.

Repairing Social Failures: Rape, Sexual Abuse, and Incest Different midrashim describe the dreadful societal failure of hiding and denying the sexual abuse of children, rape, and incest. They use familiar biblical stories, like the rapes of Dinah and Tamar, while boldly interpreting other biblical stories in a creative way, discerning there too similar phenomena, such as Noah and his sons, Ishmael and Abraham's daughter, Mordechai and Esther. The writers' aim is to show a widespread phenomenon from the days of the Bible to the present. The midrashim illuminate the respective failures of family and community and the silencing of victims precisely by the people closest to them, who thus become accomplices to the crime. For the victims, this is one more blow and one more obstacle to overcoming and healing. The midrashim demand taking immediate responsibility rather than staying silent.

Accepting the Other as a Religious and Moral Imperative Some midrashim raise a call for an accepting and open stance toward different persons and varied families in our social fabric. These midrashim work to legitimize alternative families of our day in reliance on biblical stories at the heart of social consensus. They explore the ways of life of the different families and moral potential they hold as a model for moral sensitivity and inclusion. Other midrashim deal with women who are at a socioeconomic disadvantage and urge compassion toward the children of foreign workers. The demand to embrace them is portrayed as a divine religious obligation and human moral imperative.

Conclusion

This introduction has presented the enchanted world of midrash, an ancient and unique literary genre that has enjoyed a remarkable return in recent decades thanks to women writers. The word "midrash" means searching and investigating and thus reflects as well the search and exploration of the women writers themselves—a search for their feminine identities and distinctive voices and for their equal place in a society of study and creativity. Women's midrashim, like those of the sages, forge new ties between Scripture and burning issues and contemporary questions in audacious and innovative ways.

Their writing uncovers pain, distress, dealing with loss, vulnerability, and awareness of a deeply flawed reality badly in need of repair. And at the same time, these Midrashim offer a breeze of great hope for change, or renewal, and the making of a better world for themselves and the generations to come.

Notes

1. In the Bible, the root D-R-SH appears, meaning to search for and explore after God (see, e.g., Deut 13:15, Gen 25:22). Over time, it underwent a dramatic shift to mean search for and exploring after the meaning of Scripture: *For Ezra devoted himself to search out—li-drosh—God's Torah* (Ez 7:10).

2. Mishnah Avot 5:2: Turn it over and over, for everything is in it. Talmud Yerushalmi Peah 1:1: Rabbi Menna said: *For it is no empty thing to you* (Deut 32:47)—and if it is empty, the empty one is you, and why, because you don't work at it hard enough, for *it is your life* (ibid.), when it is your life, when you are hard at work at it.

3. Midrash Bereshit Rabbah, 19:9 (Theodor-Albeck, ed., 178–79): *And Lord God called out to Adam and asked where are you?* What happened to you? Yesterday, acting by my mind, today by the serpent's! Yesterday, from one end of the world to the other, and now, hiding inside a garden tree.

4. Midrash Bereshit Rabbah, 49:9 (Theodor-Albeck, ed., 511): Rabbi Levi said: *Will not the judge of all the world do justice?* (Gen 18:25) If it is a world You seek, there is no justice. And if is it justice You seek, there is no world. You're grabbing the rope from both ends. You're asking for a world, and for justice. And if You don't relent a little, the world cannot stand.

5. Midrash Bereshit Rabbah 1:10–11 (Theodor-Albeck, ed., 8–10).

6. One must distinguish between the word "aggadah" (legend), which in modern Hebrew means a fiction or folk tale (as in the Brothers Grimm), and the word "aggadah" as used by the sages, which means nonlegal material.

7. Rivkah Lubitch, *Va-Telekh li-Drosh: Midrash Nashi Yotzer* (Ramat Gan: Bar-Ilan University/Gottesfeld Institute for the Study of Women, 2003).

8. *Dirshuni—Midrashei Nashim*, vol. 1, Nehama Weingarten-Mintz and Tamar Biala, eds. (Tel Aviv and Jerusalem: Miskal-Yedioth Ahronoth Books and the Jewish Agency for Israel, 2009); *Dirshuni—Midrashei Nashim*, vol. 2, Tamar Biala, ed. (Tel Aviv: Miskal-Yedioth Ahronoth Books, 2018).

I. Further Reading: Midrash's Enchanted World

Boyarin, D. *Intertextuality and the Reading of Midrash*. Bloomington: Indiana University Press, 1990.

Hirshman, M. "Aggadic Midrash." In *The Literature of the Sages: Second Part: Midrash and Targum, Liturgy, Poetry, Mysticism, Contracts, Inscriptions, Ancient Science and the Languages of Rabbinic Literature*, edited by S. Safrai, Z. Safrai, Joshua Schwartz and Peter Tomson. Leiden: Brill, 2006.

Kugel, J. "Two Introductions to Midrash." *Prooftexts* 1 (1983): 131–55.

Lerner, M. B. "The Works of the Aggadic Midrash and the Esther Midrashim." In *The Literature of the Sages, Second Part: Midrash and Targum, Liturgy, Poetry, Mysticism, Contracts, Inscriptions, Ancient Science and the Languages of Rabbinic Literature*, edited by S. Safrai et al. Assen: Van Gorcum; Philadelphia: Fortress Press, 2006.

Shinan, Avigdor. *The World of the Aggadah*, translated by John Glucke. Tel-Aviv: Tel-Aviv University, 1990.

Stemberger, G. *Introduction to the Talmud and Midrash*, translated and edited by M. Bockmuehl. Edinburgh: T & T Clark 1996.

Stern, D. "Midrash and Midrashic Interpretation." In *The Jewish Study Bible*, 1863–1875. Oxford: Oxford University Press, 2004.

———. *Midrash and Theory: Ancient Jewish Exegesis and Contemporary Literary Studies*. Evanston, IL: Northwestern University Press, 1996.

Visotzky, B. "The Literature of the Rabbis." In *From Mesopotamia to Modernity: Ten Introductions to Jewish History and Literature*, edited by B. Vizotzky and D. Fishman. Boulder, CO: Westview Press, 1999.

II. Further Reading: Midrash's Unexpected Return

Adler, Rachel. *Engendering Judaism: An Inclusive Theology and Ethics*. Philadelphia-Jerusalem: Jewish Publication Society, 1998.

Biala, Tamar. "A New Women's Torah, Coming from Zion." *CCAR Journal: The Reform Jewish Quarterly* (Spring 2018): 184–197.

Cohen, Norman J. "New Wine in Old Vessels: Creating Contemporary Midrash." *Living Text: The Journal of Contemporary Midrash* 1 (July 1997): 12–16.

El-Or, Tamar. *Next Year I Will Know More: Literacy and Identity among Young Or-*

thodox Women in Israel. Translated by Haim Watzman. Detroit: Wayne State University Press, 2002.

Fraade, S. "Rabbinic Polysemy and Pluralism Revisited: Between Praxis and Thematization." In *Legal Fictions: Studies of Law and Narrative in the Discursive Worlds of Ancient Jewish Sectarians and Sages,* edited by S. Fraade. Leiden: Brill, 2011.

Irshai, Ronit. "'And I Find a Wife More Bitter Than Death' (Eccl 7:26): Feminist Hermeneutics, Women's Midrashim, and the Boundaries of Acceptance in Modern Orthodox Judaism." *Journal of Feminist Studies in Religion* 33: 1 (2017): 69–86.

Kadari, Tamar. "Transformation and Innovation in Modern Orthodoxy: Jewish Women and the Study of Talmud and Halacha." In *Dialogische Theologie: Beiträge zum Gespräch zwischen Juden und Christen und zur Bedeutung rabbinischer Literatur,* edited by Alexander Deeg, Joachim J. Krause, Melanie Mordhorst-Mayer, and Bernd Schröder, 243–56. Leipzig: Evangelische Verlagsanstalt, 2020.

Myers, Jody. "The Midrashic Enterprise of Contemporary Jewish Women." In *Jews and Gender—The Challenge to Hierarchy,* edited by Jonathan Frankel, 119–41. Oxford: Oxford University Press, 2000.

Orenstein, Debra. "Stories Intersect: Jewish Women Read the Bible." In *Lifecycles: Jewish Women on Biblical Themes in Contemporary Life,* edited by Debra Orenstein and Jane Rachel Litman, 2:xi–xxviii. Woodstock, VT: Jewish Lights, 1997.

Rosenberg, Esti. "The World of Women's Torah Learning—Developments, Directions and Objectives: A Report from the Field." *Traditions* 45:1 (2012): 14–18.

TAMAR BIALA

Editor's Introduction
The Road to Women's Midrash

Realizing That the Torah Is Patriarchal

Growing up in Beersheva in the 1980s, girls like myself who wanted to learn Talmud had a problem. In that spiritual desert, a little manna descended on us from time to time, scattered pages of Talmud that an American rabbi taught us, who had recently arrived at the religious girls' high school we attended; a Talmud passage from the head counselor in our youth movement, who had come from Jerusalem, where, wonder of wonders, she had studied Talmud in high school. We even traveled to Moshav Beit Meir to meet with Chana Safrai, one of the pioneering women Talmudists in Israel, who mailed study sheets to our homes, almost like underground literature. Only later, after many years spent in Torah study in academia and various batei midrash, would I find, like many other women who entered the world of Torah study in those years, that the world we had so longed to know wasn't what we expected.

Written Jewish culture, like all other cultures, was written by men, for men, from men's life experiences. Our sacred texts were sanctified by men, interpreted by men, and renewed by men. Jewish men don't all think alike and don't experience life in the same ways, and so Jewish culture is rich, deep, and wider than the sea. After we women dove deep into study, it took a little while to get over the shock and discern that despite the breadth and force of the world that had opened up before us, we couldn't find ourselves there, at least not in the ways we understand ourselves.

As our feminist awareness grew, ominous fissures began to crack open in us. Disappointment, bitterness, and humiliation were our lot when we were exposed to the extent of the essential patriarchy in the sacred texts we studied. Many of us found ourselves in unbearable pain.

In the midrash "All the Answers and Excuses in the World," which appears

in the second volume of the Hebrew *Dirshuni*, Rivkah Lubitch captures the
dead end in which we found ourselves:

> There was a little girl who would pester her mother and ask, why do
> the males humiliate us, saying "Blessed is He Who did not make me a
> woman"? And she would bring her all the answers and excuses in the
> world, and they didn't put her mind at ease.
>
> When she got a little older she would ask her mother, why do the rab-
> bis humiliate us by saying "to teach one's daughter Torah is to teach her
> foolishness"? And she would bring her all the answers and excuses in the
> world, and they didn't put her mind at ease.
>
> When she came of age, she would ask her mother, why do the men
> humiliate us, saying we're their property, and divorce is only at their will?
> And she would bring her all the answers and excuses in the world, and
> they didn't put her mind at ease.
>
> When the days passed, and that girl became a mother, her little girl
> would pester her and ask her all the questions in the world, and she would
> bring her all the answers and excuses in the world, and they didn't put her
> mind at ease.

Over time, many of the women studying Torah learned to live with the
split between the world of their feminism and the world of their Torah study
and to more or less endure the pain. But some couldn't bear the dissonance
any longer and searched urgently for new answers and excuses.

Using the Master's Tools to Expand the Home

At about the same time, and usually unaware of each other, without knowing, some of the women who were studying Torah in different batei midrash
(houses of study) all over Israel,[1] having acquired knowledge of the tradition
and the literary tools and techniques through which the tradition is written,
women began to use these tools in their attempts to bridge the gap between
their feminism and the patriarchy of the sacred texts. They hoped that in
so doing, they still would be able to keep the sacred texts in their lives as
moral and spiritual anchors. In the language of Talmudic and kabbalistic
midrash, some of them began to express their life experiences as women,
their existential insights and theological perspectives on the matters they

had studied. Through this writing, they at last discovered a way to find themselves and their voices on the sacred Jewish bookshelf and to convey, as did the Talmudic sages (Hazal[2]) their opinions on ethical, spiritual, and legal questions, even if it was only kept for themselves.

Aside from Rivkah Lubitch, who published via the Rackman Center of Bar-Ilan University a slim volume of midrashim, which didn't make it into bookstores, they had no idea that their Torah could have a life beyond their own circles. Nor did they know about the midrashic writing by American Jewish feminists starting in the 1960s—maybe because of the geographic distance, maybe because it was in English, and maybe because the insightful, creative interpretation that American women thought of as midrash didn't read like midrash to them, unmoored as it was from the specific rabbinic techniques of close, intertextual reading of the Hebrew text. When I met Yehudah Mirsky, an American Jewish Studies scholar I later would marry, he showed me a few of these midrashim by American women and helped me translate them into Hebrew. The very fact that they had been published in different journals astonished me.

At the end of the 1990s, I became aware of a few of the midrashim written by Israeli women, who wrote mainly for themselves, and for a long time, at every place I was invited to teach (regardless of what they had asked me to teach), I made sure to present those midrashim. I presented the phenomenon with missionary zeal as the beginning of the redemption of Judaism. One night in the early 2000s, in a study session at a private home in Modiin, I met Nehama Weingarten-Mintz, who, when I was done, told me that she too had noticed this phenomenon. She too had been collecting midrashim—and they weren't the same ones that I had!

This was the beginning of a beautiful friendship between two women in the middle of life's journey, who, between births, jobs, and endless responsibilities of housekeeping and child rearing, found time to celebrate what they found and to make it endure. When we let it be known that we were collecting women's midrashim, some two hundred works somehow made their way to us, the writers happy to publish them. The abundance that showered on us left us stunned. I remember in particular one digital file sent by an acquaintance who had studied with me in Beit Midrash Elul containing midrashim she had written in Aramaic, kabbalistic midrashim, midrashim mixing traditional texts with texts from the Zionist cultural renaissance of the

xxxvi EDITOR'S INTRODUCTION

early 1900s. The sheer intensity was too much for me to bear, and I literally ran away from the computer. This sense that this kind of women's writing bore atomic energies would overwhelm me time and again over the years.

Nehama and I sought to gather these midrashim into an anthology that would take its place on the Jewish bookshelf and add the women's voices that were so long absent from it. We spent many hours editing them. We explored the ideas' originality and whether the writers' use of midrashic tools of different kinds was precise, helped convey the idea, or whether some other midrashic technique would work better. Intensive email correspondence with the writers became fascinating and very moving *havrutot*[3] where we learned about the inner worlds that they sought to express.

In order that the anthology be precise and responsible, we established an advisory committee. Two scholars of midrash, Dr. Tamar Kadari and Dr. Anat Shapira, accompanied our work, pointed out inexactitudes, and offered constructive suggestions. Nehama, who was then working at the Jewish Agency for Israel, turned to her employer, who was glad to publish the volume, and Ruhama Weiss, then editor of the Judaica series of Yediot Aharonot (and was, yes, that head counselor of my youth movement in the 1980s who had taught me some Talmud), was happy to pursue a joint publishing venture. We titled the book *Dirshuni—Midreshei Nashim* ("Dirshuni—Women's Midrash"). *Dirshuni* means "seek me" as well as "interpret me," taken from the prophet Amos (5:4): *Thus said the LORD to the House of Israel: Seek Me (dirshuni), and you shall live,* a prophetic imprimatur that this work is what God wants. In 2009, volume 1 of *Dirshuni* was published, to an ambivalent reception.

The Other Half of the Jewish Bookshelf

Dirshuni got an enthusiastic reception in various institutions of Torah study, where, to our surprise, it was shelved next to the classical works of midrash. The reactions flowing to us over the years revealed to us, happily, how wide and varied was our readership. Students and scholars alike shared with us the circumstances in which they learned of the book, or of some of its contents, and the occasions on which they taught them as Jewish texts. Sales outstripped our expectations. The enthusiastic responses made clear to us just how right we were in thinking that the time was ripe to expand the Jewish bookshelf. And how deep was the thirst among contemporary readers to hear the Torah of women.

Not surprisingly, in some quarters the book was condemned and characterized as foolish and even heretical. Some of the book reviews saw it as the beginning of the end, and one rabbi published a halakhic ruling that it is forbidden to have the book in one's home and that if a copy comes to hand, it literally has to go straight into the garbage can, even if it is full of biblical and Talmudic passages.

DIRSHUNI, VOLUME 2

Nehama and I became an address for new writers who enthusiastically inundated us with new midrashim. They dealt with power relations between men and women in the public and private spheres; the difficulties of dealing with the rabbinic establishment, especially the legal courts of the chief rabbinate; the policing of sexuality; relations between parents and children; the obstacles facing women in Torah study; the sheer joy of Torah study; and more. They also began to deal with hard questions that the writers finally had the courage to face: incest; bastardy; post-Holocaust theology; homosexuality; single motherhood and protracted bachelorhood. While the subgenre of kabbalistic midrash was represented in volume 1, we received more midrashim written by women immersed in the kabbalistic study. In these midrashim, the writers expressed, via kabbalistic and Hasidic imagery and themes, their own existential insights.

I began to edit the new midrashim for a second volume with the sensitive, expert help of Tamar Kadari, dean of the Schechter Institute of Jewish Studies and an expert on midrash and aggadah, and Hadas Achituv, an astounding literary editor with deep sensitivity and understanding of Jewish texts, who had helped us on the first volume.

I edited the second volume in Boston, where my family and I spent several years. I received invaluable material support from the Hadassah-Brandeis Institute through fellowships and, no less important, moral and emotional support. The second volume of *Dirshuni* appeared in Israel in 2018 to a welcome reception.

AN ENGLISH EDITION OF *DIRSHUNI*

During my stay in North America I was invited to teach in synagogues of all denominations, in Jewish adult education programs, and in universities. In my missionary zeal, I taught women's midrashim that I carried in my kit bag of English translations executed by my husband, Yehudah Mirsky. I was privileged to engage with rabbinical students of all denominations and wrote about the project in different venues. What's more, the financial support I received also came from Jews of all denominations. I was witnessing the fulfillment of my collaborator Nehama's vision that "from Zion will go forth women's Torah."

The response to these Israeli women's midrashim was overwhelmingly similar wherever I went: surprise and astonishment, alongside great enthusiasm and deep emotion. Some said the texts changed their attitude toward Judaism and even changed their lives. As more and more rabbis and educators asked for my materials, the idea of an English edition grew.

In 2019, when I taught in the Wexner Graduate Fellows' Summer Institute—young people pursuing their doctorates in Jewish Studies, and rabbinic students of all denominations—some of the students already knew of *Dirshuni* and viewed it as a sacred text. They even asked me to help facilitate midrash writing workshops for them. I understood I needed to hurry up and edit an English edition so that the new generation of scholars and rabbis could introduce women's midrashim to the communities and schools they soon would be called on to lead.

The Hadassah-Brandeis Institute, first under the leadership of Shulamit Reinharz and Sylvia Barack Fishman, and later Lisa Fishbayn Joffe, took upon themselves to support the English edition, and Brandeis University Press, under the editorship of Sylvia Fuks Fried, accepted it for publication. They asked me to add a commentary to each midrash to make the texts more accessible to a range of audiences unfamiliar with Hebrew and Jewish text and with the Israeli backdrop to the writers' works. We chose fifty midrashim, culled from both volumes.

Yehudah Mirsky completed the translations, and Ilana Kurshan happily agreed to translate the commentaries that I'd written for the English edition under the expert eyes of Tamar Kadari.

I remain ever grateful to an anonymous donor who grasped the importance of the project, and the joy at its heart, at her first encounter with it, and sponsored my work on this volume.

In May 2020, in the midst of the Covid-19 pandemic, a few weeks before we returned to Israel, I received an email invitation to take part by Zoom in a traditional *siyum*—the ceremony on completing the study of a sacred text—that rabbinical students at Jewish Theological Seminary (JTS) were doing for *Dirshuni*, which they had been studying that year with Professor Eliezer Diamond. It was the second siyum on a volume of *Dirshuni* to which I'd been invited. The first had taken place a few months earlier in Israel, in Herzliya, at Kehillat Torat Chayim, under the leadership of Rabbi Barry Schlesinger. Because we were in the United States, I couldn't participate in that one. This time, I wasn't going to miss the chance. The JTS students' ceremony was also attended by faculty and many guests. After the text study, they recited Kaddish De-Rabbanan and a special Hadran Alakh bespoke to *Dirshuni*, and sang *niggunim*.[4] The elation, spiritual elevation, and gratitude that swept over me were beyond words. Choking with tears, I asked if I could say something, and I sobbingly recited the Shehecheyanu.[5] Twenty years earlier, I never dreamed I would be at an occasion like this. And for that I am deeply grateful.

How Do You Edit a Book of Midrashim, and How Do You Do It in English?

The editorial work in the Dirshuni project is not fundamentally academic. It's primarily a creative process, the fruit of the writers' Torah study and, later, of the dialogue between the writers and the editors, most often by email. In this editorial work , the chief criterion for including a midrash in these collections was an estimation of its originality, whether it grappled with and illuminated the pressing questions of the day—whether the idea itself, the interpretive reading of the classical text, or the agenda were to our liking or not. So long as the midrash applied the midrashic method skillfully and succeeded in presenting the writer's idea or moral issue, I thought I had no right to censor this authentic voice. In my work with Nehama on the first volume, this acceptance, this coming to terms, did not come easily to me. But in the subsequent volumes I edited on my own, I took it on myself from the beginning.

I understood my editorial task as helping the writers express their ideas in rabbinic language and in the form and structure of classical midrash: appropriate use of the biblical and Talmudic sources, with precise use of classical hermeneutic forms (what the rabbis referred to as *middot she-ha-Torah nidreshet bahen*), concision, and proof texts that unpacked their references and allusions. I checked to see if the midrashic tools the writer was using helped her express her ideas or were getting in the way, and, as needed, I suggested ways of clarifying obscure knots in the text or passages requiring more specialized knowledge than the average reader might have. At times I felt that there was more to the idea at play than the midrash at hand conveyed and suggested to the writer additional related classical sources.

Just as the classical rabbinic midrashim are far from homogeneous in style and sophistication, so too the midrashim in this book vary in style and registers of speech and in the exertion demanded of readers. Some of the midrashim required very light editing, and others are the product of long processes of mutual learning between the writers and me. The writers were all enormously patient and dedicated, and shared their excitement in the work. I am grateful for their willingness to entrust their creations to me.

From midrash to midrash I came to realize the remarkably rich range of life experiences from which their works arose—not just that different women experience and judge the same things differently from one another, but also different and conflicting impulses and voices are at work within themselves too. I was surprised again and again to discover how a writer's perspective can be so different from mine, her experience so foreign to me, and her judgment too, and, in other words, how deeply debate and different voices are at the heart of Torah study.

HOW THIS VOLUME IS ORGANIZED

I hope that the division into different sections makes it easier for readers to find midrashim of interest, but it is far from definitive. As Nehama and I were editing volume 1 and were thinking about how to organize it, we turned to our beloved role model of midrash collection, Bialik and Ravnitzky's *Sefer Ha-Aggadah*, first published in 1911.[6] Like them, we sought to keep the order of the biblical narrative, but also to find room for thematic clusters that gather different perspectives around a common subject. So the earlier sections of the book present midrashim in the order of the biblical narratives, and the later ones present midrashim dealing with a variety of themes. At least two sections address the severe injustices resulting from patriarchal culture in both the private and public spheres, such as sexual abuse of women and children, the brutal halakhic treatment of bastards (*mamzerim*), and women seeking divorce at the hands of the Israeli chief rabbinate's court system. Patriarchy and its problems aren't the only issues dealt with in this book. Some midrashim explore post-Holocaust theology, others dive into the Megillot read at holidays (like Ruth, Esther, or the Song of Songs), and can be used in liturgies and life-cycle events.

THE SIN OF WRITING COMMENTARY

I wrote the commentaries with a heavy heart. A midrash, like a poem, can be understood in many ways and bear different meanings. An element of secrecy, holding meanings close to the chest, may be what preserves its call and power. Opening up the text through commentary risks flattening its meaning, but I hope it will open the door to more readers.

I tried in my commentaries to make the texts accessible to a range of reading audiences, without assuming much prior knowledge of rabbinic literature. In the commentaries I elucidate the references to rabbinic and later Judaic sources, embedded, or alluded to, in the midrashim. Quotations of biblical verses are in italics. The translations from the biblical and Talmudic sources are not taken from any one English translation (e.g., Jewish Publication Society, Robert Alter, Harold Fisch, Everett Fox); instead we (Yehudah, Ilana, and I) tried to figure out the best translation for each word and passage in the frame of the particular midrash on which we were working. For instance, at times a translation will incorporate some Talmudic lines from Sefaria (including their explanatory comments in parentheses), but we have also translated the biblical lines embedded in that Talmudic text. Every commentary that I wrote was checked by Tamar Kadari, who showed me additional layers of meaning worthy of attention. Afterward, Ilana, as she translated the commentaries, added emphases that seemed necessary to her, and finally, Sylvia Fuks Fried, editorial director of Brandeis University Press, added her corrections in the course of an exceptionally delightful *havruta* on every text.

A friend of mine once put the experience of midrash study like this: midrash is like a play; it takes a two-dimensional text and turns it into three dimensions as the characters pop up and turn to face the reader. "How can you ignore Sarah's voice, insisting on telling her side of the Binding of Isaac?" she asked.

In the end the commentaries tell the story that I, with my particular baggage and life experience, saw in the midrashim. I reserve to myself the right to ask of you, the readers, to ignore the commentary as you prefer and let yourselves interpret the midrashim as you would like. Similarly, I apologize to the writers if I didn't get their intentions right and caused them hurt by this.

An Answer to That Little Girl

The midrash by Rivkah Lubitch that I cited above on the little girl who asks about the conflict between feminist ethics and the tradition ends on a note of despair. But in other midrashim of hers, such as "And Your Desire Will Be for Your Man," and "Daughters of Tzelophchad," the conflict between the two is resolved by the community, or divinity, realizing the rightness in the women's claims about the injustices being done to them.

Dirshuni contributes its part to the resolution of this conflict in a multidimensional way. It renders visible the gender injustices in traditional Jewish texts and in the abusive conduct of the rabbinic hegemony, and at the same time, *Dirshuni* shifts the balance and power relations in this culture by its very presence on the sacred Jewish bookshelf. Through this work, the writers take hold of the rabbinic bookshelf, make it their own, and with their own agency build the next layer of Jewish culture. At times, more than it provides satisfactory answers to the questions of that girl/woman, it shifts the ground under the structure that gives rise to the questions in the first place and offers different perspectives on what to believe in and how to live.

Notes

1. Some in women's batei midrash; some in pluralistic batei midrash, in which women and men, religious and secular both, study together; some in academic Jewish Studies; and others as autodidacts who studied privately.

2. "Hazal" is an acronym for "Hakhameinu Zikhronam Liverakhah," which means "our sages of blessed memory."

3. Literally "fellowship," *havruta* is a traditional method of text study in which pairs of readers go through, analyze, and discuss a text together.

4. Kaddish De-Rabbanan is a special form of Kaddish recited after Torah study. A Hadran Alakh (literally, "we will return to you") is an Aramaic prayer said at a siyum. In it the participants promise that they will return to study again the text they have just finished. A *niggun* is a traditional Jewish melody.

5. A traditional blessing thanking God, "who has given us life, sustained us, and brought us to this moment."

6. *Sefer Ha-Aggadah*, a massive anthology and reworking of classical midrashim by Haim Nahman Bialik and Yehoshua Hone Ravnitzky, was reprinted many times and is a foundation stone of modern Hebrew literature. It was published in English under the title *The Book of Legends* by Schocken Books in 1992.

Translators' Notes

Yehudah Mirsky: Translations of Midrashim

Participating in this project has been more of an honor and pleasure than I can express. I am grateful to my wife Tamar, to Brandeis University Press, and above all to the remarkable writers and thinkers whose works are gathered in this book. They are many, each with a distinctive voice and perspective all her own. I have tried to honor, shade, and inflect those different voices and registers as best I can, and where I haven't, trust me, reader, *Dirshuni* in the Hebrew original is richer and more powerful than I was able to convey.

In translating biblical and Talmudic passages in the midrashim and the introductory essays of the two Tamars, I have consulted various translations (for the Bible: Robert Alter, Ariel and Chana Bloch, Harold Fisch, Everett Fox, Jewish Publication Society, King James Version; for the Talmud: Soncino and Steinsaltz), and then chose, or crafted, the one I thought best suited to the midrash at hand.

This project has become a part of me. I hope it becomes a part of you.

Ilana Kurshan: Translations of Commentaries

All translation is commentary. No two languages map perfectly onto one another, especially when one of those languages is Hebrew—at once the ancient language of the Bible and a modern tongue brought back to life less than two centuries ago. In translating the commentaries that appear in this book, I sometimes felt that I was not just rendering Tamar Biala's commentary into English; I was also commenting on her commentaries and offering my own. Our many fruitful exchanges touched on the nuances of particular turns of phrase but also on the gendered nature of language, the delights and dangers of ambiguity, the pleasures of allusion. I found myself adding my own notes in the margins, hopeful that with the publication of this English translation, a wider audience of readers would begin adding their own notes and their own comments too.

The texts of our tradition remain relevant and vibrant because they are infinitely generative: they allow for manifold interpretive possibilities. So much has sprouted and so much has bloomed from the fertile soil of our texts. We have so much more to glean, so much deeper to dig. I am humbled and blessed that my portion is among those who have merited to cultivate and coax forth this richness.

ONE

Creation of the World

Miscarriage and Creation

Pregnancy loss, and the ensuing depression and recovery, are at the heart of this midrash, which considers what God must have experienced when She lost several worlds prior to the creation of the world as we know it.

At the beginning God created the heaven and the earth. And the earth was tohu va-vohu, darkness over the face of the deep, and the spirit of God hovering over the face of the waters (Gen 1:1).

He brings everything to pass precisely in its time (Eccl 3:11). Rabbi Abahu said that we learn from here that The Holy Blessed One was building worlds and destroying them, creating worlds and destroying them, until he created these (Kohelet Rabbah, Vilna edition, sec. 3).

And God saw all Her worlds falling at Her feet, and She said to Herself: I will just let my heart fall along with them, and I *will sit in darkness, like those long dead* (Lam 3:6). Her tears and blood were scattering in space, searching for land that would absorb them, and they wept to fragments and pieces, until all of existence was the cloud and fog of the great deep. God tried to look again at the ruins of Her worlds, and just couldn't. She covered Herself with this great deep, as is written, *You made the deep, covered it as a garment* (Ps 104:6), and She beat Her chest and wailed: for *I shall be a desolation forever* (Jer 51:26).

What did She think at that moment, when She could no longer bear to look on those worlds? She remembered that it is said of Her, *You brought forth the earth and the world* (Ps 90:2) *and her womb, eternal* (Jer 20:17), and She felt her sons and daughters straining to be born so that they could say in gratitude, *for I was not killed in the womb* (Jer 20:17). She closed Her eyes, swallowed the pain lodged in Her throat, and pleaded for Herself, that She might find more loving-mercy, and faith, as is written, *I declare, a world of loving-mercy will be built, Your faithfulness will be established in the heavens* (Ps 89:3). And from that She went and created new heavens and a new earth.

When the heavens and earth stood, in wonderment and bewilderment, *tohim uvohim*, She took off the garment of the deep with which She had been covering Herself, and that deep of cloud and fog, made of Her blood and tears, went and gathered into living waters, and She hovered over them back and forth, as is written *when the earth was tohu vavohu, darkness over the face of the deep, and the spirit of God hovering over the face of the waters* (Gen 1:1).

And what was She saying at that moment? *That it should not totter and fall, forever* (Ps 104:5). And Her sons and daughters joined their prayers to Hers, and they themselves said: *That it should not totter and fall, forever; that it should not totter and fall, forever.*

Commentary

The book of Ecclesiastes teaches *He brings everything to pass precisely at its time* (3:11). In the midrash in Ecclesiastes Rabbah on this verse, Rabbi Abahu deduces that God first created other worlds that were displeasing unto God and then destroyed them, and then ultimately created this world and left it intact. Tamar Biala reads this midrash as a description of the "miscarriages" that God experienced prior to successfully "birthing" the world as we know it. Hers is thus a midrash on the midrash from Ecclesiastes Rabbah. She also links her midrash to the first verse in the Bible, which describes the creation of the world and all that preceded it. She reads this verse as chronicling God's experience of miscarriage, followed by a new pregnancy and culminating in a live birth.

The midrash opens with a description of God in a state of despair following several miscarriages. God attests that She *will sit in darkness, like those long dead* (Lam 3:6), perhaps as a way of identifying with Her miscarried babies.

The tears of Her pain and the blood that still flows forth from Her fill up the vast cavities of space and obscure all visibility because there is not yet any earth to absorb them. They are *the depths* (Gen 1:1). Since God cannot even see Her miscarried losses, She becomes even more depressed, and She envelops Herself in those depths and mourns, wailing in the words of Jeremiah, *For I shall be a desolation forever* (51:26).

But the despair and mourning of God do not last forever. As She sits there, enveloped in the depths and covered in her tears and blood, She hears, echoing within her, fragments of biblical verses that speak to the notion that She can birth a world and give rise to humanity. These voices spur Her to action again. God overcomes Her depression by associating Herself with two of the elements contained within Her, loving-mercy and faith, according to a verse from Psalms (89:3) that teaches that the world is built and established by means of loving-mercy and faith. Embracing these strengths enables God to try to conceive once more. Biala suggests that a woman mourning the loss of a pregnancy can find strength by means of loving-mercy—the desire to care for others—and faith—the awareness that there is always the hope of change and repair.

The heavens and earth that are created are as vulnerable and bewildered as newborn children. The words *tohu vavohu* are understood as a description of wondering and staring, unsure of what to expect (see Genesis Rabbah 2:2). Following Her successful birth, God gathers up the depths that represent the endless pain She has experienced so that they may become living waters. She hovers over those waters, as per the continuation of Genesis 1:1.

The midrash concludes with a prayer. God, who has experienced difficult losses, prays that the world should endure: *That it should not totter and fall, forever* (Ps 104:5). Her children join in Her prayers. At the end of the midrash, God is depicted not as a perfect, confident being immune to hurt, but rather as strikingly human: She is well-acquainted with suffering and fear, and She needs to strengthen Herself by means of prayer. She prays the same prayers as Her human children, underscoring the similarities between them.

This midrash presents a theology in which divinity is modeled on humanity. In a sense, this is the opposite of the description in Genesis, whereby God creates humanity in God's image (1:27). Biala's God is created in the image and likeness of woman, which serves not to diminish God but to strengthen Her and render Her a powerful role model.

This midrash challenges the deterministic message of the book of Ecclesiastes and points to the fact that creation and the role of God in creating and sustaining the world reflect the ability to transcend situations that seem deterministic but are not in fact so. In our own day, human creation, which involves pregnancy and birth, reflects individual choice and agency and is thus a challenge to the forces of determinism.

MIRI WESTREICH

This One Will Be Called Woman

The book of Genesis contains two accounts of Adam naming the first woman. According to Miri Westreich's midrash, these two names express a change that took place in Adam's understanding of the woman's identity while they were in the Garden of Eden. Adam's feminist consciousness evolved as he learned to appreciate that women are independent subjects who are differentiated from men.

And Adam called out names for all the livestock and the birds of the sky and the beasts of the field but for Adam there was not a helping match to be found. . . .

And Adam said, this one is it, bone of my bones—self of my self, flesh of my flesh, this one will be called woman, for she was taken from a man (Gen 2:20, 23).

And he woke from slumber and saw a self of his self, bone of his bones.

And he was hurrying to complete the work of assigning names, male and female, and said *this one will be called woman, for she was taken from a man.*

And the woman saw how he was saying *taken from a man*—that she is a part, and not a creature in her own right.

And the serpent gazed into her, added a prohibition, craftily opening Adam's sleepy eyes, and at the end of this opening—curses: crawling dirt, childbirth pain, sweat of brows.

And Adam sees: three curses—serpent, woman, man. And understands—separate curse, separate flesh, separate bone. And selfhood. This one is not just *bone of my bones—self of my self, flesh of my flesh*; this one is a *helping match* to me.

At that moment, the work of calling out names was complete, *And Adam called the name of his woman Eve (Chava), for she was the mother of all the living (em kol hai)* (Gen 3:20).

Commentary

In the account of the creation of humankind in Genesis 2:7, Adam is described as a unique creation, without a counterpart. God sees that *it is not good for man to be alone* and creates the entire natural world for him. Adam gives names to all the animals, but he does not find a "helping match" among them. At that point God causes a slumber to descend upon him and creates a woman from his rib. Adam gives her a name: *And Adam said, this one is it, bone of my bones—self of my self, flesh of my flesh, this one will be called woman, for she was taken from a man* (Gen 2:23).

Miri Westreich's midrash deals with the naming of the woman. Adam's act of naming her is deeply significant, as it is an expression of the way he regards her and therefore his relationship with her. Westreich illuminates this verse from the woman's perspective—the woman understands that Adam views her as merely a part of himself, and not as an independent entity with a mind and a will of her own.

The serpent too hears Adam's words, but it can see inside the woman's heart and understand her dissatisfaction with the way Adam views her. The serpent succeeds in opening both Adam and Eve's eyes so that they understand themselves in a different way. In dialogue with the woman, the serpent adds an additional prohibition, declaring that Adam and Eve are forbidden from eating from all the trees in the garden, and not just from the Tree of Knowledge (Gen 3:1). It thereby engages her in dialogue and manages to tempt her to violate the original divine prohibition (as in Avot de Rabbi Natan, version B, chapter 1). And so the woman's act of eating from the Tree of Knowledge may be understood as her attempt to act freely as an independent entity, distinct from Adam.

Ultimately the woman eats from the fruit and also offers it to Adam, who accepts. In response, God curses the three partners in crime: the serpent will crawl in the dust, the woman will suffer pain in childbirth, and the man will have to work by the sweat of his brow in order to eat bread. But the act of eating from the Tree of Knowledge and the curses that ensue also result in heightened discernment. Adam and Eve understand that they are naked. But Westreich adds that Adam also discerns that Eve is not a part of him.

Adam notices that God has given each of them a separate punishment. His eyes are opened, and he suddenly recognizes that the woman is an independent entity. This realization leads him to give her a new name, *And Adam called the name of his woman Eve (Chava), for she was the mother of all the living (em kol hai)* (Gen 3:20). This name is not a derivative of his name (like man-woman); rather, it highlights her unique capacity to bring new life into the world. Only at this point does Adam conclude his work of naming God's creatures.

RIVKAH LUBITCH

And Your Desire Will Be for Your Man

In the story of the Garden of Eden, Eve is punished for eating from the Tree of Knowledge and sharing the fruit with Adam. One of the punishments she receives is, *And your desire will be for your man, and he will rule over you* (Gen 3:16). This punishment portrays a woman's dependence on her husband and the patriarchal power dynamics between men and women as dating back to the beginning of human existence. The following midrash tries to come to terms with the nature of these power dynamics and to explore whether they are unidirectional.

And your desire will be for your man, and he will rule over you (Gen 3:16).

Tanot asked the Shekhinah: In Beruriah's Torah it is written, *And your desire will be for your woman and she will rule over you.*

The Shekhinah said to her: These and those words are true, and both were said in the same utterance, since whoever desires someone is ruled by them; but the Torah of Moses spoke in the language of human beings, which is to say, males.

Commentary

The verse at the heart of this midrash articulates one of the punishments that Eve received after she ate the forbidden fruit. These punishments are understood as applying not just to Eve but to all womanhood, and thus their reverberations can be felt throughout the unfolding of Western civilization.

The verse describing Eve's curse contains two aspects. The first, *and your desire will be for your man,* deals with a woman's attraction to and dependence on man. The second, *and he will rule over you,* deals with a man's power to rule over the woman. The relationship between these two aspects of the punishment creates an existential problem. Women accede to male dominance because of their strong need to live in a relationship with a man.

Lubitch's midrash unfolds as a dialogue between two heavenly figures, the Shekhinah and Tanot. The Shekhinah, in rabbinic literature, is the feminine manifestation of God in the world. Tanot is a product of Lubitch's literary imagination—she appears throughout Lubitch's midrashim and is adopted by other writers of midrash as well. According to Lubitch, she is the soul of Jephthah's daughter, who sits at the foot of the Shekhinah and enumerates the woes of the daughters of Israel (see "Tanot, Jephthah's Daughter" by Rivkah Lubitch, page 89). Tanot serves as an intermediary between heaven and earth who challenges the Shekhinah by posing moral and theological questions, most of which deal with gender discrimination.

In this midrash, Tanot presents the Shekhinah with a subversive reading of the verse describing Eve's punishment: *And your desire will be for your woman and she will rule over you.* This reading is presented as if it appears in a version of the Torah attributed to Beruriah. Beruriah, who lived in the second century CE, was the daughter of the martyred Rabbi Hanina ben Teradion and the wife of the rabbinic sage Rabbi Meir. The idea of the existence of different versions of the Torah is a rabbinic tradition. Several rabbinic midrashim propose alternative versions of biblical verses attributed to Rabbi Meir's version of the Torah (see, for instance, Genesis Rabbah 9:5, 20:21). In the spirit of this tradition, Lubitch ascribes a different version of a verse to Beruriah—not just because she is Rabbi Meir's wife but also because she is depicted as a woman learned in rabbinic sources. The verse ostensibly found in Beruriah's Torah reverses the power dynamics between men and women. Moreover, it is found in the Torah belonging to a woman who rebelled against the accepted social conventions by daring to study Torah in spite of her gender.

The response of the Shekhinah is that both versions are true, and both were spoken in the same utterance by God. As for the contradiction inherent in the two readings, the Shekhinah responds practically, with an awareness of real-life experience: Both versions exist because both are true, and both reflect a familiar reality. There is a fundamental connection between the attraction to another person, the need for that person, and the sense of being ruled by that person. Anyone who is interested in or in need of someone else becomes dependent on that person's kindness and will. This is as true of men as it is of women.

The fact that Moses's Torah articulated only the woman's attraction to man and his rule over her should not be read as implying that the power dynamics operate in only one direction. Lubitch quotes the rabbinic midrashic principle that "the Torah is written in the language of human beings," traditionally understood as signifying that the Torah speaks in human terms, the way people speak to one another, and not every word is laden with esoteric meanings. But Lubitch wittily invokes this principle to explain the gender bias inherent in the language of the biblical text. She demonstrates that this principle itself is gendered because the term for "human beings," *bnei adam*, literally means "sons of Adam." Most of the commandments in the Torah that are written in the masculine form are in fact addressed to all of Israel, and according to Lubitch, this verse from Genesis is no exception.

This midrash serves as a sort of cautionary note, like those that often appear in fine print at the bottom of legal forms or want ads that are written in Hebrew in the masculine form. Such notes explain that although the form or ad is written in the masculine, it is addressed to men and women alike.

This midrash has far-ranging implications beyond the alternative reading of this particular biblical verse, for it prevents us from attributing existential or religious superiority to men. By reading Eve's curse as applying to Adam as well, Lubitch dismantles the biblical foundation of the traditional hierarchy between men and women. She insists instead on the mutual dependence between the sexes and the essential similarity between them.

DANA PULVER

And He Will Rule over You

Offensive patriarchal references appear throughout rabbinic literature. In response, this midrash offers a commentary on the verse from Genesis in which God punishes Eve after she eats from the Tree of Knowledge: *And your desire will be for your man, and he will rule over you* (Gen 3:16). This verse contains the verb "rule," which encapsulates what we refer to as patriarchy: the organization of power dynamics between men and women such that it is the men who are invested with authority in both familial and social contexts. Dana Pulver points to another meaning of this term, which offers a new way of thinking about the gender dynamics implicit in many rabbinic metaphors.

And your desire will be for your man, and he will rule over you
(Gen 3:16).

What is the meaning of *he will rule over you* (*vehu yimshol bakh*)?

Eve was cursed through none other than the parables (*meshalim*) made of her by men.

Our rabbis, of blessed memory, compared women to everything in the world.

When they wanted to compare them to a cup, they did.

When they longed to say they were the same as meat, they did.

When they sought to analogize them to bread, they did.

When they felt like describing them as earth, they did.

Women were in their eyes like a dish, like sheep, like geese, like a human body; and like a goatskin full of one thing or the other, and a sexual provocation.

In the future to come there will be fulfilled: *I will put an end to this parable (hamashal hazeh) and it will not be used (yimshelu oto) anymore in Israel* (Ezek 12:23).

Commentary

Dana Pulver plays with the various meanings of the Hebrew word *yimshol*, whose root means both "rule" and "parable." She interprets this term as it appears in the verse from Genesis as referring not to the rule of one person over another but to the activity of making parables. However, she regards the two meanings as related, since she views the literary activity of making parables as one aspect of patriarchal rule. According to Pulver, Eve, who represents womanhood, was cursed in that men would forever make parables about her, invoking objectifying and degrading images of her to validate and justify patriarchy.

Pulver offers examples of these parables by invoking images from various Talmudic and midrashic sources in which the rabbis compared women to various objects. For instance, man is told not to drink from one cup while settling his eyes on another, meaning that he should not engage in sexual relations with one woman while thinking about another (b.Nedarim 20a). Elsewhere in that same passage, a man is told that he may do whatever he wishes with his wife, just like a customer may do whatever he wishes with the meat he purchases from a butcher.

Women are also analogized to bread (the Talmud uses the phrase "bread in his basket" to refer to the ready availability of sexual partners in b.Yoma 18b) and to earth (Queen Esther is described in b.Sanhedrin 74b as being passive as "the soil of the earth" while sleeping with King Ahasuerus). And the act of marrying a divorced woman while her husband is still alive is compared to cooking in a pot in which another person has already cooked his food (b.Pesachim 112a).

Then there are the analogies to the animal world. Rabbi Akiva's daughter is said to have followed in her mother's footsteps like a ewe follows a ewe (b.Ketubot 63a), and Rav Gidel insists that women emerging from the mikvah are as asexual to him as white geese (b.Berakhot 20a). When a woman is compared to a human body, it is to the male body; the Talmud teaches that a man is not ashamed in front of his wife because "his wife is like his own flesh" (b.Berakhot 24a). Even that is better than the image of a woman as a flask full of feces (b.Shabbat 152a) or the image of a woman as so provocative that even an exposed handbreadth of her flesh constitutes nakedness (b.Berakhot 24a).

The midrash closes with words of consolation, declaring that in the future, the punishment of Eve will be revoked, meaning that men will stop invoking such objectifying and degrading parables. This message of consolation is based on a verse from Ezekiel in which the prophet foretells that God will put an end to a parable that will no longer be invoked. In its original context, this verse refers to God's promise to put an end to the parables invoked by false prophets so as to persuade Israel that there is no hope of any significant improvement in their situation. Instead God promises the fulfillment of prophecies of truth that speak of hope and change. Dana Pulver invokes this verse to suggest that God will someday put an end to the use of patriarchal parables, and social change will pave the way to a more egalitarian reality.

Pulver's deep familiarity with Talmudic literature and the authority with which she invokes a discourse that was in the past considered to be the province of men alone serves in itself as a critique of the images of femininity so prevalent in these sources.

TAMAR BITTON

Why Was It Given to Her?

Three commandments are associated with women in Jewish tradition: *niddah* (menstrual purity), *challah* (separating a portion of bread dough for the priests), and kindling the Sabbath candles. Tamar Bitton explains why these commandments were given specifically to women. Unlike the sages, who claimed that these commandments were punishments meted out to Eve (in Hebrew, *Chava*) on account of the destruction she brought to the world by eating the forbidden fruit in the Garden of Eden, Bitton suggests that these commandments are a reward for Eve's contributions to the creation, formation, and fashioning of human life.

Why was she given the mitzvah of niddah? Because she shed the blood of Adam. That is why the mitzvah of niddah was given to her.

Why was she given the mitzvah of challah? Because she ruined Adam who was the challah [beginning] of the world. That is why the mitzvah of challah was given to her.

And why was she given the mitzvah of the Sabbath light? Because she extinguished the soul of Adam. That is why the mitzvah of the Sabbath light was given to her (Genesis Rabbah sec.17:8).

Why was she given the mitzvah of niddah?

Because she moved us to wanderings (*nidudim*) that sped up the heartbeat and quickened the pulse, to live, to experience, *lichyot, u-le'chavot*, and that is why her name was *Chava*.

And why was she given the mitzvah of challah?

Because she initiated (*hechelah*) choice in the world, as is written, *the first of your kneading bowl, a round loaf, challah you will give* (Num 15:20), and because she was the yeast in the dough, the ferment that drives creation.

And why was she given the mitzvah of the Sabbath light?

For it is written, *God's candle is man's soul* (Prov 2:27), *and a spirit sweeps forward from her and souls she has made* (after Isa 57:16), as is written, *I have acquired a man with God* (Gen 4:1).

Commentary

The commandments of niddah, challah, and kindling the Sabbath lights are identified by the rabbinic sages as women's commandments. The first, niddah, is the injunction not to engage in sexual relations during menstruation and the obligation to immerse in a body of living waters before resuming intimacy. The second, challah, is the commandment to set aside a portion of the finished dough for the priests when baking bread. The third refers to the commandment to light candles at the start of the Sabbath and festivals. Although these commandments can be performed by men, they are identified as women's mitzvot, which women are responsible for and which women perform. The mishnah states that a failure to fulfill these commandments properly will cause a woman to die in childbirth (Mishnah Shabbat 2:6). The tragedy of death in childbirth is thus portrayed as a punishment.

In the rabbinic midrash in Genesis Rabbah, these three commandments are presented as obligations incumbent on women since the time of Eve, the first woman (see Genesis Rabbah 17:8). They are described as punishments given to Eve for eating from the Tree of Knowledge, because, as the mishnah teaches, each involves an element of life-threatening danger. Adam and Eve were warned, *On the day you eat from it you shall surely die* (Gen 2:17), and indeed following the banishment form the Garden of Eden, they became mortal creatures with finite life spans. This midrash blames Eve for Adam's sin and for bringing death into the world. Consequently, she was punished with these three commandments, each of which fits the nature of the crime.

According to Genesis Rabbah, the commandment of niddah, which is about menstrual blood, was given to Eve because she shed Adam's blood. The commandment of challah, which involves separating a portion of bread dough once it is finished, was given to Eve because she ruined Adam, who was the "challah of the world," the pinnacle of creation and the sign that God had finished making the world. The commandment to kindle the Sabbath lights was given to Eve because she extinguished Adam's soul, and the soul of a human being is likened to a candle in the book of Psalms (20:27).

Bitton's midrash was written as a counterargument to the traditional midrash in Genesis Rabbah. Bitton depicts Eve and all other women as role models and sources of blessing in the world. The three commandments associated with women are presented as compensatory rewards given to Eve as a reward for her good deeds.

The commandment of niddah was given to Eve as a reward for causing human beings to wander the earth. Bitton plays with the phonetic similarity between "niddah" and "n'dudim" (wanderings). The banishment from the Garden of Eden caused Adam and Eve to go forth into the world, to wander, to discover new vistas. Thanks to Eve, they experienced newfound excitement, and their hearts began to race. Eve intensified humanity's sense of vitality, and for this reason, Bitton claims, she was called Eve, which comes from the same root word as "life" and "experience."

The commandment of challah was given to Eve as a reward for modeling the power of choice and the force of human initiative. Eve was the first to choose, and challah signifies beginnings, according to the commandment to give *the first of your kneading bowl* (Num 15:20). Furthermore, every batch of dough contains yeast that ferments the dough and causes it to rise; so, too, Eve was endowed with an effervescence that animated her, drove her to eat from the forbidden fruit, and inspired her to act independently to forge a new reality.

The commandment to kindle the Sabbath lights was given to Eve as a reward for bringing life into the world. Like God Himself, who created new life and fashioned new souls, Eve gave birth to children, bringing new souls into the world. When she gave birth to her firstborn son, Cain, she gave him a name that expressed her ability to create like God. Thus, the candle, which symbolizes the soul, merited to be lit by her.

The act of eating from the Tree of Knowledge, the first sin recorded in the Bible, led to harsh punishments for humanity. Historically the blame has been placed on women, since Eve was the first to eat the fruit and then seduced Adam to follow her example. In this midrash, Bitton offers an alternative to the narrative of the Garden of Eden in which Eve is presented as an impressive woman with a mind of her own—one who is not afraid to try new experiences. She is bold and effervescent. The act of eating from the Tree of Knowledge and the exile from the garden are a blessing for humanity because it enabled people to wander the earth and discover new and exciting worlds. Eve is blessed with the God-like ability to give life. The three special commandments that were given to Eve, and to all other women, capture their unique attributes and the blessings they evince.

TAMAR BIALA

The Ever-Turning Sword

Man is created in the image of God, according to the account at the beginning of the book of Genesis (1:27). Jewish philosophy has dealt exten-
sively with the meaning of the term "image of God" and with the question
of how humanity resembles God. Tamar Biala's midrash explores this
analogy while asking a daring and revolutionary question: How does God
resemble the human being He created? In the book of Genesis, man is
created as a lone, incomplete creature in need of assistance in order to
discover his feminine side—a description that can serve to shed light on
the nature of divinity. Biala's feminist theological reading contends that
like man, God is also a lone, incomplete being waiting for the work of creation to be concluded so that God too might become complete.

*And He stationed east of the Garden of Eden the cherubs and the fiery
ever-turning sword* (Gen 3:24).

Tamar said: *For I am nearly limping on my side, and my pain is with me always*
(Ps 38:18).

The Holy Blessed One planted Adam in the Garden of Eden and said:
Let the one created in My image come and do all that I did; work it, as is
said of Me: *And God saw all that He had made* (Gen 1:31); guard it, as is
said of Me: *God protects the simple* (Ps 116: 6); let him not eat of the Tree of
Knowledge, so that he not die, as is said of Me: *And the Lord God truly is a
living God* (Jer 10:10). At the moment that The Holy Blessed One said to
him: *do not eat of it* (Gen 2:17)—that Adam not feel—so that he not die.
Adam fell silent, and his soul fell silent too.

The Holy Blessed One said: *It is not good for Adam to be alone; I will make
a helping match for him* (Gen 2:18). God fashioned from the ground all the
beasts of the field and all the birds of the sky and said: Let the one created
in My image come and do all that I did, and give them names, as is said of
Me: *And he declared their name Adam on the day they were created* (Gen 5:2).

Adam declared names but did not find a helping match for himself, and he spiraled downward and downward into silence until he found himself in a great crater, alone.

The Holy Blessed One could not bear to witness His own suffering reflected back to Him. The Holy Blessed One brought sleep down upon Adam. Once Adam's limbs relaxed, The Holy Blessed One took an ever-turning sword and cut him along his side. He brought the female side to the male side and stood from afar to see what would become of them. And God was left, alone. And the male side turned to the female side and said in relief and wonder: *This one is it, bone of my bones and flesh of my flesh ... this one will be called woman* (Gen 2:23–24). And they became one flesh.

And He wailed and beat His heart, *For I am nearly limping on my side, and my pain is with me always* (Ps 38:18). How can I, alone and by myself, meet My other side? Let the one created in My image come and do all that I did, draw the sword and slice me in half and bring the other side to me ... *And the Lord God called out to Adam and said: Where are you?* (Gen 3:9).

And He stationed east of the Garden of Eden the cherubs and the fiery ever-turning sword (Gen 3:24).

And He waited.

Commentary

This midrash is structured as a *petihta*, a literary form frequently employed by the ancient rabbis in aggadic midrash. It begins with a quote from Psalms, *For I am nearly limping on my side, and my pain is with me always* (38:18), and only after a long and extensive exegesis does the midrash finally conclude with a return to this verse by way of a verse about the fiery ever-turning sword in the Garden of Eden (Gen 3:24).

Biala links the verse from Psalms with the description of the creation of man and woman. God asks man, who was created in His image, to imitate Him and engage in acts similar to those that He performs: to work, to guard and protect, and to refrain from eating from the Tree of Knowledge so that he might live forever. The midrash suggests that the prohibition on eating from the Tree of Knowledge stems from the concern that partaking of this fruit will awaken in man feelings and desires that will ultimately lead to his death. God tries to protect humanity so that they will not experience life in a manner that will culminate in death.

But this protection comes at an unexpected cost: Man, who was placed in a safe bubble, ultimately lost his vitality.

God is aware of the consequences of His actions and does not want man to remain in this "not good" place (see Gen 2:18). In order to improve Adam's situation, He creates animals. He commands Adam to give names to the animals, which is a way in which Adam imitates God and continues the divine work of naming. But Adam does not find a "helping match" for himself, his life force dwindles, and his loneliness deepens.

God finds it difficult to bear witness to man's situation, because it mirrors His own loneliness and pain. And so God takes a fiery, ever-turning sword and splits Adam into two "sides," an allusion to a classical midrash (Genesis Rabbah 8:1) in which Adam is created with two halves, one male and one female, connected back-to-back. According to this classical midrash, God cut Adam into two, and thus the bond between man and woman represents complementarity and completion. Biala describes how these two sides encountered one another for the first time, while God watched from afar to see what would happen to Adam. The male side recognized the female side and the two became one flesh, and thus Adam said, *flesh of my flesh* (Gen 2:23).

At this point Biala offers a surprising shift in perspective, turning our attention to what happened to God at that moment.

God's loneliness, which was previously reflected in man's loneliness, has only deepened. Perhaps the goal of the creation of man was to alleviate God's loneliness, but instead man found companionship in woman and God remained alone. At this point, the connection to the verse from Psalms has become apparent: God attests that He is "nearly limping on my side," namely, that He is ready to meet His other half, because in His current state, "my pain is with me always." God admits that He needs help so as to meet His other side. God also needs to be split so that God's two sides can encounter one another.

At this point, the petiḥta concludes by circling back to the verse from Genesis about the fiery, ever-turning sword. The petiḥta thus serves to juxtapose two verses from different points in the Bible, one from Genesis and one from Psalms.

At the conclusion of the midrash, God turns to man to request that man imitate God and use the fiery ever-turning sword to split God into two halves that may encounter one another. God calls to Adam and asks

Where are you? Even after Adam and Eve are no longer in Eden, the question continues to resound. God places the cherubs and the fiery ever-turning sword at the entrance to Eden so that Adam and Eve will someday return and understand that it is their role to use that sword to redeem God. To this day, according to the midrash, God continues to wait for humanity to redeem the fullness of God.

This midrash proposes that we understand divinity by means of the man created in His image. According to this theology, God resembles humanity—He is needy, complex, and multifaceted. Just as God is responsible for humanity, God expects humanity to be responsible for God. Moreover, our patriarchal conception of God reflects just one aspect of divinity; if we are content with this conception of God alone, we have only a partial understanding of God's nature. God needs humanity in order to reveal the feminine side of God. Only then, through the encounter between both aspects of divinity, can God become whole and can God's full identity be revealed to His people.

TWO

Matriarchs and Patriarchs

RUTI TIMOR

The Tears of Salt

This midrash deals with the conflict between a divine command and natural human instinct. In the biblical story Lot and the members of his family are instructed to flee Sodom and its environs because The Holy Blessed One is about to overturn the city and destroy its foundations. Lot is commanded not to look back when he flees. The Torah describes how Lot's wife violates this injunction and looks back. As a result, she is punished: she is turned into a pillar of salt. The rabbinic sages regarded Lot's wife as emblematic of all the sinners in her city, who were notoriously abusive to strangers. In this midrash, Ruti Timor offers a refreshing reading, suggesting another explanation for her transformation into a pillar of salt. Timor's explanation serves to exonerate Lot's wife, claiming that she was unaware of the injunction not to look back. The midrash offers a sympathetic reading of her behavior as a mother who experienced tremendous loss and never managed to overcome it and portrays her as a worthy and rational woman who met a tragic fate.

And as they were bringing them out, he said: Escape for your life, do not look behind you and don't stand still anywhere on the plain, escape to the hill country, lest you be slain (Gen 19:17).

As the flames began to devour the houses of Sodom, Lot said to his wife, quick, get some bread and a skein of water and we'll run for our lives or be killed.

She said, we'll save ourselves, and our daughters will stay here?

And how do we know Lot had other daughters who stayed behind? At the outset it says *And the men said to Lot: Who else have you here? A son-in-law? Your sons? Your daughters?* (Gen 19:12) And later it says *Get up, and take your wife and your two remaining daughters* (Gen 19:15). We learn from this that the married daughters stayed behind with their husbands.

He said to her: Quiet, woman! Do as I say!

She was silent.

And the angels took them out of the city, and Lot did not say to his wife a word of what they said. He walked sure-footed, and she lagged behind him. Her heart was heavy upon her, she looked back and saw her city, her family, and her property going up in flames.

And his wife looked behind, and became a pillar of salt (Gen 19:26). Tear after tear dripped from her eyes, and the tears grew fuller and fuller, stronger and stronger, until they became a pillar of salt. She stumbled and fell, and stirred no more.

And Lot did not look back.

Our Sages of Blessed Memory said, *with salt she sinned and with salt was she punished.* And I say, she sinned not, but was punished all the same.

Commentary

This midrash struggles with the negative attitude toward Lot's wife that pervades rabbinic literature. Timor concludes her midrash with the words, "With salt she sinned and with salt she was punished," an allusion to a midrash (Genesis Rabbah 51:5) that teaches that when the angels came to Lot's house, his wife refused to welcome them into her home. The midrash relates that in an attempt to notify all the city's inhabitants of the visitors' arrival so that they would torment the newcomers, she went from neighbor to neighbor asking to borrow salt so as to prepare food for her guests. And so it came to pass: The people of Sodom surrounded Lot's house and demanded that he release his guests so that they could rape them. The midrash in Genesis Rabbah concludes that Lot's wife was therefore punished measure-for-measure. Since she sinned with salt, her punishment was that she was transformed into a pillar of salt. She died like the other inhabitants of her city and was not among the survivors.

Ruti Timor chooses to consider the story of Lot's wife from a different angle, empathically identifying with her as a woman. She imagines a dialogue between Lot and his wife during those frightening moments when they had to flee from Sodom quickly. Lot explains to his wife that they are risking their lives if they do not flee quickly. Lot's wife finds it difficult to accept that they are supposed to save themselves and leave their two married daughters behind.

Timor bases her reading on a midrash (Pirkei d'Rabbi Eliezer 25) that teaches that Lot had four daughters, two of whom were married and two of whom were single. This midrash is based on a close reading of the biblical story. Lot declares, *Look, I have two daughters who have not known a man* (Gen 19:8), thereby attesting that he has two unmarried daughters. But later the Bible relates that Lot's daughters are married: *So Lot went out and spoke to his sons-in-law, who had married his daughters, and said, "Up, get out of this place, for the Lord is about to destroy the city." But he seemed to his sons-in-law as one who jests* (Gen 19:14). The midrash resolves this contradiction by explaining that Lot and his wife had two single daughters who fled the city with them and two married daughters who were left behind. Timor explains that Lot's wife turned into a pillar of salt after she turned back to see what became of her married daughters.

By engaging in her own close reading of the biblical verses, Timor offers an original interpretation of the story. When the angels command Lot to flee, they tell him, *Flee for your life! Do not look behind you, nor stop anywhere in the plain; flee to the hills, lest you be swept away* (Gen 19:17). This injunction in Hebrew is stated in the singular, addressed only to Lot, and the entire exchange takes place only between him and the angels. Timor thus concludes that Lot did not inform his wife of what he had been told, and thus she was unaware of the injunction not to look back.

Timor emphasizes the distinction between Lot, who remained safe because he heard and heeded the angels' instructions, and his wife, who lagged behind him with a heavy heart. Lot's wife's weeping bespeaks the suffering of all those who bear witness to a tragedy that they are unable to prevent.

According to Timor, Lot's wife was not transformed into a pillar of salt as a form of punishment but rather as a natural consequence of her weeping. Her tears, which gained force and continued to accumulate, turned her into a pillar of salt. Her ability to feel pain, or perhaps her inability to avoid it, stands in contrast to her husband's stony forward gaze.

The pillar of salt in this midrash serves to represent the way in which a person's heart can turn to stone after great loss. As Emily Dickinson wrote, "After great loss a formal feeling comes / The Nerves sit ceremonious, like tombs / The stiff Heart questions." Lot's wife was shattered by her pain, and she was unable to keep living or to start over after the tragedy.

According to Timor, Lot's wife was not guilty of sin, and yet she was nonetheless afflicted. She was a victim of injustice, for she innocently and unknowingly violated a divine injunction. The midrash thus offers an empathic portrayal of a mother who was unable to overcome the loss of her daughters, encouraging us to suspend our harsh judgment of others and to judge all men and women generously.

NAAMA ELDAR

Sarah's Trials

> *And it came to pass after those matters God tested Abraham* (Gen 22:1). The story of the binding of Isaac begins with these words, but the sages asserted that Abraham was tested with ten trials, all of which he passed (Avot 5:3). The sages were trying to understand why Abraham was chosen to be the forefather of the Jewish nation and to portray him as a paragon of virtue for future generations.
>
> In her midrash about Sarah's trials, Naama Eldar presents ten parallel trials that Sarah withstood. Eldar seeks to correct the imbalance in those stories in the book of Genesis that place Abraham front and center. She relays various stories from Sarah's perspective, thereby offering new moral, existential, and theological perspectives on familiar tales. In so doing, she expands and enriches the significance of what it means to successfully endure a divine trial, and she presents Sarah too as a paragon of virtue—one who is worthy, in her own right, of becoming the foremother of the Jewish nation.

Ten times was Abraham our father put to the test, and he withstood them all. This tells how great was the love of our father Abraham (Mishnah Avot 5:3).

Ten times was Sarah our mother put to the test, and she withstood them all. This tells how strong she was, and how great was her hope.

That she was barren and without a child;

And she was taken from her birthplace and father's home to an unknown land;

That she was asked to lie on Abraham's behalf on coming to Egypt and being taken to Pharaoh's home where there was done to her what was done to her;

That her Egyptian maidservant bore a child for Abraham her man;

And her maidservant made light of her;

And her man said to her *do with her as you see fit* (Gen 16:6);

That she heard from the opening of the tent the news of Isaac's birth;

That she waited many years for Abraham her husband to return from his journeys and wars;

That she was asked to lie on Abraham's behalf on coming to Gerar, and being taken to Avimelekh's home where there was done to her what was done to her;

That her son was taken from her to be sacrificed on the altar.

Commentary

In her narration of the stories of Genesis, Eldar identifies ten trying circumstances in which Sarah had to make a difficult decision about how to conduct herself. Eldar notes that in each case, Sarah behaved appropriately and withstood the trial.

The first trial Sarah had to endure was her barrenness, which involved two challenges: she had to deal with her public image as a barren woman, as well as with the private pain of not having a child. There are various ways in which a woman could respond under such circumstances, and Eldar notes that in this case, as with all subsequent trials, Sarah's response was exemplary.

The second trial was that Sarah agreed to leave her homeland and her father's house and to travel to an unfamiliar land. In general, it is Abraham's greatness in heeding God's command that is emphasized, but Eldar notes that Sarah too had to agree to come along. She could have chosen instead to stay back.

The third trial relates to Abraham and Sarah's descent to Egypt in the wake of the famine in Canaan. Sarah chose to cooperate with Abraham and say that she was his sister, even though this meant that she was taken into Pharaoh's palace, despite her being a married woman. Eldar regards Sarah's willingness to lie and to live in close quarters with a strange man in order to save her husband's life as an act of heroism and as another trial that Sarah withstood.

Sarah passed her fourth trial when she took the initiative to give her maidservant Hagar to Abraham so that he would be able to have children with her.

The fifth trial was the disparagement she endured from Hagar after her maidservant learned that she was pregnant. Sarah had to deal with the painful and perhaps unanticipated emotions that Hagar's pregnancy awakened in her, a development that undermined her own status and her place in Abraham's household.

Sarah's sixth trial was when Abraham charged her with the responsibility to decide how to respond to Hagar's hurtful treatment.

Sarah's seventh trial was the news that she would become pregnant at age ninety, which she overheard casually while standing at the entrance to the tent, as if she were merely peripheral.

The eighth trial that Sarah endured was the years in which she waited patiently at home while Abraham journeyed through Canaan and fought against the four kings. Eldar calls our attention to the underappreciated challenges faced by those women back on the home front, as it were.

The ninth trial Sarah endured was when she and Abraham arrived at Gerar and he asked her to say that she was his sister. The Torah does not describe what Sarah endured in Avimelekh's home, but Eldar suggests that Sarah was confronted with a trying situation, as was the case when she was taken to Pharaoh's palace.

The tenth trial was the binding of Isaac. In her description of Sarah's last trial, Eldar focuses on the experience of women whose children's lives are endangered on account of a system of beliefs or values. What is the significance of the fact that Sarah withstood this trial? Did she pass the test because she did not prevent Abraham from taking Isaac to the altar? Is she being applauded for her silent compliance? Or perhaps it was that she did not fall apart in spite of her staunch opposition to Abraham's blind obedience? Eldar invites us to consider the role that women must play under such circumstances.

RIVKAH LUBITCH

Sarah and the Sacrifice of Isaac

The story of the binding of Isaac is a foundational tale in Jewish tradition. Commentators in every generation have tried to address the profound questions this story raises: What does God ask of us as believers? How can we understand Abraham's readiness to sacrifice his son? Rivkah Lubitch's midrash fills in a gap in the biblical story. She describes what happened to Sarah throughout this incident and furnishes her with a significant role in the proceedings. Lubitch proposes that Sarah was the first one confronted with this trial, and she refused to obey the divine command. When she discovered that Abraham was on his way to sacrifice Isaac, she entreated God in prayer, asking mercy for her husband who, as she saw it, acted inappropriately. It was thanks to her prayer that tragedy was averted and Isaac was spared.

The midrash presents an unorthodox theological stance regarding the place of sacrifice in religious life. Lubitch proposes an alternative model for the relationship between humans and God, one based on the experience of parenting. As she sees it, the responsibility for one's children is the ultimate value, and it cannot be contradicted by any divine command.

And it came to pass after those matters (Gen 22:1).

Those matters, the matters with Sarah. And God tested Sarah.

And the angel said to her: *Take your son, your only one, whom you have loved, Isaac, and take him to the land of Moriah, and offer him up* (Gen 22:2).

And Sarah said: No. Because a mother does not slaughter her child.

And early in the morning, Sarah awoke, stunned to see that neither Isaac nor Abraham was there. She lifted her arms to God in heaven and said: Master of the Universe, I know that one who slaughters his son in the name of God will in the end be left without a son or God. Forgive Abraham, who was mistaken about this. Please remember that it did not occur to a mother to offer her son up to God, and save the boy from him.

At that moment *Abraham stretched out his hand to the knife to slay his son* (Gen 22:10). And the angel of God called out to him and said: *Do not lay your hand on the boy, and do not do anything to him, for now I know that you are God-fearing* (Gen 22:12), even though you did not withhold your son. And this is why it was said *whatever Sarah tells you, heed her voice* (Gen 21:12) and as a result *for in Isaac your seed will have a name* (Gen 21:12).

Commentary

The story of the binding of Isaac begins with the words, *And it came to pass after those matters.* The Hebrew word for "matters," *dvarim,* can also mean discussions. The midrash in Genesis Rabbah (55:4) asks about the nature of the discussions that preceded and precipitated the trial of the binding of Isaac. Various answers are proposed: There was a dialogue between Abraham and God, or between Ishmael and Isaac. Rivkah Lubitch provides her own answer to this question, and it is one that involves Sarah in the biblical narrative. According to Lubitch, the exchange of words that preceded the binding of Isaac took place between Sarah and God. God tested Sarah, commanding her exactly as He then commanded Abraham: *Take your son, your only one, whom you have loved, Isaac, and take him to the land of Moriah, and offer him up.* Sarah, reacting immediately and decisively out of a clear maternal instinct, refused to accede to the divine command. As Lubitch sees it, Sarah passed the divine test.

The next morning, Sarah is horrified to discover that Abraham and Isaac are nowhere to be found. She understands that God must have given the same command to Abraham and that Abraham thought that in order to fulfill the divine command, he had to overcome his own emotions and sacrifice his son. Sarah takes immediate action. She lifts her arms to God in prayer, insisting that Abraham has acted wrongly, and that in the end, he will lose both his son and his faith. As Sarah sees it, people attribute cruel instincts to God in order to justify their own terrible behavior, which in fact contradicts the true will of God. According to this theological stance, God furnished us with parental responsibility and with a love for our children, which also serve as the basis for God's relationship with His believers. Thus, the paternal and maternal instincts are also deep religious instincts that should guide our behavior in relation to God. For a father to sacrifice his son is religiously problematic because it destroys the relationships within a family and the connection with God. Sarah is so certain of the rightness of her perspective that she pleads with God to forgive Abraham and spare Isaac by the merit of her own refusal.

At that very instant, God stops Abraham from sacrificing his son. The angel explains to Abraham that even though he did not withhold his son, He still knows that Abraham is God-fearing. But Sarah was in the right, and thus God reminds Abraham *Whatever Sarah tells you, heed her voice* (Gen 21:12). By the merit of Sarah's intervention, Isaac was saved, and Abraham's seed would endure.

Lubitch's midrash incorporates women into the foundational tales of our tradition. According to the theological stance that underlies her version of the binding of Isaac, the maternal instinct and the sober, clear-eyed perspective of women are fundamental elements of Jewish existence and of the religious experience more generally.

Stirrings

In Jewish culture, the story of the binding of Isaac has become a symbol of the human being's readiness to sacrifice that which is most precious to us on account of his or her faith in God. In this midrash, Bilha Kritzer Ariha challenges this reading. She criticizes the biblical Abraham for the alacrity with which he obeyed God's command to slaughter his son. She also indirectly criticizes God's decision to test Abraham in this manner. In this midrash, Kritzer Ariha elaborates on the biblical story, enabling us to hear other voices that she imagines inside Abraham's heart. She also gives voice to the various angels who challenge the appropriateness of this trial and its consequences and may in fact reflect other voices within God.

And Abraham woke up early in the morning and saddled his donkey and took with him his two lads (Gen 22:3).

Don't read his two "lads," *ne'arav,* but rather *ne'urav,* his awakenings—for two voices stirred in him.

One voice saying, "Here I am."

And another voice saying, "And what about Isaac? Will he too say, 'Here I am'? And Sarah, will she say it as well? If You seek to test me, then test away, but don't lay a hand on the boy!"

And the first voice says, again, "Here I am."

And the second voice says, "Here I am, for generations. That all Israel should learn from my deed. And if I sacrifice the boy, Israel will sacrifice their children in all the generations to come. Sacrifice to Moloch, to rebelliousness, to war, to stubborn-headedness."

And the first voice says, again, "Here I am."

And the two of them walked together (22:18).

Something else: Don't read *and Abraham saddled (va-ya-chavosh) his donkey (chamoro)* but rather *he overcame (va-yikhvosh) his mercies (rachamav).*

For Abraham was holding back his tears as he went, but they broke through from his eyes and ascended all the way to The Master of the Universe, and said before Him "look at Your servant Abraham, see his lowliness before You, see that he isn't begging for mercy for himself and his son, like he did for Sodom, because of his trust in You. Please, revoke Your decree."

And there Abraham built the altar, and laid out the wood (Gen 22:9).

And the angels on high gathered together group by group. These saying, "he'll slaughter," and those saying, "he won't slaughter."

These saying, "test him" and those saying, "have mercy on him."

And he bound Isaac his son and placed him on the altar above the wood (22:9). And the voices of the angels on high grew stronger, and Abraham's tears burned, and seraphs and holy creatures rose aloft in great tumult, and the ministering angels flapped their wings.

And only one of the lesser angels got up and departed from the Heavenly Throne and called out "Abraham! Abraham! . . . Do not raise your hand against the boy."

Some say, of this it was written, *He confirms the word of His servant and fulfills the counsel of His angels* (Isa 44:26).

And some say, of this it was written, *For He commands His angels to you, that they watch over you in all your pathways* (Ps 91:11).

Commentary

The verses in Genesis 22 describe how Abraham engaged very matter-of-factly in the preparations to fulfill the divine command to sacrifice his son. Kritzer Ariha reads the word *ne'arav* (his lads) exegetically as signifying *ne'urav* (his awakenings), a reference to the inner struggle that she imagines took over Abraham's consciousness on that terrible morning. Those awakenings, or voices, express conflicting positions regarding the divine command. Abraham debates whether he should answer the divine command affirmatively and decisively by saying, "Here I am," or whether he should reject the possibility of sacrificing his son entirely.

Abraham's dilemma is presented in conflicting inner voices. The argument against has significant force: Abraham does not know if Isaac and Sarah are ready for this act. Moreover, Abraham, the father of the Jewish nation, is a role model for his descendants. That same inner voice warns him that in sacrificing his son, he will be setting a detrimental educational, religious, and moral example for future generations. In spite of these misgivings, the voice that says, "Here I am," answers back repeatedly, reflecting the part of Abraham that responds to God immediately and seeks to fulfill the divine command. This voice wins out, and Abraham sets out on his journey. Kritzer Ariha understands the Bible's words *and the two of them walked together* (22:18) as referring not to Abraham and Isaac but to the two voices within Abraham accompanying him as he fulfills the divine decree.

The dilemma within Abraham intensifies in Kritzer Ariha's exegesis on the verb "saddled" in the phrase *And Abraham saddled his donkey.* Employing a familiar midrashic technique, Kritzer Ariha substitutes one Hebrew letter for another, Chet for Kaf—both of which sound the same—thereby changing the verb to mean "restrain" or "overcome." Deploying yet another midrashic technique, she flips the letters in *chamoro* ("his donkey") so the word instead reads *rachamav* (his mercies). The dry description of saddling the donkey becomes a description of the drama unfolding within Abraham, who is fighting back tears. Although Abraham tries as hard as he can to restrain himself from opposing the divine command, he is unable to stop crying. On account of his ambivalence, his tears rise to the heavenly throne and plead with God to have mercy on Abraham and his son and avert the decree of the divine command. Even though Abraham ultimately sets off to sacrifice his son, the midrash describes him as a torn and conflicted figure, plagued by doubt and questions.

The second part of the midrash deals with the dynamic that takes place in the heavenly realm while Abraham prepares the altar to sacrifice his son. The biblical story relates that an angel of God prevents Abraham from slaughtering his son (Gen 22:11, 15). The midrash in Genesis Rabbah (56:8) describes how the angels gather "group by group" and cry out in panic and despair at the prospect of the imminent slaughter. Kritzer Ariha invokes this image, but she places other words in the angels' mouths. She suggests that the angels were not a united front but divided into two opposing camps— much like the opposing voices within Abraham. Some of the angels assume that Abraham will fulfill the divine command and slaughter his son, while others assume that he will not go through with it. Some of them turn to God and encourage Him to continue with the trial, whereas others plead with God to have mercy on Abraham and put an end to it. As Abraham gets closer and closer to performing the act, the voices grow louder, both in heaven and within Abraham, who cries while preparing the altar. The tension reaches a climax.

Amid all this confusion and chaos, Kritzer Ariha describes how one small angel departs from the heavenly throne and decides to take action. The angel calls out to Abraham to stop the sacrifice, thereby preventing him from slaughtering his son. Kritzer Ariha's description of this angel's departure from the heavenly throne implies that this angel is part of the divine rather than a separate entity. And so, it seems that the various angels and the confusion they create are depicted as a sort of internal confusion within God. The verb used for "depart" (*poresh*), which refers to separating oneself from a crowd, heightens how unusual this act is. In the face of an internal struggle taking place in the human realm and another internal struggle taking place in the divine realm, only one small angel bestirs to take action.

The midrash concludes with "Some say" and "And some say." According to the characteristic style of rabbinic midrash, this is a later addition, offering two different interpretations of the conclusion of the midrash. The first references a verse from Isaiah's prophecy of consolation (44:26) that describes how God, in response to the advice of His servant and His angels, will once again establish and redeem Jerusalem. This dynamic is applied to the story of the binding of Isaac to explain how God, in spite of commanding Abraham to sacrifice his son, accepted the advice of the angel and put an end to the trial. Isaiah's statement that God "fulfills the counsel of His angels" is read as implying that by answering to the inner voice that the angel represents, God in fact fulfills that part of divinity that wished to revoke the original charge to Abraham.

The second interpretation is bolder. It is based on a verse from Psalms (91:11) that describes how God commands His angels to watch over human beings in all their ways. But when applied to the story of the binding of Isaac, the meaning of the verse is turned on its head: God commands His angels to watch over God's own ways. The small angel, who watched over God's ways, intervened at the moment of truth and prevented the sacrifice that God had demanded.

Bilha Kritzer Ariha presents us with a complex, multifaceted world in which there are no clear and easy answers. The different voices and the internal conflicts are very real and very much warranted, and they in no way reflect a lack of faith. At the same time, the conclusion of the midrash attests that sometimes it is necessary to break away and depart to silence the inner voices and act in a way that will redeem both the upper and lower realms.

TAMAR BIALA

And Where Was Sarah?

The biblical story of the binding of Isaac recounts the actions of Abraham and his son and is silent about Sarah, Isaac's mother. This midrash offers five different accounts of Sarah's role in that story. These accounts are attributed to five biblical women who are very different from one another. Each one tells a story about Sarah that reflects her own life and is influenced by her own inner struggles and her moral and theological stance.

And Abraham rose early in the morning and saddled his donkey and took his two lads with him, and Isaac his son, and he split wood for the offering, and rose and went to the place that God had said to him (Gen 22:3).

And where was Sarah at the time that Abraham gathered the donkey, the lads, and their son Isaac, and split the wood, when the only thing he did not take with them was a sheep?

Jezebel said: Sarah was of one mind with Abraham and she too sought not to withhold her only son, whom she loved. For Abraham and Sarah both worshipped the same God, and would convert people to Him; he the men, and she, the women.

Dinah said: Sarah was in the tent and didn't know of their departure, for ever since she had returned from the palace of Avimelekh, her husband had told her, *All the princess's treasure is inward* (Ps 45:14). She would hide within the tent and no longer took notice of other people.

The Great Woman of Shunam said: Sarah hurried after Abraham to stop him from slaughtering their son, but judges and officers at the gates prevented her, as is written, *Then the watchmen found me as they went about the city; they beat me, they bruised me, they tore the shawl off my shoulders, those watchmen of the walls* (Song 5:7) until she returned to her tent and buried herself in it.

Hagar came and said: Sarah did not go looking for her husband Abraham

or her son Isaac at all, and God knew it would be like that. When the Holy
Blessed One saw that she sought to send away Abraham's first son to the
desert, mercilessly, He feared that she wouldn't have mercy on her own son
either, her only one, and so He spoke to Abraham with precision: *take your
son, yours, and not hers, for through Isaac, seed will be called by your name*
(Gen 21:12). By your name, yours and not by hers.

And Tanot, Jephthah's daughter, said: That's not how it was. Sarah was
a prophetess, for she foresaw by the Holy Spirit that fathers would in the
future sacrifice their children, and that High Priests in the future would look
from afar and not undo those vows and beliefs, and she saw how between
the two of them those sad ones would be lost to the world and she didn't
know how to protect those children, and was silent. And this was her mis-
take. For the Holy Blessed One had told Abraham *Whatever Sarah says to
you, listen to her voice* (Gen 21:12), but He had not said those words to her.

Commentary

Sarah is not mentioned in the biblical story of the binding of Isaac in Genesis 22, and this midrash seeks to fill in the gaps. The midrash opens with
a question: Where was Sarah when Abraham and Isaac left the house?
According to the biblical account, it took a while to get organized for the
trip: Abraham saddled his donkey, split the wood, and took along Isaac
and his lads. It's hard to believe that Sarah was oblivious to it all. In Biala's
midrash, five women attempt to answer this question: Jezebel, Dinah, the
Great Woman of Shunam, Hagar, and Tanot.

The first answer is suggested by Queen Jezebel, the wife of Ahab king
of Israel, who incited her husband to join her in worshipping Ba'al and in
building idolatrous altars (see 2 Kgs 16:31). She proposes that Abraham and
Sarah were essentially of one mind. The midrash in Genesis Rabbah (39:14)
explains how Abraham and Sarah worked together to convert the people
who joined them. Jezebel notes that here, too, Abraham and Sarah saw eye
to eye, and Sarah agreed to sacrifice Isaac in accordance with the divine
command. Child sacrifice is regarded in the Torah as a form of forbidden
idolatrous worship (Deut 18:1), but Jezebel viewed it as a deep expression
of the desire to give of oneself to God.

The second response is suggested by Dinah, the daughter of Leah and

Jacob, who was kidnapped and raped by Shechem, the son of Hamor (Gen 34). Dinah identifies with Sarah, who was also forcibly taken to the castle of a foreign king (Gen 20). She attributes a sort of posttraumatic response to Sarah, similar to her own response to her experience with Shechem. Both women seek to hide inside their tents and do not want to have to look at men. Abraham encourages this behavior in Sarah, quoting a verse from Psalms: *All the princess's treasure is inward* (Ps 45:14). Sarah's confinement in the tent left her depressed and indifferent to everything that was taking place in the world outside, and so she did not object when Abraham left with Isaac on that fateful morning.

The third answer is proposed by the Great Woman of Shunam, who, like Sarah, experienced a prolonged period of barrenness before ultimately meriting to birth a son (2 Kgs 4:14). But one day her son fell ill and died suddenly, and the Great Woman of Shunam went to cry out to the prophet for help and was repulsed by his assistant (27). When the Great Woman of Shunam offers her account of the binding of Isaac, she envisions Sarah recreated in her own image, running after Abraham in an attempt to save her son's life. But Sarah does not manage to reach Abraham in time because she is stopped by judges and officers at the gates. Unlike the Great Woman of Shunam, who was ultimately able to save her son, Sarah returned empty-handed and sank into a deep depression.

The fourth answer is offered by Hagar, Sarah's maidservant. Hagar questions Sarah's maternal instincts and her love for her son Isaac, since, after all, she banished Abraham and Hagar's son Ishmael to the wilderness and showed him no mercy (Gen 21). According to Hagar, God deliberately directed the commandment to Abraham alone because He did not trust that Sarah would protect her son. It is for this reason that when God promised Abraham that his descendants would be from Isaac's line, God used the second-person singular rather than the plural, which would have implied Sarah: *For through Isaac, seed will be called in your [singular] name* (Gen 21:12).

The fifth and final answer is offered by Tanot, the daughter of Jephthah, who first appears in Lubitch's midrash about Jephthah's daughter (see page 89). Tanot argues that Sarah was a prophetess, a claim advanced in the Talmud as well (b.Megillah 14a). In her prophecy, Sarah foresaw the fate of Jephthah's daughter, whose father would take a vow to sacrifice the first creature to exit his house when he returned victorious from battle. She knew that, tragically, it would be Jephthah's daughter who would be the first to emerge. She also foresaw what the sages would describe in the midrash (Tanhuma Behukotai 7), namely, that there was in fact a halakhic way in which to invalidate the vow. Jephthah could have sought out the assistance of Pinchas, who was the High Priest at the time, but he was too proud to turn to him for help and instead waited for Pinchas to come to him. Pinchas, in turn, waited for Jephthah to seek his aid, and "between the two of them, that poor woman perished from the world." The Tanhuma describes a situation in which neither the parents nor the rabbis were able to find a way to put a stop to child sacrifice, a tragedy that drove Sarah to despair and rendered her unable to act. But the midrash concludes that Sarah was in fact unaware of her own power to change reality. Biala blames God for telling Abraham alone that "whatever Sarah says to you, listen to her voice" (Gen 21:12). God did not ensure that Sarah, too, overheard this charge.

This conclusion cries out against a patriarchal reality in which women truly do have the power to intervene and avert catastrophe, in both the domestic and the political spheres, and yet they fail to do so because they are so convinced of their existential oppression that they are unaware of their own strength.

HAGIT RAPPEL

In the Presence of His Wife

Isaac and Rebecca experienced infertility before they were granted a child. The midrash addresses the loneliness that spouses sometimes feel in their married lives, the difficulty of accepting one's partner's shortcomings, and the sense of distress when one's partner does not share in one's sorrow.

Only when God teaches Isaac and Rebecca to look compassionately at one another and to accept one another's deficiencies do they develop a deep bond that leads to their shared prayer. Only when their own relationship is repaired do they become fertile and conceive.

And Isaac appealed to God in the presence of his wife, for she was barren, and Rebecca his wife conceived (Gen 25:21).

And Rebecca was barren. She had no sons or daughters. In the nights, her tears would dissolve the pillow beneath her head, and in the days, she wished she were like one of the sheep in Isaac's sheepfold, for God had granted him many lambs.

She whispered countless prayers, but her lips alone moved, and her voice was not to be heard. Not on earth, and not in heavenly vaults.

And Isaac? He would go off to meditate in the fields, devoting his heart and soul to establishing the afternoon minhah prayer, and there was no room left in his heart for his wife's tremulous tears.

And she took the veil and covered up (Gen 24:65).

She dropped to the ground, took her veil, and covered her face, partitioning her from her husband, so that none of *her waves and breakers can surge* (Ps 42:8) toward him, and whatever flaw she may have, he wouldn't accept.

Rebecca did as all women do: a candle burned in the tent from one

Sabbath eve to the next; there was blessing to be found in her dough; and a cloud rested atop the tent as it was in Sarah's days. Rebecca comforts Isaac on the death of his mother, but there is no comforter for her.

And Isaac appealed to God in his wife's presence, for she was barren . . .

He would stand in his corner and pray, and she would stand and pray in hers, and they were not answered, because their prayer was divided, not flowing from one spring. The Holy Blessed One saw their distress and opened up their eyes. Isaac and Rebecca stood face to face; he in the presence of his wife and she in the presence of her husband. They removed the partitions between their hearts and saw eye to eye. Rebecca saw Isaac's splendor but also his flaws—he does not dig wells like his father Abraham did, but merely preserves them. And Isaac saw his partner in marriage, her beauty, and purity of heart, but also her flaws, the suffering of her barrenness, the pain of the words people used to speak about her: "a daughter of evil, and a sister of evil too."

They took upon themselves to live in love, in togetherness, in peace, in friendship. And some say: it was from that wave of mercy that their son Jacob drew the strength to roll that big stone off the top of the well.

And Rebecca conceived.

Commentary

The first part of the midrash describes Rebecca's distress on account of her barrenness. She is dealing with her pain and hardship on her own, assailed both night and day by her anguish. Her prayers are silent and voiceless, like Hannah's prayer for a child (see 1 Sam 1:13). Rebecca's husband Isaac is unaware of her pain and does not come to her aid because he is too preoccupied with establishing the afternoon minhah prayer (see b.Berakhot 26b). Toward that end, he goes out to the fields for long stretches of time alone.

The second part of the midrash underscores the rift between Rebecca and Isaac, based on the description of Rebecca covering herself in a veil when she first sees Isaac (Gen 24:64–65). Rappel reads this description as part of an ongoing dynamic in their relationship. The veil is a symbol of the divide between them. Isaac does not look at Rebecca, and thus he is unaware of her distress and pain. Rebecca, for her part, continues to conduct herself like all other women, following in Sarah's footsteps with the candle burning in her tent, the blessing in the dough she bakes, and the cloud above her tent (see Genesis Rabbah 60:16). Rebecca consoles Isaac after the death of his mother, but Rebecca herself remains unconsoled (Gen 24:67).

The third part of the midrash begins with a description of the rift between the couple: they pray separately, each standing in a different corner (as per Rashi's explanation of Gen 25:21). According to Rappel, this is the reason that the prayers of two such righteous individuals are not answered. Their physical barrenness becomes, for Rappel, a sign of their spiritual barrenness as well.

The change takes place when God intervenes in their lives and opens their eyes, the way He opened the eyes of Adam and Eve (Gen 3:7) and of Hagar (Gen 21:19). God causes Isaac and Rebecca to face one another and remove the barriers between them. From the moment they look at one another and accept one another's weaknesses, they succeed in establishing a fertile union. Rappel explains the verse *And Isaac appealed to God in his wife's presence* as signifying that only after Isaac stood in his wife's presence and saw the extent of her suffering on account of her barrenness did God answer his prayers. The change that takes place is not in God but in the two members of the couple. Rebecca does not just see Isaac's greatness and his splendor; she also accepts his shortcomings and his deficiencies: unlike Abraham, who dug new wells, Isaac is more passive and is primarily responsible for the upkeep of his father's wells. Isaac too is able not just to see Rebecca's beauty and innocence but also to accept her deficiencies: she is unable to move past her own pain, caused by her barrenness and by a society that mocked her because her father and brother were thieves (see Genesis Rabbah 63:4).

The ability to see the other and express empathy are what make Rebecca's pregnancy possible. The midrash concludes with the notion that in the future, these same forces of empathy and love will empower their son, Jacob, to roll the stone off the top of the well when he recognizes the suffering of those who have come to draw water (Gen 29:10). In the next generation, too, a display of empathy will ultimately give way to a fruitful marital bond.

RIVKAH LUBITCH

And Dinah Went Out

Dinah was the only daughter born to Leah after she gave birth to six sons. Dinah was also the only daughter born to any of Jacob's four wives. These midrashim examine Dinah's birth, and her rape, from a feminist perspective to illuminate issues related to raising young women in a patriarchal society, the silencing of women, and the response to rape.

And Leah conceived and bore a son ... And she conceived again and bore a son ... And she conceived again and bore a son ... And she conceived again and bore a son. . . . and she conceived and she bore Jacob a fifth son ... And Leah conceived again and bore a sixth son to Jacob ... And afterward she bore a daughter (Gen 29–30).

What is "and afterward"? After all these sons, she had a daughter.

Some interpreted "afterward" as a language of pain, others of joy.

A language of pain, for Jacob made no feast when she gave birth to Dinah, and Jacob didn't come when her mother named her; rather the call went out, a daughter is born to Jacob, and the world went on as usual.

A language of joy, for Leah had longed for a daughter. Until then, she had wanted to make her husband happy with male children and outdo her sister with sons. Once she had given birth to all these sons, she asked for nothing for herself but a daughter.

And Dinah, Leah's daughter, who she had born to Jacob (Gen 34:1).

Why did the Torah announce here, and not earlier, that Dinah was Jacob's daughter? Dinah had sat with her mother all her days until she had matured. When she came of age, she left the tent to go see the daughters of the land. Jacob said to Leah: My grandmother, Sarah, and mother, Rebecca, would stay in the tent always, a candle would be lit there, and a cloud of divine glory tied atop it. This girl's a nosy one, going to see the daughters of the land; she isn't mine. That is why the Torah said, *And Dinah, Leah's daughter, who she had born to Jacob.*

And Dinah went out (Gen 34:1).

Some interpreted this to mean, like mother, like daughter; others, to mean like father, like daughter.

Like her mother, as it says, *And Leah went out toward him* (Gen 30:16). Just as this one went out toward her husband for an act of mitzvah, so this one went out to find a husband.

Like her father, as it says, *And Jacob went out* (Gen 28:10). Just as this one went out on account of his brother, Esau, so this one went out, on account of her brothers, to find a place for herself.

And Dinah went out to see the daughters of the land.

Dinah always tagged along with her brothers. When she grew up, she saw her place wasn't with them and went out to see the daughters of the land. As it says, "Either friendship, or death."

And Dinah went out to see the daughters of the land.

Dinah was a quiet person and had no voice. Why to such an extent? Because the members of her household did not listen to her and didn't engage her in conversation, as the sages said: "Do not engage in excessive conversation with the woman." And that is why she went out to see the daughters of the land.

Dinah was like a mute, as it says, *And Dinah went out . . . to see . . .* She went out to see, not to hear. What's more, it says, *and he bedded her and abused her* and it doesn't say "and Dinah cried out." Is it conceivable that she did not? But it's as if she was a mute, out of the pain and the shame she hushed up and fell silent.

And he took her and bedded her and abused her (Gen 34:2).

In Beruriah's beit midrash, opinions differed if this was what she wanted or if it was against her will.

Some said it was against her will, since, after all, the verse says *and he took her* (Gen 34:2), teaching us that Shekhem kidnapped her. And what's more, Scripture says, *and he bedded her*—and not *with her*, teaching us that he forced himself on her. And the meaning of *and he abused her* is just like it says.

And some said this was by her will, as is written *and he took her* and *taking* is none other than matrimony, as is written *when a man takes a woman* (*as wife*) (Deut 24:1). And what's more, the meaning of *and he bedded her* is just like it says. And what's more, it says *abused her* (*vaya'anehah*), he came to her in her time of her wanting (*be'onatah*). Or perhaps that he answered her *'anah lah*—that she asked and asked her brothers and they shunted her and they made fun of her, until Shekhem came, and answered her.

Dinah's silence resounds from one end of the world to the other. It is the scream of the heart.

Two women were raped, and their silence resounded from one end of the world to the other. Dinah and Tamar, the sister of Amnon. Of Tamar, Scripture says, *and she went walking and screaming and her brother Avshalom said to her . . . be silent, my sister, he's your brother, don't take this to your heart and Tamar sat down, desolate* (2 Sam 13:20).

Commentary

The book of Genesis (chapters 29–30) recounts that Leah gave birth to six sons for Jacob, *and afterward she bore a daughter* (Gen 30:21). Rivkah Lubitch interprets *and afterward* (*v'achar*) as referring not to a period of time but to a change. What was different about the birth of Dinah? Lubitch offers two possible answers: pain and joy. According to the first, the birth of Dinah was a source of disappointment to Jacob, who would have preferred another son. Therefore, he did not celebrate her birth the way he celebrated the birth of his sons. He did not make a party and was not present when she was named. According to the second answer, *and afterward* (*v'achar*) refers to a joyous transformation. Dinah's birth was a source of tremendous joy to Leah because she had been hoping for a daughter. After having six sons, she felt that her status with Jacob was secure and now wanted joy for herself.

The midrash goes on to ask why the Bible refers to Dinah as Jacob's daughter in the verse describing how she went out to see the daughters of the land. According to Lubitch, Jacob tried to renounce all connection to Dinah when he saw that she was so curious and was so often out and about. Jacob regarded Dinah's frequent excursions as unbefitting, since a woman's place was in the tent—a notion reflected in various rabbinic sources (e.g., Genesis Rabbah 8:12). Jacob informs his wife, Leah, that in his family, women traditionally stayed inside the tent, as was the custom of his grandmother, Sarah, and his mother, Rebecca. According to one famous midrash, the blessing associated with the matriarchs was a lit candle and a cloud above the entrance to their tent (Genesis Rabbah 60:16). Lubitch thus essentially critiques the rabbis' deliberate decision to associate such domestic images with the matriarchs. Given these associations, Jacob insists that Dinah, who so often left the home, was not really one of his own. According to Lubitch, the Torah expresses opposition to Jacob's renunciation of Dinah by emphasizing the connection between Jacob and Dinah in the very same verse that describes Dinah's habit of going out.

Lubitch explores the verse beginning with *and Dinah went out* and offers an interpretation that differs from the classical midrashic understanding.

In some traditional midrashim, the phrase *and Dinah went out* was invoked to hold Dinah accountable for the rape, arguing that she went out in the hope that the men around her would take note of her beauty and, in so doing, she attracted the attention of Shekhem, the son of Hamor (Midrash Tanhuma Buber, ed., Vayishlach 19). In other midrashim, this phrase was invoked as a way of linking Dinah's unseemly behavior with the midrashic account of how Leah "adorned herself like a whore" when she went out to greet Jacob after the incident with the mandrakes (Genesis Rabbah 80:1). The phrase "like mother, like daughter" (see Ezek 16:44) appears in these midrashim in a derogatory context.

In contrast to these rabbinic midrashim, Lubitch reads *and Dinah went out* as expressing the value of the behavior that parents model for their children and that children in turn imitate—not just the value of "like mother, like daughter" but also, by extension, the value of "like father, like daughter."

The first midrash, like Genesis Rabbah, draws a parallel between the two phrases *and Dinah went out* (Gen 34:1) and *and Leah went out* (Gen 30:16), arguing that we can learn about the purpose of Dinah's "going out" from the purpose of Leah's "going out." Leah went out to greet her husband, Jacob, in order to fulfill the commandment of having children with him. Therefore, Dinah's "going out," too, must have been for the sake of fulfilling that same commandment—to seek out an appropriate life partner so that she too might marry and have children.

The second midrash focuses on imitating the behavior of the father. The midrash draws a parallel between the phrase *and Dinah went out* (Gen 34:1) and the phrase *and Jacob went out* (Gen 28:1), arguing that we can learn about the purpose of Dinah's "going out" from the purpose of Jacob's "going out." Jacob left Be'er Sheva and went to Haran on account of his brother, Esau, who sought to kill him after he stole his birthright. Therefore, Dinah's "going out" must also have been related to the behavior of her brothers (as the subsequent midrashim will explain) and her desire to find a place for herself in which she could flourish independently. Thus, Dinah is portrayed as a young woman whose behavior was blameless, particularly when it came to the brutal rape she endured. The midrash goes on to explain the reason that Dinah did not find her place in her family and sought to go out to see among the daughters of the land. As the youngest of her siblings and the only daughter born after six brothers, she felt extraneous and insignificant. Lubitch quotes the rabbinic saying, "Either friendship or death," to convey that Dinah's search for companionship was perfectly natural and healthy. As the rabbinic saying suggests, one who has no friends is better off dead (b.Taanit 23:1).

Throughout the entire biblical story, Dinah never speaks. Lubitch links Dinah's silence in the home to her silence during the rape. As Lubitch reminds us, Dinah grew up among six brothers. The men in her home probably did not listen to her, did not appreciate what she had to say, and did not speak with her, in accordance with the rabbinic dictum, "Do not increase conversation with the woman" (Mishnah Avot 1:5). Thus, Lubitch says, Dinah fell mute.

It is for this reason that the verse says that Dinah went out "to see" and not "to hear" or "to be heard." Later, during the rape, Dinah's silence is even more resounding on account of her pain and shame. Lubitch asks, "Is it conceivable that Dinah didn't cry out?" The fact that she presumably did not cry out for help during the rape recalls the laws of rape in the book of Deuteronomy (22:23–27). The Bible assumes that a woman who was raped would cry out, thus proving that the act was committed against her will. But in keeping with modern psychology, Lubitch understands that many women are rendered speechless when they become victims of such a crime. She describes rape in a way that absolves the victim of any responsibility. Dinah's silence begins at home and continues in her life outside the home, and it speaks to her lack of recourse and to the enormity of the injustice committed against her.

The midrash on the words *And he bedded her, and abused her* (Gen 34:2) presents a debate that arose between the women sages in Beruriah's beit midrash, a fictional women's study house headed by Beruriah (see page xxiii) that Lubitch invented to parallel the all-male beit midrash. The women sages in this beit midrash try to figure out what really happened between Dinah and Shekhem. Was it truly a rape, or was it consensual?

One group of women sages argues that it was indeed rape, calling our attention to the various verbs used to describe the incident: Shekhem "took" Dinah," "bedded" her, and "abused" her, suggesting that Shekhem was the active player whereas Dinah remained passive. These women sages interpreted the Torah's use of the unusual phrase "and he bedded her" rather than "and he slept with her" as implying that the act was not consensual and that he did indeed "abuse" her, as the Torah states.

The second group of women sages argues that Dinah slept with Shekhem because she was interested in marrying him. They interpret the very same biblical phrases as implying that Dinah participated consensually. The term *and he took her* is interpreted by juxtaposition with the phrase *when a man takes a woman* (as a wife) (Deut 24:1). The term *take* refers to marriage, which requires a woman's consent, and thus the women sages conclude that in the story of Dinah, Shekhem's act of "taking" was consensual. Likewise, they interpret the phrase "and he bedded her" as a reference to consensual sexual relations. Finally, they interpret the phrase "and abused her" as deriving from the biblical term *'onah*, which, in rabbinic parlance refers to the frequency with which a husband is supposed to provide his wife with sexual relations (see Exod 21:10; Kiddushin 18b). Furthermore, the verb *la'anot* (to abuse) also means "to respond"; whereas Dinah's brothers used to mock her instead of responding to her, Shekhem was the first to take interest in her, listen to her, and respond accordingly, and thus she was eager to forge a connection with him. (The midrash in Genesis Rabbah 80:11 explains that the brothers had to drag Dinah from Shekhem's home against her will.)

Lubitch concludes with a discussion of the suffering of women who were raped and were unable to give voice to their pain, whether because of an internal psychological barrier or because their community was not interested in hearing their cry. Lubitch draws a parallel between two biblical women who were raped and remained silent. The first is Tamar, the daughter of King David, who was raped by her paternal brother Amnon (2 Sam 13). Following the rape, Tamar went out to the streets and wailed and yelled, but her brother Avshalom silenced her. The second was Dinah, whose voice was not heard at all. Lubitch refers to this silenced pain as "the scream of the heart," which cannot be heard but nonetheless resounds from one end of the world to the other.

AYALA TZRUYAH

The Daughter of Dinah

This midrash invokes Jacob's daughter, Dinah, and the daughter born to Dinah as a consequence of rape, as a way of dealing with a family and community's attitudes toward a victim of rape. Ayala Tzruyah regards the rape victim not as blameworthy or as "damaged goods" but rather as someone deserving support and compassion.

And these are the names of the children of Israel who entered Egypt: Jacob and his sons, Jacob's first born was Reuven. And the sons of Reuven . . . And the sons of Shimon . . . And the sons of Levi . . . And the sons of Yehudah . . . And the sons of Ysachar . . . And the sons of Zevulun . . . These are the children of Leah who bore them for Jacob in Padan-Aram, and Dinah his daughter, all souls, his sons and daughters, thirty-three (Gen 46:8–15).

A man and his house, his spouse and his children, went down to Egypt.

And only Dinah, in her loneliness, without a man or children.

And her brothers couldn't speak to her a kind word.

They did not speak to her when she was young, thus *And Dinah went out . . . to see the daughters of the land* (Gen 34:1).

They didn't speak to her after Shekhem seized and abused her and didn't even ask her what she wanted, as is written, *And they killed Hamor and Shekhem his son by the sword, and took Dinah from Shekhem's house and went* (Gen 34:26) . . .

And didn't speak to her once she was pregnant, but sought to kill her, as is written *And they said, will our sister be treated like a whore?* (Gen 34:31) They'll say all through the land, that there's a whore in Jacob's tents?

Jacob's sons called Dinah's daughter Osnat—that the disgrace of her birth should be remembered and that her mother remember her disaster (*ason*) and her rape (*ones*), that she went out to see the daughters of the land.

And Jacob *took note*. He said, don't call her Osnat, but At-Nes (lit. You are a miracle). And he marked her with a gold frontlet. And he dressed her in a coat of many colors to save her from them.

And when the day of Jacob's death drew near, he repaired his sons' deeds, as is written *And to Joseph were born, in the land of Egypt, Menashe and Ephraim, whom Osnat the daughter of Potifera, priest of On, had born to him* (Gen 46:20), *And Jacob said to Joseph . . . and now your two sons born to you in the land of Egypt before I came to you to Egypt, are mine, Ephraim and Menashe will be like Reuven and Shimon to me* (Gen 48:3–6).

And a redeemer comes to Dinah.

Commentary

Genesis 34 relates the story of the rape of Jacob's daughter Dinah by Shekhem, son of Hamor. The Torah does not elaborate on Dinah's fate. We do not know if she ever married after the rape or if she bore children. Midrash Pirkei d'Rabbi Eliezer fills in this gap by linking the story of the rape of Dinah and the birth of a girl shortly after to Joseph's marriage to Osnat, the daughter of Potifera. According to the midrash, Dinah became pregnant as a result of the rape and gave birth to a daughter whom her brothers named Osnat. Dinah's brothers were concerned that Osnat's presence in Jacob's tent would be misconstrued as proof of Dinah's licentiousness, and thus they set out to kill the infant. But their father, Jacob, prevents them from doing so, and ultimately Osnat arrives at the home of Potifera and his wife in Egypt, where she marries Joseph. This midrash resolves the problem of Joseph's marriage to an Egyptian woman, because Osnat was in fact Joseph's niece, as follows:

> Jacob's daughter was a tent-sitter. What did Shekhem the son of Hamor do? He brought playful young women around her tent, beating on tambourines, and she went out to see the daughters of the land and he seized her and lay with her and she became pregnant and gave birth to Osnat. And Jacob's sons thought to kill her. They said, they'll say all through the land that there's a whore girl in Jacob's tents?! What did Jacob do? He wrote the Holy Name on a frontlet of gold, placed it on her neck and let her go. And all was seen before the Holy Blessed One, and the angel Michael descended, and picked her up, and brought her down to Egypt to the

house of Potifera . . . and Potifera's wife was childless and raised her like a daughter. And Yosef took her as a wife (Pirkei d'Rabbi Eliezer, Higger edition, chapter 37).

Tzruyah expands and elaborates on the midrashic tradition in Pirkei d'Rabbi Eliezer, focusing on Jacob's daughter, Dinah. In the description of Jacob's family's descent to Egypt (Gen 46:8–15), Dinah is mentioned on her own, without any mention of a husband or children. According to Tzruyah, Dinah suffered from loneliness because her brothers "could not speak a friendly word to her," a phrase that appears in the Bible in the context of the brothers' difficult relationship with Joseph (Gen 37:4).

Dinah's brothers could not speak a friendly word to her either before or after the rape, and they sought to kill her daughter. In a manner characteristic of rabbinic midrash, Tzruyah offers various interpretations of the name Osnat. For the brothers, it is a derogatory term for the infant, a reference to the tragedy (*ason*) of the rape (*ones*) of Dinah. With this appellation, they seek to immortalize the miserable fate of both mother and daughter as punishment for the mother's wretched behavior.

Jacob is presented as an oppositional force to his sons. He knew about the rape and birth, but he "kept the matter to himself" (Gen 37:11), just as he did when it came to the strained relationship between Joseph and his brothers. For Jacob, the name Osnat is a sign of honor. He interprets the name by shifting around the letters, calling her *At-Nes*, meaning "you are a miracle." This name does not just empower Osnat by conferring legitimacy on her existence but also regards her birth as miraculous. And thus "out of the strong came something sweet," to quote Samson's riddle (Judg 14:14). Jacob bestows two gifts on Osnat. First, he places a frontlet of gold upon her neck, according to the midrash in Pirkei d'Rabbi Eliezer. And second, he gives her a coat of many colors, which is Tzruyah's invention but which of course is reminiscent of Jacob's special treatment of Joseph, therefore also a reference to her future husband. In addition, the mention of this garment recalls the story of Amnon's rape of Tamar, in which Tamar is described as wearing an ornamental tunic, like all virgins wear, prior to her rape (2 Sam 13:18). With this allusion, Jacob's gift signifies that Osnat is unique and regal, and in his eyes she is a pure and unsullied virgin.

According to Tzruyah, the final corrective measure took place at the very end of Jacob's life. He blesses Joseph's sons and Osnat, conferring on them the same legal status as his own sons. And thus, as Tzruyah writes, "a redeemer comes to Dinah," which is an allusion to Isaiah's prophecy, *And a redeemer comes to Zion* (Isa 59:20).

Ayala Tzruyah highlights various human responses to rape and to the fruits of such an illicit union. Jacob's noble and impressive behavior becomes a model for others. He is not afraid of what other people will think; he acts independently to cleanse Osnat's reputation and secure her place in society, thereby sparing her from the fate that would otherwise have befallen her.

HAGIT BARTOV

Let Your House Be Open Wide

A mishnah from Pirkei Avot begins with the phrase, "Let your house be open wide." This midrash focuses on two biblical families that were "not like those of most people." One was the family of Abraham, who fathered a son with his wife, Sarah, and another with her maidservant, Hagar. The other is the family of Jacob, who fathered children with two sisters and with their maidservants. Hagit Bartov examines the emotional lives of the two barren women, Sarah and Rachel, to offer guidance on building a healthy alternative family.

Ishmael, the son of a maidservant was he; Dan, Naftali, Gad, and Asher—the sons of maidservants were they. Why did Ishmael despise Isaac, while Dan and Naftali and Gad and Asher are sons of Israel and merited to inherit the Land?

Sarah was barren. Rachel was barren.

Of Sarah it does not say *and she was jealous,* and it doesn't say, *give me children or I shall die* (Gen 30:1). Sarah's pain and hurt lay like a stone on her heart, and since she did not allow her anger to abate, there was no room left in her heart. Sarah said, if I did not merit a son from my loins, I will take a son not from my loins, and will be built through another woman. She took her maidservant and gave her to Abraham, her man, as his woman.

And a family that is unlike those of most other people needs more love and compassion, and needs the humility and concession that come from a light heart, a heart that has endured its pain and has been healed. But Sarah, once Abraham had come to her maidservant and made her pregnant, had no place in her heart for the family she had made, which was unlike that of most other people—and her pain threatened to destroy the whole world, and she brought destruction down onto her home. For thirteen years, she tormented Hagar, and yet her mind had not been calmed until she merited a son herself and until she chased out the maidservant's son, as if chasing out that one would make her family a family like all the others.

And she did not succeed. And Abraham took up the cleaver. And Ishmael despises Isaac.

And of Rachel it is said, *and she was jealous* (Gen 30:1), and of Rachel it is said, *give me children or I shall die* (Gen 30:1). And even so, the sons of the maidservants were like sons of Rachel and Leah.

And how did this happen? For the families of Rachel and Leah, too, were not like those of most other people, for it's usually not the way of sisters to marry the same man, and since they were accustomed to things that most people called "strange," they found room in their hearts also for the different and irregular people within their own families.

And so the sages said, "Let your home be open wide."—When is it "your home"? When it is open wide to the expanses hidden in what most of the people think is irregular. For even if it is not like others' homes, it is open wide; in an instant, it's your home.

Commentary

The midrash begins with a description of the commonalities between the personal stories of two biblical matriarchs, Sarah and Rachel. Both were barren, both offered their maidservants to their husbands, and ultimately both had children of their own. In light of all these similarities, the midrash questions why the family dynamics in each of these complex families were so different. Sarah ultimately banished her maidservant Hagar along with Hagar's son, Ishmael. According to the traditional midrash (Psikta d'Rav Kahana, Nachamu 16:5), Sarah's son, Isaac, and Hagar's son, Ishmael—both of whom were sons of Abraham—became sworn enemies. By contrast, in Jacob's family, the sons of the maidservants Bilhah and Zilpah were accepted and embraced by Jacob's wives, Rachel and Leah, such that they became an integral part of the people of Israel and were even allocated portions of land in Israel.

Hagit Bartov attributes these differences to the very different ways in which Sarah and Rachel dealt with the pain of their barrenness and with the members of the alternative families they established as a result.

Sarah kept all her pain and anger bottled up inside throughout the years of her barrenness. She tried to create an alternative family for herself by bestowing her maidservant Hagar upon Abraham so that she might have a son, without giving voice to the distress she felt about her bitter fate. But her repressed emotions poisoned the atmosphere in her home and led her to treat Hagar with cruelty and violence. This atmosphere also influenced Abraham, as evident from his willingness to sacrifice his son, Isaac. A legacy of cruelty and violence continued to shape the relationship between Ishmael and Isaac's descendants.

In contrast, Rachel gave voice to her pain and frustration throughout her barrenness. And so she learned over time to contain and accept her own emotions. The fact that she shared her husband with her sister, Leah, enabled her to open her heart to the maidservants as well. The descendants of this family became the twelve tribes of Israel.

The midrash concludes with a quote from the mishnah in Avot 1:5: "Yose ben Yochanan, man of Jerusalem, says: Let your home be open wide." Bartov interprets this mishnah as referring not only to the openness of the house but also to the openness of the heart. When we open our hearts wide, we will succeed in transforming even our very different kinds of families into a home. Family ties are not necessarily based on bloodlines but on the bonds of the heart, which are forged with an open heart unafraid to experience pain or joy.

THREE

Exodus

ORNA PILZ

The Midwives Saw and Feared

This midrash considers the source of belief and trust in God and the power of that faith to inspire individuals to act morally, and to make bold and daring choices that transform reality.

The book of Exodus opens with a description of the Israelites' enslavement in Egypt. Pharaoh, who realizes that the harsh labor that he has inflicted on the Israelites has not led to any decrease in their numbers, decides to take more drastic measures. He commands the Hebrew midwives to kill off any male babies at birth. The God-fearing midwives defy Pharaoh's decree and allow the male babies to live. This midrash seeks to understand the source of their faith. Where did they muster the courage to spurn Pharaoh?

He [the king of Egypt] said [to the midwives]: When you deliver the Hebrew women, look (u'rei-ten) at the birth stool. If it is a boy, kill him; if it is a girl, let her live. The midwives feared God in awe (va-tir-ena) and did not do as the king of Egypt had told them. They let the boys live. (Exod 1: 16-17).

The midwives were asked: Where did you get your fearful awe of God?

And they answered: From the great and deep things that we saw at the birth stool, from the mystery that embraces us morning and evening: human being after human being coming into the world; where does he come from and what does she bring with her? The goodness that her mother sees in him, the compassion and the love that she awakens, crying babies bursting forth from exhausted bodies, and the soft seal of God's finger imprinted on their faces.

The midwives were challenged:

But didn't it happen at Sinai that *All the people saw (ro-im) the thunder and the lightning and the voice of the Shofar and the smoking mountain and the people saw it and trembled and stood far off . . . and Moses said to the people do not fear (al ti-ru), for God has come to test you, to keep the fearful awe of God (yir-a-to) before you so that you will not transgress* (Exod 20:15–17). The fearful awe of God comes from the place of thunder and lightning!

And the midwives answered:

There is fearful awe (*yir-a*) that comes from external seeing (*re-i-ya*) and there is fearful awe that comes from internal vision (*re-i-ya*); a person can be frozen in terror, witnessing a supernatural miracle, which awakens and strengthens her sense of fearful awe. But for us, it doesn't work like that. Our fearful awe is *not in the heavens* (Deut 30:12). Our fearful awe of God arises precisely from within nature, from within the pain of what we witness on the birth stool. From there we learn to choose what is good, to protect life, to fight against death, and to resist evil.

Commentary

The biblical story relates that the Hebrew midwives violated the edict issued by Pharaoh and refused to kill the male babies. As the Bible explains, *The midwives feared God in awe and did not do as the king of Egypt had told them. They let the boys live* (Exod 1:17). The Hebrew word for "feared God in awe" can be interpreted in two ways: it may come from the root word for "awe," or it may come from the root word for "vision." Orna Pilz plays with the two meanings of this term, linking vision with faith.

According to Pilz, it was because the midwives "saw" that they came to "fear" and believe. Their God-fearing behavior was a product of what they saw.

The midrash opens with a question posed to the midwives: Where did they get the fear of and trust in God, which led them to act with such exceptional courage? The midwives explained that their faith developed from their work as midwives—from beholding the mystery and wonder that surrounds new life, and the love and compassion between mother and infant, and the seal of God's finger imprinted on each child's face.

They are then asked: But doesn't the Torah teach that fear of God develops from experiences of fear and trembling, like the revelation of an exalted, transcendent God at Sinai?

The midwives explain that there are different types of experience that inspire faith in God. There is fear of God that is awakened by an encounter with a transcendent God and supernatural miracles, as with the revelation on Sinai. And then there is fear of God that springs from an encounter with an immanent God and the wonders of nature, as with the midwives, whose experience of the natural process of birth instilled in them a sense of God's wondrousness. In witnessing birth, they came to appreciate life amid pain, which awakened their love and compassion and led them to choose life and to follow the path of goodness.

GILI ZIVAN

Bityah, the Daughter of God

The story of Bityah, the daughter of Pharaoh, draws Gili Zivan to explore our compassion toward those who are different from us and with the deeper meaning of our compassion toward foreign workers. In the biblical story, Pharaoh's daughter rescues a baby she discovered in the Nile and named him Moses. In spite of her father's decree to kill all the children of the Israelites and although she knew that he was the son of slaves, she decided to adopt him and raise him in her home. In order to highlight the moral greatness of Pharaoh's daughter, Zivan juxtaposes the verses that describe her discovery of Moses in the Nile with the verses in the book of Isaiah in which the prophet lists the acts of kindness incumbent on us to perform toward the underprivileged members of society, including slaves. These verses are chanted in synagogue on the morning of Yom Kippur, to make the point that the central call of the day is not the fast but the humane behavior that must accompany it. Zivan presents the injunction to treat the children of foreign workers with compassion as a religious commandment that is an aspect not just of human morality but also of God's will.

And Pharaoh's daughter went down to bathe in the Nile, and her maidens were walking along the Nile. And she saw the ark in the reeds and sent her slave girl and took it—and she opened it, and she saw the child, and it was a young lad, crying, and she took pity on him and said, "this is a child of the Hebrews" (Exod 2:5–6).

And these are the children of Bityah, daughter of Pharaoh (1 Chron 4:18).

Lo, this is the fast I desire. Open the manacles of evil, untie the ropes of the yoke, let the oppressed go free, and break every yoke. Share your bread with the hungry, and the wretched poor, take them in to your home. If you see someone naked, clothe them and do not ignore your own flesh (Isa 58:6–7).

Bityah, daughter of Pharaoh (1 Chron 4:18)—Pharaoh's daughter or God's daughter? [Bit-Yah = Bat-Yah = daughter of God].

Well, she took herself out from under her father's authority, for she pitied the boy, even though she knew her father had commanded *every newborn boy, you will cast into the Nile* (Exod 1:22).

The Holy Blessed One said: She who took pity on my child, will be my daughter, and that is what it says: "Bityah."

And how does pity happen?

Go and see what the prophet Isaiah learned from the deeds of Bityah, Pharaoh's daughter:

> *And she saw*—she saw and did not look away, as is written, *If you see . . . someone naked, clothe them, and do not ignore your own flesh* (Isa 58:7).
>
> *And she sent*—she sent her slave girl and did not shutter the blinds of her heart, as is written, *Send the oppressed free* (Isa 58:6).
>
> *And she took*—she took the ark and did not fear for her own life and say, "what has he to do with me?" As is written, *and the wretched poor, take them in to your home* (Isa 58:6)
>
> *And she opened*—she opened her heart to a foreign child and did not say, "he isn't one of ours," as is written, *Open up the manacles of evil* (Isa 58:6).
>
> *And she saw him, the child*—and she saw again, that she returned and looked in his eyes, as is written, *If you see someone naked, clothe them* (Isa 58:7).

The Holy Blessed One said to Pharaoh's daughter, you, with the Torah of kindness on your lips, and your mouth opened with wisdom, you taught my sons and daughters the secret of opening the heart, as is written *and she opened*; who taught the gaze that sees in the child the lad that he will become, as is written *and she saw him, the child, and it was a young lad* and you taught the secret of listening to the weeping of foreign children, as is written *this is a child of the Hebrews*—you will be taken in under my wings and you will be a daughter to me, and your name in Israel will be Bit-Yah.

And not only that, but the Holy Blessed One commanded her, and said, go and teach that secret of compassion to all who come to this world, you who rebelled against the idols of your father's house, the idols of racism.

Commentary

This midrash deals with the story of Bityah, the daughter of Pharaoh, who violated her father's decree and saved the life of a Hebrew baby. She adopted him and raised him as her son, even though he was a son of the Hebrews, who were slaves in Egypt. And she gave him the name Moses. The midrash relates that the Holy Blessed One said to Pharaoh's daughter, "Moses was not your son, but you called him your son. So too, you are not my daughter, but I am calling you my daughter" (Leviticus Rabbah 1:3).

Pharaoh's daughter's name is not mentioned in the biblical story in Exodus, but the rabbis called her Bityah, identifying her with a figure who lived several hundred years later and is mentioned in the book of Chronicles: *And these are the children of Bityah the daughter of Pharaoh* (1 Chron 4:18). Since the Bible does not contain vocalizations, the name Bityah may also be read as Batyah, meaning daughter of God. It is against this backdrop that Gili Zivan asks whether Bityah was the daughter of Pharaoh or the daughter of God.

Zivan's response is that although she was Pharaoh's daughter, "she removed herself from her father's domain" with her act of compassion for the Hebrew baby she found in the river. Zivan invokes quasi-halakhic language, implying that her act had real-world implications. The Holy Blessed One bore witness to her compassion and had compassion for her. Just as she adopted Moses, God adopted her and accepted her into His domain. Just as Bityah named Moses, The Holy Blessed One gave her the Hebrew name Bityah.

Zivan's midrash, which like many classical midrashim has a chiastic structure of repetiton in reverse order, then shifts to an exegesis of biblical verses before returning to an imagined dialogue between The Holy Blessed One and Pharaoh's daughter. The middle part of the midrash is closely patterned on verses from Exodus 2 that describe Pharaoh's daughter's actions: *And she saw ... and she sent ... and she took ... and she opened ... and she saw.* By focusing on these verbs, Zivan emphasizes Pharaoh's daughter's active role in rescuing Moses.

In order to shed light on the nature of Pharaoh's daughter's acts of kindness, Zivan uses the midrashic technique of juxtaposing verses from different contexts by means of a word that recurs in both. She compares the verbs used in Exodus 2 with the prophecy of Isaiah 58:1–2. The choice of Isaiah is not incidental. In this chapter, Isaiah rebukes the people for their moral depravity in stringently observing the rites of fasting without changing the way they treat their slaves and other disempowered members of society. As Zivan demonstrates, Isaiah chooses to describe the compassionate behavior that God desires by means of the same verbs used in Exodus 2 to describe Bityah's compassion in rescuing Moses:

> "And she saw"—"If you see"
> "And she sent"—"Send the oppressed free"
> "And she took"—"Take them in to your home"
> "And she opened"—"Open up the manacles of evil"
> "And she saw him, the child"—"If you see"

This section of the midrash conveys the notion that Isaiah regards Bityah's behavior as an act of kindness that has significance far beyond her own personal context. For Isaiah, her actions become a model of the behavior expected of all the people of Israel.

The final section of the midrash returns to the imagined dialogue between God and Bityah. Isaiah's words are understood not as the prophet's personal insight but rather as a prophetic expression of God's will.

God's words are expressed by invoking terminology that appears in "A Woman of Valor," the description of an ideal woman that appears in Proverbs 31. God enumerates Bityah's virtues and explains that she who has "the Torah of kindness" on her lips and her "mouth opened with wisdom" is the one who taught all of Israel the values of empathy and responsibility toward "foreign children," and thus God adopts her as a daughter. The term "foreign children" serves to connect the biblical story with the political reality in contemporary Israeli society. One of the great moral problems confronting Israel today is how to deal with the children of foreign workers residing illegally in Israel, who face the constant threat of expulsion. By means of this midrash, Zivan demands that Israeli society treat these children with compassion and embrace them.

God sanctions Bityah's moral rebellion against her father. The midrash reaches beyond the understanding in the Babylonian Talmud, Sotah 12b:

And the daughter of Pharaoh came down to bathe [lirhotz] in the river (Exod 2:5). Rabbi Yohanan says in the name of Rabbi Shimon ben Yohai: "She came down to cleanse from her father's idols." Zivan's phrasing, "You who rebelled against the idols of your father's home, the idols of racism," identifies idolatry with racism and the religious dimension with the moral.

TAMAR BIALA

The Giving of the Ten Commandments

Much of the Jewish biblical and midrashic tradition is addressed to men alone and regards their spiritual experience as the totality of Jewish religious life. This midrash focuses on the revelation at Sinai, the foundational spiritual experience of the covenant between the Jewish people and God. The verses describing the revelation at Sinai and the language of the Ten Commandments are addressed to men alone, as if to suggest that women did not take part in the revelation and that the commandments were not also given to them. Tamar Biala grapples with these questions by constructing a frame narrative that imagines a discussion between The Holy Blessed One and a young woman who has just heard these verses chanted in the synagogue. The midrash depicts the biblical revelation as an experience that was only partial, in the sense that it did not convey the fullness of God's voice. God's intention was for women to be included in revelation and for them to be obligated in the commandments just like their male counterparts.

This is a story of a young woman who was sitting in synagogue while the Ten Commandments were being read. The Reader was chanting so expertly that the young woman felt as though she was hearing them for the first time. And she was astonished at what she heard, and her heart became aggrieved.

She asked in her heart, what is the nature of *Remember the Sabbath to hallow it* (Exod 20:8), of which it is said *You shall do no work, you and your son and your daughter, your male slave and your slave girl and your beast and your sojourner who is within your gates* (Exod 20:10)—and his wife, what about her, is she not commanded to hallow the Sabbath?

And what is the nature of *You shall not covet*, of which it is said, *You shall not covet your fellow man's wife, or his male slave, or his slave girl, or his ox, or his donkey, or anything that your fellow man has* (Exod 20:14–7)—and his wife, what about her, did the Torah not command her, too, not to covet that which is her fellow woman's?

The young woman was pious, and not until that day had she had a single foreign musing or doubt regarding the truth of Torah. At that moment of questioning, her heart was wrapped in fear, beating and beating until she thought everyone in synagogue could hear its rhythm. The tears that rose in her throat had the taste of the deep, and the taste of the sea that drowned the Egyptians, and she was shaking and aghast, and her soul fled.

The Holy Blessed One gathered up her soul in the palm of His hand and was looking and smiling at her. He said to her: How long have I waited for you to come and ask Me, so that I might reveal to you that which has been hidden away with Me for three thousand years! She cast her eyes downward and asked: Did The Holy Blessed One not speak with women at Mount Sinai, and not command them the same things He commanded men with thunder and lightning?

The Holy Blessed One lifted up her head and said, when Moses ascended I commanded him: *And have them make themselves ready for the third day, for on the third day, God will come down before **all the people** on Mount Sinai.* (Exod 19:11). Since Moses distanced himself from women, for he separated from his wife, Zipporah; he brought only men near the mountain, as is said, *And Moses brought **the people** toward God from the camp* (Exod 19:17).

And at that time, when Moses heard the commandments, and there were only men around him, he heard *You shall do no work* and said to himself, "and who will be punished for doing work, if not the man? And whose are the slaves and slave girls, chattel and children, whom he can command to do work, or to rest, if not the man's?"

And so Moses bade the men to keep the Sabbath, in the masculine pronoun. And because he was not *me'urav 'im haberiyot*, engaged with people, *beriyot*, in the feminine, for he had not been with his wife, Zipporah, for a long time, he did not remember that women too have desire, and so he did not include them in the prohibition not to covet.

The young woman asked The Holy Blessed One, if so, and Moses who separated from women could not hear those words which The Holy Blessed One ordained for them, will a sage who has not separated himself be able to hear?

The Holy Blessed One's countenance became grave, and He answered her thus: Any beit midrash that has no women—My word will not emerge from there whole.

Commentary

The midrash depicts an earnest young woman distressed to discover a problem with the biblical description of the revelation at Sinai in the book of Exodus. The commandments to keep the Sabbath and not to covet are worded in the masculine form, as if addressed to men only. This leads her to a deeper and more broad-ranging question: Did women not take part in the precious, foundational experience of the revelation at Sinai?

The ancient rabbis were aware of this problem as well, and they offered a solution through their midrash on Exod 9:3: *This you will say to the house of Jacob, and you will tell the children of Israel.* In Exodus Rabbah 28:2, the rabbis suggested that the expression "the house of Jacob" referred to the women, and the expression "the children of Israel" referred to the men. The midrash explains that the women heard the commandments, but they understood them only partially; only the men, who were more learned, were capable of hearing and understanding the full depth and detail of the commandments.

Tamar Biala's midrash offers an alternative solution to the problem in the biblical text. According to this midrash, the young woman who is so distressed that her soul flees her body finds herself gathered into the palm of God's hand. God explains that the gendered language of revelation is a product of its human conduit. The commandments were conveyed to Israel through Moses, a flesh-and-blood human being.

The Holy Blessed One explains to the young woman that in spite of God's instructions to bring *the entire nation* to stand at Sinai (Exod 19:11), Moses brought only *the nation* (Exod 19:17), that is, only the men. The Holy Blessed One explains that Moses lost the capacity to be sensitive to women after he withdrew from his wife and surrounded himself by men alone, according to the midrash Sifrei Bamidbar. He no longer regarded women as independent subjects who, like men, could be held accountable for fulfilling these two commandments.

Moses associated the commandment to keep the Sabbath with men alone for two reasons: first, since the punishment of having to work the land was decreed to Adam in the Garden of Eden, then not working on Sabbath must surely be directed to men. And second, since God also commanded that one must ensure that one's children, servants, and animals desist from work as well, then the command must apply exclusively to men, who were the only masters of children, servants, and animals in Moses's time. Moses therefore did not think to apply the Sabbath commandment to women as well. Nor did he associate the prohibition on covetousness with women because his own withdrawal from his wife led him to forget that women too have a sexual drive that can be dangerous and destructive.

The midrash concludes with God's declaration that any study house that excludes women cannot possibly purport to be conveying the full word of God. If women are not channeling the voice of God as well, then revelation is only partial.

This midrash serves as a historical corrective, as it depicts a personal, private revelation to a single woman alone. The Holy Blessed One reveals Himself to this woman and informs her of His original intentions through an experience of shared revelation and study. The fact that God was anticipating her question for three thousand years indicates that God is pleased with her response. God's declaration that His full voice can be heard only in a society in which both men and women take part in Torah study serves to validate the young woman's distress, while also calling for a revolution in the world of Torah learning so that women's Torah may be heard and studied.

FOUR

Israel in the Desert

RIVKAH LUBITCH

Daughters of Tzelophchad

The book of Numbers describes how the daughters of Tzelophchad turn to Moses on the eve of the Children of Israel's entry into the land of Israel as the land is being divided up among the tribes. Tzelophchad's daughters request a portion of land for themselves, explaining that their father died leaving no male heirs. They express their concern that if they do not inherit his portion, his name will go unremembered. Moses turns to God to inquire about the legal precedent in such a case, and God approves of the daughters' request, ruling that henceforth women shall inherit in cases where their fathers have no male heirs.

Lubitch's three midrashim about the daughters of Tzelophchad deal with the feminist demand for equal rights. What conditions allow for the equality of women, and when is this demand met with opposition? Lubitch examines the classical patriarchal opposition to women gaining power, which involves casting suspicion on the motives of feminists, particularly those who campaign on behalf of women's equality in the religious sphere. She also considers the role of God in the patriarchal social order.

1

And the daughters of Tzelophchad drew near ... and these are his daughters' names: Machlah, Noa and Choglah and Milkah and Tirtzah (Num 27:1).

Why were they referred to, first, as "the daughters of Tzelophchad" and only afterward by their own names?

Because of the *Tzel* and *Pachad*, shadow and fear, that was in them at first. For at first they dwelled in their father's shadow, and feared to raise their heads. Once they drew near to one another, they were empowered, and known by their own names, as is written, *And the daughters of Tzelophchad drew near ... and these are his daughters' names.*

2

Rightly (ken) do Tzelophchad's daughters speak (Num 27:7).

Tanot asked God: If Tzelophchad's daughters spoke the truth, why didn't you write that in Your Torah in the first place, for after all, You are truth and Your Torah is truth, and Your word endures forever?

God answered, *Truth will grow from the ground* (Ps 85:12).

Tanot asked, but is it not written *God's Torah is whole?* (Ps 19:8).

God answered her, I already wrote in My Torah, *Be wholehearted with God your Lord* (Deut 18:14). And what's more, I wrote, *walk before me, and be wholehearted* (Gen 17:1).

There is truth that descends from on high, and there is truth that grows from below. Blessed is the generation in which truth from above meets truth from below. And this is what Scripture means when it says *Truth will grow from the ground, and justice look down from Heaven* (Ps 85: 12).

3

The cynics of the time said: Tzelophchad's daughters are hypocrites.

They said: they're doing this for their own power, their own prosperity, to make themselves men's equals when it comes to inheritance. They aren't doing this for the sake of Heaven.

That is why the Torah says, *ken*, "rightly" as in "honest" (*kenut*), and "rightly" as in "correct" (*nakhon*). They act for their own power, they act for their prosperity, they act to make themselves men's equals when it comes to inheritance, they act for the sake of Heaven.

Commentary

The first midrash describes what the daughters of Tzelophchad went through before they managed to express their unusual request to Moses, Elazar the high priest, the leaders of the tribes, and the entire people. Lubitch reads this verse closely, noting that the daughters are mentioned twice, in two different ways: First they are referred to collectively as "the daughters of Tzelophchad," and then their names are listed individually. Lubitch reads these two references as reflecting the stages that the daughters went through in searching for their own independent voices and mustering the courage required to stand before a group of men.

A Tannaitic midrash in Sifrei Bamidbar (133) relates that the daughters of Tzelophchad gathered to consult with one another. Lubitch continues this literary thread and dramatizes it further, describing the difficult inner struggle that motivated the daughters' request. She interprets the name Tzelophchad by means of a midrashic technique named "acronym," in which one word is broken down into two shorter words: Tzelophchad becomes *tzel* (shadow) and *pachad* (fear). According to her interpretation, the daughters at first dwelled in their father's shadow and feared to raise their heads and make their request. The patriarchal society in which they lived dictated their role as subservient to the rule of men, including their father and the leaders of the people. But in the wake of the problem created by the division of the land, they gathered to consult with one another. Finding strength in numbers, they were able to consolidate their identities as individuals as well. And so, by the end of the verse, after they mustered the courage to appear before the entire congregation, they are referred to by their first names: Machlah, Noah, Choglah, Milkah, and Tirtzah.

When they joined together and supported one another, they were able to bolster their self-confidence, identify their needs as women, and make their voices heard in the public sphere.

The second midrash opens with a question posed to God by Tanot, a literary figure created by Lubitch to personify the soul of Jephthah's daughter (see page 89). In this midrash, Tanot asks God: If Tzelophchad's daughters spoke the truth, why didn't God enshrine the ruling about women's inheritance in the biblical text from the outset?

This same question is raised by the sages of the mishnaic period in a rabbinic midrash on the book of Deuteronomy (Midrash Tana'im Deut 1:17), where the rabbis explain that the incident with the daughters of Tzelophchad served to punish Moses for his pride. When Moses set up the judicial system, he said that the elders should bring difficult matters before him and he would adjudicate. Instead, he should have said that God would adjudicate in such cases. The midrash explains that God sought to rebuke Moses for this error. Moses's punishment involved the simple case posed by the daughters of Tzelophchad, in which the ruling was so obvious that even a child would know the answer. Moses was shamed for not knowing how to respond to a group of women; instead, he had to consult with God. This rabbinic response serves to detract from the significance of the legal precedent and from the wisdom of Tzelophchad's daughters, who serve merely as a means of punishing Moses. This midrash also does not relate to the pain and suffering caused by the lack of any such legal precedent.

Lubitch offers another answer to the question of why the Torah did not enshrine this ruling in the laws of inheritance from the outset. Tanot asks: It is written in the book of Psalms (19:8), *The Torah of the Lord is whole*, meaning that it is complete as is. If so, how can its legislation be lacking? Until the daughters of Tzelophchad appealed to Moses, part of the laws of inheritance had not yet been enshrined. Was the Torah then lacking?

The Holy One Blessed Be He responds in kind. The Torah states, *Be wholehearted with the Lord Your God* (Deut 18:13) and *Walk before Me and be wholehearted* (Gen 17:1). Human beings are commanded to be perfect with God and to fulfill His commandments in a way that renders the Torah perfect. They must walk before God and fill in any gaps in the law so that the Torah will become whole.

This midrash concludes with the insight that there is a truth that descends from on high, from a transcendental realm, and a truth that grows from below, from a place of immanence. Ideally the two meet in between, so that both have their place and complete one another.

In the final midrash, Lubitch describes the communal response to the episode with Tzelophchad's daughters. The cynics among the people look unkindly at the daughters' request. They claim that they are hypocrites who ostensibly are asking for a portion of land so as to keep their father's memory alive, when in reality they are trying to gain power, possessions, and status. Lubitch is depicting one of the classic strategies employed by those who oppose the feminist demand for equality: they question the motivations and try to undermine the integrity of those who speak up.

To silence these slandering voices, the Torah uses the words *Rightly [ken] the daughters of Tzelophchad have spoken* (Num 27:7). Lubitch interprets the word *ken* as meaning both "honest" and "correct." The daughters of Tzelophchad have spoken honestly, from a place of integrity devoid of hypocrisy. And the daughters have spoken correctly, in the sense that they are right.

The conclusion of Lubitch's midrash is surprising. She explains that the daughters' request for power, prosperity, and economic status is justified. The midrash reflects the desire for a deep, systemic reform, and with the words *rightly the daughters of Tzelophchad have spoken*, God approves of the daughters' call for equality between men and women in the legal, economic, and social spheres.

TAMAR BIALA

Death by a Kiss *Miriam's Passing*

Miriam the prophetess, the older sister of Aaron and Moses, played a major role in the story of the exodus from Egypt. But unlike the Torah's description of her brothers' deaths, the Torah describes Miriam's death very tersely: *The Israelites arrived the entire community at the wilderness of Zin on the first new moon, and the people stayed at Kadesh. Miriam died there and was buried there* (Num 20:1). The sages too, who expounded at length on the final moments of Moses's and Aaron's lives and the different ways in which they passed away, did not elaborate on Miriam's death. While the sages note that all three siblings died with the kiss of God—which was thought to be the ideal way to die, devoid of suffering—they thought it was indecent to describe The Holy Blessed One kissing a woman. In a midrash on a verse from the Song of Songs, they explain that this is why Moses and Aaron are described in the Bible as dying "at God's word," and literally "at God's mouth," whereas Miriam is not.

In this midrash, Tamar Biala offers a detailed description of Miriam's final days, filling in the gap in the biblical and midrashic records. Biala portrays the unique way in which Miriam took her leave of the world and the reaction of the community of women to her death. Her midrash describes Miriam as dying at the kiss of God, thereby serving as a corrective to the more understated depiction of her death in the classical rabbinic midrash.

Oh, let him kiss me (*yishaqeni*) *with the kisses of his mouth* (Song 1:2).

The Holy Blessed One said their desire (*meshuqayuton*) is for me; and the Rabbis say: These ones' souls will be taken with a kiss. Rabbi Azariah said, we found that Aaron's soul was taken by none other than a kiss, as is written *And Aaron the Priest went up on Hill's Hill,* **at God's word** [*al-pi Hashem*, lit. by God's mouth], *and died* **there** (Num 33:38). And from where do we know as regards Moses's soul? As is written, *And **there** died Moses, the servant of God, **at God's word*** [*al-pi Hashem*, literally *by God's mouth*] (Deut 34:5). And from where do we know as regards Miriam? Since it is written, *And Miriam died **there*** (Num 20:1). Just as the **there** later on [with Aaron and Moses] is by God's mouth, so too here; but it is indecent to spell it out (Shir Ha-Shirim Rabbah 1:5).

From the day that Miriam returned to the encampment, God's statement about her, *would she not be disgraced?* (Num 12:14), was fulfilled, and she hid in the tent and no longer revealed herself to the Children of Israel. Like the moon, which, too, sought to reign as an equal and was told "Go and diminish yourself," she would emerge only at the time when darkness would descend, and hurry to that well that The Holy Blessed One had left them, which rolled along with them on their journeys.

Miriam sat alone, as the people were scared of her leprosy, lest it return, and she herself waited for that leprosy to come and destroy her face and take her soul.

And what would she do every night at the time that she would come to the well? She would lean down to those very same waters, to see if the delicate splendor of her face had dimmed. She wanted to know if the skin pendent on it had been devoured, and her eyes sunk again in their graves. When at that time she would see that the light still flowed from her countenance, that she had asked for forgiveness and been forgiven—she wept for her face, which nobody ever saw or kissed any longer, not her beloved, not her brothers, not her friends.

One night, at the time she usually went to the well to check her speculum, the full moon that hung above her appeared to her in the water. Her tears dripped into the well, and the reflections of her face and of the moon mingled one with the other.

As she cried, the waters began to recede. She wanted to know what they were up to and she doubled over the mouth of the well and her heart sank, as her image was no longer visible in the water. She strained her eyes into the waters and the moon rose in them again in all her fullness. The moon trembled in the waters, and her visage hid and revealed itself and seemed like that of her mother, Yocheved.

Miriam's heart rose up, as the longings imprisoned in her from the day that her mother had died broke the floodgates of her heart. She wanted to look at her more, sink her head into the well until she felt a mouth kissing her on her lips.

Her empty pitcher slipped to the ground and shattered.

At first light, the one called the morning star, the daughters of Israel came to fill their pitchers at that same well and found it dry. They said, let's call our sister Miriam to raise the waters, since this well has been given to us in our wanderings only because of her.

They said, "Who will go into that tent?" since they were scared to do so.

Zipporah said: "I will, since after all, this disease infected her because she tried to bring my husband back to me."

She found her lying in her bed, draped in a gentle light, her eyes closed, and her lips pursed like a baby's.

She said, "We will return to you, my sister."

She exited and told them.

Some say that as they were preparing her body for burial, they wailed over her, *Who is she that shines through like the dawn, beautiful as the moon?* (Song 6:10). And some say they wailed *Oh, let him kiss me (yishaqeni) with the kisses of his mouth* (Song 1:2).

Commentary

After Miriam's triumphant song and dance at the parting of the Red Sea, she appears in the Torah's narrative only once more before her death.

Numbers 12 recounts that Miriam challenged Moses's authority, insisting that both she and Aaron also had prophetic powers. This same passage relates that Miriam spoke negatively about Moses' dark-skinned wife. As a result, Miriam was punished with leprosy for seven days, and she had to live outside the Israelite camp until she recovered.

Biala in this midrash relates to the consequences of this incident, which will affect the rest of Miriam's life and eventually bring about her death.

In order to understand these consequences, Biala uses two recurrent leitmotifs, the moon and the well. Both figure in rabbinic midrash as symbols of femininity.

In Genesis 1, the sun and moon are initially both described as the "two great lights," but then immediately after, they are described as the "greater light," the sun, and the "lesser light," the moon. The Babylonian Talmud in Hullin 60b explains this shift in terminology by relating a story about the birth of hierarchy and patriarchy. The moon is initially described as being equivalent in size to the sun, and then as the "lesser light," because the moon was punished for challenging God theologically. The moon asked God, Is it possible for two kings to serve with one crown? Her (the moon, *levanah*, is gendered feminine in Hebrew) question challenges the monotheistic conviction that there is room for only one figure at the top of the hierarchical pyramid. In response to the moon's insolence, God says, "Go and diminish yourself," thereby commanding that the moon be diminished in size and the sun alone reign in the daytime sky. Similarly, in this midrash, Miriam who challenged Moses's sole authority, is "diminished" by the punishment of leprosy for seven days, having to live outside the camp.

The midrash opens with the remark that although Miriam was permitted to return to the camp, she continued to isolate herself in her tent because of her disgrace. Like the moon that shines only at night, Miriam emerges from hiding only at night, when she draws water from the well.

The motif of the well is a symbol of femininity in the midrash, but it is also explicitly connected to Miriam in Numbers Rabbah 1. There, the sages ask why immediately following Miriam's death, the Torah goes on to relate an incident involving a lack of water in the wilderness. The sages explain that the lack of water was a consequence of the disappearance of the well that used to roll with the people throughout their wilderness travels and was given to them by the merit of Miriam. When Miriam died, the Israelites lost that merit, and thus the well disappeared (Tosefta Sotah 11:1).

In her midrash, Biala focuses on the last night that Miriam will go to the well where she will meet her death. That night, when Miriam was gazing into the well, she no longer saw her own reflection and saw instead a vision in which her face was replaced by that of the full moon, and of her mother, until she felt a mouth kissing her own. And thus she died with the death of a kiss.

The next day, the daughters of Israel discovered that the well had dried up, which led them to learn of Miriam's death. They wanted to call for Miriam's help, since the well had been given to them on account of Miriam's merits, but they were also scared to enter her tent. Zipporah, Moses's wife, took upon herself the task of entering the tent. She felt responsible because when Miriam had spoken negatively about Moses, it was in an attempt to reunite Moses with Zipporah after he had separated from her (according to Sifrei Bamidbar 99).

Zipporah discovers that Miriam has died. She takes leave of Miriam with the words, "We will return to you," a phrase traditionally recited when completing the study of a tractate of Talmud, which serves as a promise that the tractate will never be forgotten and will be studied again in the future.

The entire community of women prepares Miriam's body for burial, and they eulogize her by invoking verses from the Song of Songs. Some praise her beauty by comparing her to the moon, while others quote a verse that serves to affirm that she merited to die by a kiss. These eulogies memorialize Miriam for her sensitivity and her willingness to fight on behalf of others, while also celebrating her closeness to God, who valued her and her brothers equally.

FIVE

Prophets
and
Writings

RIVKAH LUBITCH

Tanot, Jephthah's Daughter

The judge Jephthah, described in the eleventh chapter of the book of Judges, was asked to lead Israel in a war against the Ammonites. He vowed that if he was successful in battle and returned home safely, he would sacrifice the first creature to come out of the door of his home. Following the Israelites' victory, Jephthah's daughter came out to greet her father, who had returned from battle to a chorus of drumming and dancing. As a result, she was fated to die in her youth, never to marry and bear children. In this midrash, Lubitch invents a mythical literary figure named Tanot, the soul of Jephthah's daughter who ascended to the heavens, where she presents the troubles of the daughters of Israel before the Shekhinah, the feminine form of God in rabbinic literature. Tanot gives voice to the pain and distress of women who live in a patriarchal society. When she prays for them and serves as their advocate before the Shekhinah, she transforms their destiny.

She was an only child, he had no other son or daughter (Judg 11:34).

The Shekhinah said to Jephthah's daughter: Jephthah had no progeny from you, and on earth they don't know that a woman has a name of her own, even without having a son or daughter. Sit with Me in heaven, and weep for this. On earth they call you "Jephthah's daughter," and I will call you "Tanot."

And why was she called "Tanot"? Because it is written, *And so since long ago, the daughters of Israel go to wail (le-Tanot) for the daughter of Jephthah the Gileadite, four days a year* (Judg 11:40). And they said, Tanot does not mean wailing but is the name of Jephthah's daughter. And what does she do? She sits in heaven and listens to the stories of the earthly daughters of Israel, and then sits by the Shekhinah and bewails their sorrows in Her ear, prays for them, and pleads their righteousness.

Commentary

This midrash opens with a description of the transformation of Jephthah's daughter into a heavenly figure who advocates for the daughters of Israel before God. After her soul ascended to heaven, a dialogue ensued between her and the Shekhinah. The Shekhinah, the feminine form of God, bemoans the mistaken way in which men on earth perceive the status of women. As men see it, women do not have names of their own, and their existence is meaningless if they have not born children. Jephthah's daughter is not given a name in the biblical story, and she is still unmarried and childless. She was also Jephthah's only child. The Shekhinah invites this young woman to sit beside Her in heaven. She gives her the name Tanot as a way of protesting the injustices of the patriarchy.

Lubitch, employing the Talmud's style of discourse, asks why she was called Tanot. The answer given by her midrash invokes the verse that describes the fate of Jephthah's daughter: *And so since long ago, the daughters of Israel go to wail (le-Tanot) for Jephthah's daughter, four days a year* (Judg 11:40).

Lubitch reads the Hebrew word for "to wail" as a reference to Jephthah's daughter, such that the daughters of Israel go out to, or for Tanot, Yiftach's daughter. (Both senses of the prefix *le-* are possible in Biblical Hebrew.) As this name suggests, Jephthah's daughter gives voice to a permanent existential state of pain and lamentation. As the victim of unforgivable injustice, Tanot is uniquely suited to identify with and to understand the pain of all women, to pray on their behalf, and to intercede with the Shekhinah to improve their situations.

Tanot is a recurrent figure in Lubitch's midrashim (see, for instance, her "And Your Desire Will Be for Your Man" and "The Daughters of Tzelophchad," in this collection), as well as in the midrashim of other writers (see for instance Tamar Biala's "For Love Is as Fierce as Death" on page 110 and "Where Was Sarah?" on page 40).

YAEL LEVINE

I Will Build You Up Again

The book of Judges describes the tragedy that befalls Jephthah's daughter, whose father vowed that if he returned from battle victorious, he would sacrifice the first creature that came out of the doors of his home. Very unfortunately, the first to come forth was his daughter, and as the Bible relates, Jephthah fulfilled his vow. In this midrash, Yael Levine proposes a happy ending to the story of Jephthah's daughter that takes place in the "time to come." In keeping with the prophecies of consolation, Levine envisions a future in which Jephthah's daughter will rise from the dead and sit at the head of a beit midrash for women, becoming an inspirational role model for women scholars. She will be surrounded by other women who suffered unjust, bitter fates in this world, and together they will merit a better life in which the wrongs committed against them will be redressed.

I will build you up again, and you will be rebuilt, O virgin of Israel.
Again you shall take up your tambourine and go forth in a circle of dancers
(Jer 31:3).

Scripture was referring to Jephthah's daughter in the days to come.

Jephthah of Gilead had taken a vow to God: *If you deliver the sons of Ammon into my hands, then whatever comes out my door to meet me when I return in peace shall be the Lord's and shall be offered by me as a burnt offering* (Judg 11:30–31). When he came home, his daughter came out of his door to meet him, as it is written: *And his daughter came out to him with tambourine and circles of dancers; she was an only child, he had no other son or daughter* (Judg 11:34). Jephthah meant to keep his oath, so she went to the hills, she and her friends, to weep for two months for her virginity.

And the sages said: Once Jephthah decided to make an offering of her, his daughter wept and began to engage him back and forth with words of

Torah, insisting that he might annul his vow, but he would not consent. She saw he would not listen to her, so she went to the Sanhedrin, and the Sanhedrin found no way of undoing his vow.

———

God gave Jephthah's daughter a memorial and a name in this world. The daughters of Israel would go out four days a year to wail for Jephthah's daughter, as is written, *From days of old the daughters of Israel go to wail for the daughter of Jephthah of Gilead, four days a year* (Judg 11: 40).

But in the days to come, at the time that God will rain down on Jephthah's daughter the dew of rebirth, like our father Isaac when bound on the altar, and like the people of Israel when they received the Torah, at that time He will raise and exalt her. Of her, Scripture says, *I will build you up again and you will be rebuilt.* And of her, it is written, *Fear not, you shall not be shamed. Do not cringe, you shall not be disgraced. For you shall forget the shame of your youth* (Isa 54:4).

And there will come a time when Jephthah's daughter will wed a man, and The Holy Blessed One will bless her and enlarge her bounds with sons and daughters. *Jerusalem is surrounded by mountains, and God surrounds His people* (Ps 125:2). And her sons and daughters will congregate all around her, and she will delight in them. And Jephthah's daughter, whose father was a worthless bumpkin and a pauper in Torah, who went to the Sanhedrin to seek out their counsel, will merit to become learned in Torah. And she will sit and contemplate Torah day and night, and of her it was said, "Take care with the children of paupers, for the Torah will emerge from them."

And her husband will also study Torah day and night, as it is written: "A woman is not joined to man, other than by his deeds."

And the Torah she could not lay hold of in her lifetime, she will merit to learn in just a short time and she, the daughter of Jephthah, the mighty hero, will excel in the world of learning.

And her good name in Torah study will cast its scent afar, to the ends of the earth.

And her Torah will spread forth, as it is written: *And you will burst to the west and to the east, to the north and to the south* (Gen 28:14).

And she will sit at the head of the beit midrash in Jerusalem the Holy City, and the women of Israel will come flocking to her from each and every place, to hear Torah from her mouth.

And each and every day she will study and expound on the laws of vows and examine them in depth, and develop wondrous interpretations.

And all her sons and daughters will contemplate Torah as well, and of her it is said: *And all your sons shall be disciples of the Lord, and great shall be the happiness of your children* (Isa 54:13). "Don't read sons (*banayikh*) but builders (*bonayikh*)" of insight. And this is what Scripture meant by *I will yet build you up and you will be rebuilt, O virgin of Israel*, and she is included among them.

And the four days of the year that the daughters of Israel would go to wail for Jephthah's daughter will become days of joy and happiness and festivals for Israel.

And the daughters of Israel will lay rest their handiwork, and go to the beit midrash of Jephthah's daughter, and there will be ample space for them all.

And Jephthah's daughter will sit in all her majesty, in all her splendor and all her radiance, and teach Torah in public.

And she is the one and only of her Father in Heaven, as it is written, *And his daughter came out to him with tambourine and circles of dancers; she was an only child, he had no other son or daughter*, and his daughter is none other than the daughter of The Holy Blessed One.

———

And not only Jephthah's daughter will be redeemed, for in each and every generation there are daughters of Israel like Jephthah's daughter.

Some never married, and some had husbands who went off to war and never returned, some were abandoned by their husbands and were left as living widows, and other such strange and varied happenings of the generations over time.

These will be redeemed along with Jephthah's daughter in the future to come, just as many barren women conceived at the same time that Sarah our foremother became pregnant and of these women and of Jephthah's daughter, Scripture says *for I am God, I built the ruined ones* (Ezek 36:36).

And these women will also rest in the shade of Jephthah's daughter and study Torah in her presence in the beit midrash in Jerusalem, and they will sit to her right and learn.

And at that hour, Jephthah's daughter will go forth with tambourines and dancing circles, as it is written: *Again you shall take up your tambourine, and go forth in a circle of dancers*, she and the women of Israel with her and so

Scripture says: *Then the virgin will rejoice in dancing circles* (Jer 31:13). And what song will they sing? *God's right hand is heroic, God's right hand is raised up high* (Ps 118:15–16).

And this is what Scripture meant by: *I will build you up again, and you will be rebuilt, O virgin of Israel. Again you shall take up your tambourine, and go forth in a circle of dancers.*

Commentary

This midrash quotes a verse from Jeremiah's prophecy of consolation: *I will yet build you up and you will be rebuilt, O virgin of Israel, you'll yet take up your tambourine, and go forth in a circle of dancers"* (Jer 31:3). This description of going forth in dancing circles is reminiscent of the description of Jephthah's daughter, *and his daughter came out to him with tambourine and circles of dancers* (Judg 11:34), and the phrase "virgin of Israel" is read as alluding to Jephthah's daughter, *who wept for her virginity on the mountains* (Judges 11:38). According to the midrashic tradition, Jephthah's daughter is described as a disciple of the sages who presented legitimate halakhic arguments to counter her father when he sought to fulfill his vow and offer her as a sacrifice. But her father was an unlearned boor, and the Sanhedrin and the High Priest did not accept her arguments on account of interpersonal conflicts and other political reasons (Tanhuma Bechukotai 5).

The core of the midrash involves a fantastical feminist vision set in "days to come," a redeemed world in which the dead will come back to life and Jephthah's daughter's fate will merit a corrective. Levine writes that the dew of rebirth that will descend on Jephthah's daughter will bring her back to life (Pirkei d'Rabbi Eliezer, Higger edition, 33).

In describing Jephthah's daughter's return to life, Levine invokes verses of consolation from Isaiah and Psalms to describe her positive fate: she will no longer be embarrassed and ashamed, but will deserve to renew her world and rebuild her life. Elaborating on the rabbinic midrash, Levine describes Jephthah's daughter's future: she will become a disciple of the sages who sits at the head of a beit midrash for women and specializes in the laws of vows. The traditional midrash teaches that her father was "a bumpkin" (Tosefta Rosh Hashanah, Lieberman ed., 1:18) and "poor in Torah learning" (Tanhuma, Buber, ed., Bechukotai 7). In response, Levine argues that the rabbinic injunction to "take care with the children of paupers, for the Torah will emerge from them" (b.Nedarim 81a) was referring to Jephthah's daughter. She will also experience a reversal of fortune in her personal status: she will marry a Torah scholar, in keeping with the rabbinic statement that "a woman is not joined to man, other than by his deeds" (b.Sotah 2a). And her children will be Torah scholars as well, as it is written: *and all your children are learned of God and great peace to your sons* (Isa 54:13). Levine explains that Jephthah's daughter's scholarly children will be those who "rebuild" her, ascribing to them the midrash on the words "your sons" (Isa 54:13) from b.Berakhot 64a: "Don't read sons (*banayikh*) but builders (*bonayikh*)" and so invoking the verse, *I will yet build you up and you will be rebuilt, O virgin of Israel* interpreting "virgin of Israel" as referring to Jephthah's daughter.

Levine goes on to describe Jephthah's daughter as a spiritual and intellectual leader of the women of Israel. She employs an additional midrash to show that Jephthah's daughter was especially close to God, who regarded her as his singular and special daughter.

The final section of the midrash develops this vision of consolation for additional women who suffered bitter fates "like Jephthah's daughter." Levine alludes to the rabbinic midrash that teaches that when God remembered Sarah and enabled her to conceive, the divine blessing also descended on other barren women and other women with physical defects, and they were remembered and redeemed alongside her (Genesis Rabbah 53:8). Levine interprets Ezekiel's prophecy that God will build the ruined ones (36:36), which originally referred to the destroyed cities of Judea, as applying also to these other women. The midrash concludes with an enchanting description of the climax of this redemption in which Jephthah's daughter, along with these women, will go out together dancing and singing songs of praise. Unlike Jephthah's daughter's original dance, which ended in tragedy, she will now perform a true victory dance celebrating her redeemed fate and that of all those Jewish women who merit being rebuilt and to live their lives anew, with joy, Torah study, and closeness to God, in fulfillment of the verse, *I will yet build you up and you will be rebuilt, O virgin of Israel, you'll yet take up your tambourine, and go forth in a circle of dancers* (Jer 31:3).

A Woman of Valor

The verses that conclude the thirty-first chapter of the book of Proverbs are known as the "Woman of Valor" passage. These verses praise an ideal woman who is wise, industrious, gifted, engaged in both commercial and domestic labor, concerned for the needs of her family, compassionate toward the poor, and esteemed by those around her. This section of Proverbs, written as an alphabetical acrostic, is attributed by the rabbis to King Solomon. In many Jewish communities, it is customary to chant this passage in the home on Friday nights before reciting the Kiddush blessing.

In this midrash, Adi Blut offers two possible identifications of the Woman of Valor. First, she identifies her as Batsheva, the mother of King Solomon, who King David forcibly took as a lover and then married after orchestrating her husband's death in battle. Second, she identifies her with Jewish women throughout history, reading the biblical passage as a historic description of the advances in women's status from biblical times to our own day.

A woman of valor, who can find her? (Prov 31:10).

This is Batsheva, mother of Solomon. And why call her valorous?

In the beit midrash they said, do not read it *chayil* (valorous) but *chayal* (of a soldier)—for Batsheva was the wife of Uriah the Hittite, one of King David's soldiers.

Her husband placed his heart's trust in her (31:11), when he went out to battle, that she'd keep faith with him until he returned home. And she *dealt him good and not evil* (31:12), and while he was away, she kept their home—*laying hold of the distaff and taking the spindle in hand* (31:19), *sought out wool and flax* (31:13) and *selling fine cloth* (31:24) to all takers. *Her candle did not go out in the night* (31:18); maybe he'll come home today, she'd say, and she'd wait for his return every single night.

And David *oversaw her ways* (31:28) and saw her *misleading charm and fleeting beauty* (31:30) and lay hold of her with his arms and took her and slept with her. And when she conceived by him, he sent her husband into the face of battle, till there he fell.

And she returned to her home and was waiting for her husband's return, tending the lamps every night, and he didn't come back.

When he was late in returning *she girded her loins in strength* (31:17) and went out to look for him. She passed among the soldiers, asking *who has found* (31:10) him? She would describe to them how he looked, his dimensions, and his voice, and her husband was unknown. On returning home she heard that he'd died in the war. At once she tore her clothes and walked and wept for all seven days of mourning, until David swept her to his palace and took her as a wife. The Holy Blessed One saw her sorrow, heard her weeping, and was good to her—for from her came royalty.

———

A woman of valor, who can find her? (31:10)—Scripture spoke here in none other than parable, for all that women have undergone through the generations, and all that they will:

For first, women were in their homes, engaged in housework *working gladly with their hands* (31:13), as we taught "it is a woman's way to be at home" and *all the princess's treasure is inward* (Ps 45:14).

As they went on, and women *were like merchant ships* (31:14), they went out of their homes for give and take with people, as we have found "in these times, that women are legal guardians, and storekeepers, and negotiate, and borrow and lend, and pay and are paid, and make and receive deposits ... and a woman in this time has business capacity ... even a married woman."

And in the end, they engage in Torah: Her *lips open with wisdom, and the Torah of kindness is on her tongue* (31:26) as we were taught "a woman can serve as the leader, and even the great figure of her time ... and lay down norms with authority."

First, *her sons rose to declare her blessed* and after them, *her husband sang her praise* (31:28), and after him, all recognized her wisdom, as is written *and her deeds will sing her praises in the gates* (31:31).

Commentary

Adi Blut's first midrash identifies the Woman of Valor as Batsheva, based on an exegetical tradition that attributes this biblical passage to King Solomon, who wrote it for his mother (Midrash Mishlei, Buber, ed., 31). But Blut offers an entirely different justification. She reads this passage as alluding to aspects of an earlier stage of Batsheva's life when she was the wife of Uriah the Hittite (see 2 Sam 11). In so doing, she proposes a new reading of the difficult story of the sin of David and Batsheva. In the biblical account, Batsheva is depicted as a submissive, obedient wife, subservient to the king. She is even compared to a docile sheep. But Blut depicts Batsheva as an industrious woman with a mind of her own who sought to remain faithful to her husband and free of sin.

The opening lines of the midrash insist "do not read it," a common midrashic technique whereby the vocalization of a word is changed so as to support an alternative reading. Batsheva is not a "valorous woman" (*eshet chayil*) but rather the "wife of a soldier" (*eshet chayal*), since she was married to Uriah the Hittite, a soldier in David's army. The book of Samuel relates that King David saw Batsheva bathing on the roof of her home. He took her and slept with her when her soldier husband was away at the front. When David learned that she was pregnant, he sought to cause Uriah to sleep with his wife so as to cover up for what he had done. But he was unable to persuade Uriah to return home. So instead David adopted the strategy of dispatching Uriah to a fatal battle, where indeed the soldier was killed, and in so doing, David incurred God's wrath.

Adi Blut reads the passage from Proverbs as describing various aspects of this narrative. The phrase *her husband placed his heart's trust in her* (Prov 31:11) is read as a description of Batsheva, whose husband, Uriah, trusted her to remain faithful until he returned from battle. He was right to trust in her, because she *dealt him good and not evil* (31:12), caring for the home in his absence, according to the next few verses in Proverbs. The phrase *her candle didn't go out in the night* (Prov 31:18) is interpreted as describing the candle that Batsheva kept permanently lit in hopeful anticipation of her husband's imminent return.

In contrast to Batsheva's laudable behavior, the phrase *oversaw her ways* (31:27) is read as attributed to King David, who observed Batsheva's many virtues and desired her. Blut writes that King David "saw her misleading charm and fleeting beauty," an allusion to a verse from the end of the passage in Proverbs: *Charm is misleading and beauty is fleeting, but a woman who fears God will be praised* (31:30). David did not concern himself with fearing God, and thus he was drawn to that which is false and ephemeral. He didn't just commit adultery; he also sent a man to his death.

Blut reads the rest of the passage as describing what Batsheva underwent when she did not know of her husband's death. She *girded her loins in strength* (31:17) and went out to search for her husband, the missing soldier. The line "her husband was unknown" is an ironic allusion to the verse from Proverbs stating that *her husband is known in the gates of the city* (31:23). Ultimately, when she learns the truth, she is forced to confront the enormity of her loss. Blut thus depicts Batsheva as a faithful wife who was a victim of King David's corruption. On account of her virtue and integrity, God chose her to be the mother of royalty.

The second midrash reads the "Woman of Valor" passage as a representation of Jewish women throughout the generations, tracing the advances in women's status from biblical times to our own day. Blut reads the first few verses, which describe the labors that the woman performs in the domestic sphere, as referring to the rabbinic period. She quotes the rabbinic sages, who viewed the home as the proper place for a woman: "It is a woman's way to be at home, and a man's way to go out to the marketplace and learn discernment from human beings" (Genesis Rabbah 18:1). She also quotes a verse from Psalms (45:14), *All the princess's treasure is inward*, from which the rabbis deduced that a woman is praised for her humility and for staying in the home (Leviticus Rabbah 20:11; Tanhuma Vayishlach 6).

Blut describes the changes that women underwent throughout the Middle Ages by invoking the next few verses in the passage from Proverbs. The woman was *like merchant ships, bringing her bread from afar* (31:14) and *she sees that her business thrives* (31:18)—a description of a woman who engages in commerce in the public sphere. Blut also quotes a halakhic responsum from Rabbi Elazar ben Natan, the Ra'avan (Germany, 1090–1170), who was one of the early Tosafists, creative and authoritatice Talmud commentators from medieval Franco-Germany. In light of the social reality of his day, in which women were active in the commercial sphere much like their husbands, the Ra'avan ruled that a woman's commercial transactions are valid, and if she buys or sells property for her husband, the gains and losses are incumbent upon him as well.

Finally, Blut describes the changes that have taken place in women's status in our own day by means of the final verses of the chapter in Proverbs: *her lips open with wisdom, and the Torah of kindness is on her tongue* (31:26). She quotes the famous and controversial statement of Rabbi Eliyahu Bakshi-Doron, who served as Sephardic Chief Rabbi of Israel from 1993 to 2003, and who taught that "a woman can serve as the leader, and even the great figure of her time" (She'elot u-Teshuvot Binyan Av, I: 65). Blut concludes by asserting that there are wise women in our own day who are known as disciples of the sages and are praised publicly by their family members, as the final verse indicates: *Her deeds will sing her praises in the gates* (31:31). The end of the midrash expresses the hope that the great learned women of our own generation will receive the widespread public recognition they deserve.

SIX

Sexuality, Love, and Marriage

RIVKAH LUBITCH

More Bitter Than Death

Frustration and bitterness that sometimes develop between the members of a couple may in turn lead to depression. The Talmud (b.Yevamot 63a) relates that Rav's wife caused her husband great distress, leading him to experience a bitterness worse than death. Lubitch describes this relationship from the woman's perspective. She expands the Talmudic story by accounting for Rav's wife's behavior, effectively turning the story on its head and placing the responsibility for their difficult relationship squarely on the shoulders of Rav, who fails to understand his wife. By means of this midrash, Lubitch sheds light on the high toll exacted by patriarchal power relations on both members of a couple.

And I find woman more bitter than death (Eccl 7:26).

Rav was perplexed: Is there anything that is worse than death? He went, examined, and found: *And I find woman more bitter than death.* Rav's wife would aggravate him. When he would say to her: Prepare me lentils, she would prepare him peas; if he asked her for peas, she would prepare him lentils (b.Yevamot 63a).

But why?

Not because Rav would sometimes tell her he'd be coming home early from the beit midrash and come after nightfall, and his wife would sit there in her humiliation, and wait for him until she became vexed and angry; and sometimes he'd tell her he'd be getting in late from the beit midrash and then come early, and his wife would have to run back and forth to fix his supper.

And not because he sometimes hinted they'd dine together, and he'd bring home a bunch of students, and they'd sit and eat and enjoy themselves, while it fell to her to serve them, and she worked hard at it, and they would talk pleasantly in matters of Torah, wisdom, and wit, and at the end, bless

God; and sometimes he'd tell her he was bringing guests, and she would lay out a lovely repast, and in the end he'd come alone.

But because when Rav knew his wife had cooked lentils he would ask for peas, and when she'd cooked peas, he'd ask for lentils. And she remained silent, and didn't say a word, and just gave him what she'd cooked in the pot.

And this unfortunate woman didn't know why he would do this to her; after all he was the entirety of her world, and of her work. And so she was bitter all her days and almost wanted to die.

And it was about things like this that her friends would say to her:
And I find woman more bitter than death (Eccl 7:26).

Commentary

In the Talmud, the story of Rav and his wife serves to explain and account for Rav's statement, taken from the book of Ecclesiastes: *And I find woman more bitter than death*. The Talmud describes a miserable situation in which Rav's wife never cooks the dishes he requests.

Lubitch offers various explanations for the miserable dynamic between Rav and his wife, all of which serve to account for Rav's wife's behavior. These explanations reflect the daily life of a couple in a patriarchal society. Rav spends his days studying Torah, surrounded by colleagues and flocked by disciples. In contrast, his wife is ensconced in the home, where she is responsible for preparing meals for her husband and his guests. She cannot even enjoy the words of Torah they exchange. The couple is so estranged from one another that Rav does not understand or appreciate that his wife's life is entirely dictated by his lifestyle and his daily patterns. But in spite of the woman's ongoing distress and frustration, Lubitch insists that these are not the reasons for the wife's seemingly antagonistic behavior in the kitchen. Rather, as she ultimately reveals, it is not that Rav's wife prepares the opposite of what her husband requests, but rather that he requests the opposite of whatever she has already prepared.

With this midrash, Lubitch may be hinting at another story that appears in the continuation of this passage and focuses on the relationship between Rav's son and his wife:

When his son, Hiyya, grew up, he would reverse the requests Rav asked him to convey to her, so that Rav would get what he wanted. Rav said to his son Hiyya: Your mother has improved now that you convey my requests. He said to Rav: It is I who reverse your request to her.

Lubitch offers a new interpretation of the verse from Ecclesiastes. The one who finds the woman more bitter than death is not her husband but the woman's own friends, who find her tragically embittered. It is not that the husband is disappointed in and frustrated by his wife, but rather that the wife's friends empathize with the woman who is suffering at the hands of her husband.

The general category of "woman" referred to by Ecclesiastes is represented by the intimate portrayal of one particular woman. The midrash offers a window into her daily life within the social and familial contexts, exposing the terrible, unbearable injustice that many women experience under similar circumstances.

RIVKAH LUBITCH

After Twenty-Four Years

Rivkah Lubitch suggests various alternative endings to the story of Rabbi Akiva and his wife, which appears in the Babylonian Talmud in Ketubot 62b–63a. She explores the effect on a relationship when one member of a couple enjoys a rich intellectual and spiritual life, while the other forfeits her own self-fulfillment for the sake of her partner. The various alternative endings represent the range of possible outcomes when both members of the couple strive to learn and grow and influence the world.

This midrash is attributed to the women sages in Beruriah's beit midrash, an imaginary women's study house led by the second-century sage Beruriah, who was the daughter of Rabbi Hanina ben Teradion and the wife of Rabbi Meir.

What became in the end of Rabbi Akiva and his wife, who was the daughter of Kalba Savua, and who married him in secret then sent him off for twenty-four years to learn Torah?

In Beruriah's beit midrash, some said it all worked out, and some said it did not.

It all worked out: that on his return, they sat for days, telling one another about all those years that she had been at home and he in the beit midrash, and at night, he would teach her his Torah.

It didn't work out: she grieved for all those years that she never conceived, never gave birth, and would sit and weep for all those babies who could have been born, until her tears ran dry and she wished she were dead. In vain would he try to conciliate her, and tell her *am I not better to you than ten sons* (1 Sam 1:8)?

Another version: It worked out, for when Rabbi Akiva returned home from the beit midrash after twenty-four years, he sent his wife off to learn Torah too, in the beit midrash for women. And when she returned, aged, they would sit together, basking, he in her Torah and she in his, and they had many, many students.

And some say, that is indeed what they did, but it didn't work out.

And Sigal said, that's not how it was. When Rabbi Akiva returned after twenty-four years with twenty-four thousand students, he wanted to come home, stood on the threshold, and couldn't enter. His wife told him: The door of your house is not open to you. Go back to where you came from.

Commentary

The title of this midrash echoes the title of an O. Henry short story, "After Twenty Years," an ironic tale whose surprise ending upends our understanding of the entire story. In this midrash too, the various surprise endings change the way we understand the Talmud's account of the relationship between Rabbi Akiva and the daughter of Kalba Savua, shedding new light on this ancient tale.

The Babylonian Talmud (b.Ketubot 62b–63a) contains the story of the marriage of the shepherd Akiva with the daughter of Kalba Savua, one of the wealthiest men in Jerusalem. Kalba Savua's daughter pledged to wed Akiva on the condition that he go off to study Torah. When her father learned of their marriage, he disinherited his daughter and cut off all connection with her. Akiva fulfilled his wife's condition. He left home for twenty-four years of study and became one of the most important and famous sages.

Here is the story as it appears in Sefaria's English rendering of the Talmud:

Rabbi Akiva was the shepherd of ben Kalba Savua, one of the wealthy residents of Jerusalem. The daughter of Kalba Savua saw that he was humble and refined. She said to him: If I betroth myself to you, will you go to the study hall to learn Torah? He said to her: Yes. She became betrothed to him privately and sent him off to study. Her father heard this and became angry. He removed her from his house and took a vow prohibiting her from benefiting from his property. Rabbi Akiva went and sat for twelve years in the study hall. When he came back to his house he brought twelve thousand students with him, and as he approached, he heard an old man saying to his wife: For how long will you lead the life of a widow of a living man, living alone while your husband is in another place? She said to him: If he would listen to me, he would sit and study for another twelve years. When Rabbi Akiva heard this he said: I have permission to do this. He went back and sat for another twelve years in the study hall. When he came back he brought twenty-four thousand students with him. His wife heard and went out toward him to greet him. Her neighbors said: Borrow some clothes and wear them, as your current apparel is not appropriate to meet an important person. She said to them, "A righteous man understands the life of his beast" (Prov 12:10). When she came to him, she fell on her face and kissed his feet. His attendants pushed her away as they did not know who she was, and he said to them: Leave her alone, as my Torah knowledge and yours is actually hers.

In this midrash Rivkah Lubitch presents a discussion that ostensibly took place among a group of women studying the story of Rabbi Akiva and the daughter of Kalba Savua. The students suggest five alternative endings to the Talmudic story, all of which describe the life the couple shared after Rabbi Akiva returned from his twenty-four years of study.

The first two endings describe a reality in which Rabbi Akiva and his wife continue to live together in their home. The first ending describes how the couple manages to rebuild their relationship and overcome their years of separation by jointly sharing in all the spiritual treasures that Akiva has gleaned from his years of study. The second ending, which is tragic, describes how Rabbi Akiva's wife sinks into a deep depression on account of the terrible price she paid in separating from her spouse for so long. Rabbi Akiva tries to comfort her by invoking the same words that Elkana spoke to comfort Hannah in her barrenness: *Am I not better to you than ten sons?* (1 Sam 1:8).

The second pair of endings suggested by the students describe an egalitarian relationship in which following Rabbi Akiva's return, his wife sets off for a long period of study and returns home only when they are both very old. According to the first idyllic ending, the two share the knowledge that they each acquired. According to the second tragic ending, their relationship never recovers.

The midrash concludes with a fifth possibility that is most surprising of all: Rabbi Akiva returns home and his wife refuses to let him in—implying that their years of separation destroyed the home they had built together.

This midrash critiques a story that is traditionally regarded as a model of ideal love.

The midrash exposes the costs incurred by a patriarchal society that encourages and enables men alone to develop spiritually and take on leadership roles. By proposing an egalitarian alternative, this midrash heightens our awareness of and invites our response to developments we are witness to today, in which women strive to cultivate their own rich spiritual lives on par with those of their male counterparts.

TAMAR BIALA

For Love Is as Fierce as Death

Two models of intimate relationships appear in the book of Ezekiel and in the Song of Songs respectively. Whereas Ezekiel describes a patriarchal relationship based on power and ownership, the Song of Songs depicts an egalitarian partnership based on reciprocal trust and desire. Tamar Biala's midrash juxtaposes these two models to suggest that the book of Ezekiel, though morally problematic, was included in the biblical canon so as to bring about a much-needed reckoning with the unjust nature of patriarchy.

Rav Yehuda said: Indeed, that man is remembered for good, and Hananya ben Hizkiya was his name, were it not for him, the book of Ezekiel would have been suppressed, for its words contradicted the words of Torah. What did he [Hananya ben Hizkiya] do? They brought up to him three hundred barrels of oil, and he sat in an upper chamber and expounded it [to reconcile its teachings with those of the Torah] (b.Haggigah 13a).

Rabbi Akiva said, Heaven forbid! No one in Israel ever disputed that the Song of Songs renders the hands impure, since nothing in the entire world is worthy but for that day on which the Song of Songs was given to Israel; for all the Scriptures are holy, but the Song of Songs is the Holy of Holies! (Mishnah, Yadayim 3:5).

Tanot asked the Shekhinah: What did Ezekiel say that contradicted the words of the Torah?

She answered: He did not fulfill, when it came to women, *love your neighbor as yourself* (Lev 19:18). For when he wanted to tell Israel how God chose them for a people and how they betrayed Him, and to comfort them—that terrible things would befall them one day out of the blue and they would again be loved by Him—he told them all this through a parable, and that parable was cruel and humiliated the women of the world.

Tanot asked: And what were the three hundred kegs of oil that they brought up to him, to Hananya ben Hizkiya, so that he would interpret Ezekiel?

She said: They brought him the Song of Songs, as is written: *Your oint-ments smell sweet, your name is like finest oil, that is why the maidens love you* (Song 1:3).

Tanot asked: And how can one interpret Ezekiel with the Song of Songs?

The Shekhinah answered: Ezekiel said: *You were still naked and bare when I passed by you and saw that your time for love had arrived. So I spread my robe over you and covered your nudity and I swore a covenant to you—declares the Lord God—and so you were mine* (Ezek 16:7–8).

Comes the Song of Songs and says: *Let us rise early to the vineyards, we'll see if the vine has flowered, if the pomegranates have bloomed, there I'll give my love to you* (Song 7:13).

Ezekiel said, *Like mother, like daughter; you are your mother's daughter, she who rejected her man and children* (Ezek 16:44–45).

Comes the Song of Songs and says: *Until I brought him to my mother's house, to the chamber of she who conceived me* (Song 3:4) *I would lead you, I would bring you to my mother's house* (Song 8:2). *Under the apple tree I roused you, it was there your mother conceived you* (Song 8:5).

Ezekiel said: *I clothed you ... put shoes on you ... covered your head ... and cloaked you ...* (Ezek 16:10).

Comes the Song of Songs and says: *Let me see your face* (Song 2:14). *Turn back, turn back that we might gaze upon you* (Song 7:1).

Ezekiel said: *And you will be too ashamed to open your mouth again* (Ezek 16:63).

Comes the Song of Songs and says: *O you who linger in the garden, a lover is listening, let me hear your voice* (Song 8:13).

Ezekiel said: *Now I will raise my arm against you ... and give you over to your enemies* (Ezek 16:27). *I will direct bloody and passionate fury against you; I will deliver you into their hands and they will tear down ... and level ... and strip you ... and take ... and gather a mob and pelt you with stones and pierce you with their swords ... and punish you* (Ezek 16:38-41).

Comes the Songs of Songs and says: *A king is held captive in the tresses* (Song 7:6) and says: *Let me be a seal upon your hand* (Song 8:6).

Ezekiel said: *Confident in your beauty and fame, you played the whore* (Ezek 16:15).

Comes the Song of Songs and says: *If you don't know, O fairest of women, go out* . . . (Song 1:8) and added *Arise my darling, my fair one, come away!* (Song 2:10).

Ezekiel said: *I will establish my covenant with you* (Ezek 16:62), and *Your beauty won you fame among the nations, perfected through the splendor which I bestowed on you—declares the Lord God* (Ezek 16:14).

Comes the Song of Songs and says: *O would that you were my brother* (Song 8:1) and *My beloved is mine and I am his* (Song 2:16).

And so it was that the Shekhinah said to Tanot: *Draw me after you, let us run!* (*narutza*) (Song 1:4). Do not read it as "let us run" (*narutza*), but rather "let's desire" (*nirtzeh*). For there is no love where there is no will, and there is no faithfulness where there is no trust, and all the Scriptures are holy and Song of Songs is the holy of holies.

Commentary

This midrash begins with a question posed to the Shekhinah by Tanot (see page xxvi). Tanot wonders which elements of Ezekiel's prophecy were regarded by the sages as contradicting the laws of the Torah, on account of which the sages hesitated whether to include it in the biblical canon. Unlike the explanations provided by the sages (see, for instance, b.Menachot 45a), the Shekhinah responds to Tanot that the contradictions all pertain to the prophet's relationships with women, which violate the injunction to *love your neighbor as yourself.* Later it becomes clear that Tanot is referring specifically to the parable that appears in Ezekiel 16, in which the people of Israel are analogized to a young girl abandoned in a field and drawn up compassionately by The Holy Blessed One, who tended to her physically and emotionally, raised her, and took care of her until she reached maturity. When her "time for love" arrived, The Holy Blessed One took her as His wife. But instead of expressing gratitude and acting faithfully, she began to betray him. Her promiscuous behavior—acts of infidelity with various other lovers—is described in great detail in the subsequent verses, along with the harsh punishments that God will bring upon her. The history of the Children of Israel, from the birth of the nation until the historical circumstances in the time of Ezekiel, is explained by means of this extraordinarily tempestuous and violent parable in which Israel's suffering is attributed to her unfaithfulness to God.

The Babylonian Talmud recounts that Hananya ben Hizkiya rendered the book of Ezekiel fit for inclusion in the biblical canon by means of three hundred kegs of oil, which were used for food or light. But according to Biala's midrash, these kegs of oil were the verses from the Song of Songs, which mentions various fragrant oils. The Song of Songs led Hananya ben Hizkiya to a better understanding of the book of Ezekiel and its place in the biblical canon. As depicted in this midrash, Hananya ben Hizkiya compared the common themes in these texts and concluded that their role, when placed in the same biblical corpus, is to present different possible models of relationships between men and women in our world. Biala's juxtaposition of verses from each of these biblical books leads to a preference for the model presented in the Song of Songs, which is based on egalitarianism and trust.

From this point on, the midrash juxtaposes the descriptions of various aspects of relationships in the book of Ezekiel with the descriptions of these same elements in the Song of Songs:

- *The sense of obligation created between the members of the* couple: In Ezekiel, the man owns the woman—*you were mine*—whereas the Song of Songs describes this relationship as one of giving voluntarily.
- *The connection between the members of the couple and their parents*: In Ezekiel, the man spurns and repudiates his spouse's family of origin, and denigrates his spouse as a result; in Song of Songs, the woman's family of origin is a source of support, closeness, and pride.
- *The status of the individual*: In Ezekiel, the relationship between the man and woman is described as existentially weakening the members of the couple, whereas in Song of Songs it strengthens each of them.
- *How one is permitted and prohibited to conduct oneself vis-à-vis one's partner*: Ezekiel describes violence and displays of force, whereas the Song of Songs describes a relationship of restraint, self-control, softness, and gentleness.
- *The degree of trust and faith in the partnership*: Ezekiel depicts a relationship of suspicion manifested in an act of infidelity, whereas in the Song of Songs, each partner gives the other the space and encouragement to develop a social life beyond their partnership.
- *The power dynamic between the members of the couple*: Ezekiel describes a relationship of ownership in which the man is controlling of his partner and feels proprietary toward her body—*the splendor which I bestowed on you*—in contrast to the Song of Songs, which describes an egalitarian

partnership in which the man affirms the presence of his partner—*O would that you were my brother*—and *My beloved is mine and I am his.*

The midrash concludes with an exegesis on the verse *draw me after you, let us run* (Song 1:4). The Shekhinah interprets the term *let us run* (*narutza*) as coming not from the word "run" (*rutz*), but rather from the word "desire" (*ratzon*). The beloved expresses her desire to follow her partner. Her desire carries significant weight in the unfolding of their relationship. The Shekhinah explains to Tanot that love and faithfulness depend on mutual desire and trust and cannot be forced. Thus, the Song of Songs surpasses all other holy books in its depiction of the ideal relationship between a couple. In the immortal words of Rabbi Akiva: The Song of Songs, more than the other holy books, is the Holy of Holies.

AVITAL HOCHSTEIN

The Ways of Marriage

In the Bible, marriage is described using the verb "take": *Should a man take a wife and possess her* (Deut 24:1). The Bible does not describe what form this legal process uniting two people is supposed to take. It was the rabbis who formulated this process as it is practiced to this day. On account of the verb "take," they understood the act of marriage as one of acquisition.

The Mishnah (Kiddushin 1:1) described the act of tying the knot between two members of a couple as an acquisition that requires the initiative of the groom alone. He plays an active role, designating his bride for himself, whereas the bride is passively "acquired." In the following extended midrash, Avital Hochstein expands the Talmudic discussion of this mishnah in a style of language reminiscent of Talmudic discourse, weaving her insights with the original rabbinic texts. Hochstein critiques the use of acquisition as the basis for the connection between human beings as well as the lack of reciprocity in the marriage ceremony. She suggests basing the connection between the members of a couple on another concept that is mentioned in the Bible in this context: the act of clinging.

A woman is acquired in three ways, and she acquires herself in two ways. She is acquired through money, through a writ of marriage, and through sexual intercourse . . . And acquires herself through a bill of divorce or through the death of the husband (Mishnah Kiddushin 1:1–2).

1

They were asked—In our Mishnah we teach "a woman is acquired in three ways: through money, through a writ of marriage, and through sexual intercourse." A Hebrew slave is acquired how?

We taught there: "A Hebrew slave is acquired through money and through a writ of enslavement."

And large animals?

We taught: "by being handed over."

And property—How does a woman differ from property?

Property is "through money, bill of sale, and possession"—and a woman, "through money, bill of sale and intercourse."

What's more—property does not acquire itself, and the woman "acquires herself" through the death of the husband.

And why should he die?

We're telling him: if you acquired your wife as you did the rest of your property then "she acquires herself . . . through the death of the husband," as we taught. And if the man *takes leave* of acquiring a woman *and clings* to his wife (after Gen 2:24), then he does not die when she "acquires herself," as is written *savor life with a woman* (Eccl 9:9).

2

Michal the daughter of Saul asked: How does here, where we taught "the woman is acquired," differ from there, where we taught "the man betroths" (literally, consecrates)?

They said to her: It says here "is acquired through money," as is written *they will acquire fields with money* (Jer 32:44), and it says *the field which Abraham acquired* (Gen 25:10). And there we taught "the man betroths/ consecrates" for he is, after all, making her forbidden to the entire world, like a consecration.

Michal said: Making her forbidden—who exactly has made her forbidden?

The sages said: He who acquires her.

Michal said: Yet Scripture says, *and he will cling to his wife* (Gen 2:24). If it would have said "and she will cling to her husband," then she'd be forbidden to the entire world. Now that it says *and he will cling to his wife*—isn't it he who is forbidden to the entire world like a consecration?

The sages were silent.

3

We taught in a baraita: "Rabbi Shimon says: Why does the Torah say *should a man take a woman* (Deut 22:13) and not 'should a woman be taken unto a man'? And some say: Why did the Torah say *should a man take a woman* and not 'should a woman take a man'? Because it is the way of a man to pursue a woman and not the way of a woman to pursue a man. It's like someone who loses something, who goes looking for whom? The owner of the object goes looking for what he has lost."

Michal the daughter of Saul said: But it's written *for from a man was this person taken* (Gen 2:23)—she wasn't lost, or is a lost object, but rather *this person will be called woman* (2:23).

They said to her: If it's not a case of lost-and-found, what is the meaning of *the man betroths/consecrates*?

Michal said: Betrothal is the adhering of one to another, as we learned "anywhere that there's a distinction the Mishnah refers to 'ways' and anywhere that there is no distinction it refers to 'things.'" And there we teach a woman is acquired in three *ways*.

And what should the "distinction" be when it comes to betrothal?

Distinction—is a conjoining of things that are separate from one another. The way of kiddushin is like the way of the etrog [citron]. How? "An etrog is akin to a tree in three ways and to vegetation in two." An etrog shares with a tree in one way, with vegetation in another—there is distinction within the whole, in the etrog, in the one. So too with kiddushin, there is a way he shares with her, a way she shares with him—there's distinction within the union, the couple, the one.

What's more, the power of distinction is greater, as it written, *The two are better than one* (Eccl 4:9). One falls, and the other lifts up, one is cold and the other gives warmth, as is written, *For if one should fall and there is none to lift him up . . . and as for one, how will he be warm?* (Eccl 4:10–11)—That is the adhering of the two!

Commentary

1

The first section of Hochstein's Talmudic discussion refers to the first mishnah in Tractate Kiddushin (1:1): "A woman is acquired in three ways: through money, through a writ of marriage, and through sexual intercourse." The mishnah defines the three acts by means of which a man can "acquire" (i.e., marry) a woman: he can give money to the woman (such as the gift of a ring), he can sign a document that obligates him to provide for various needs of hers, or he can sleep with her, which constitutes the consummation of the marriage. The performance of any one of these three acts indicates that he has performed the act of acquisition and married the woman.

The lack of reciprocity is very pronounced in this mishnah. The woman cannot engage in a parallel act of acquisition so as to wed a man. However, the woman may extricate herself in two ways. She may either receive from her partner a bill of divorce, which is a document that attests that he is releasing her from the bonds of marriage of his own volition, or she may extricate herself from marriage by means of her husband's death, which puts an end to his ownership of her.

The mishnayot in the continuation of the chapter deal with additional acquisitions that the man may engage in, such as the purchase of a slave or an animal. The acquisition of a slave takes place by paying money or signing a contract, namely, a writ of enslavement. The acquisition of an animal takes place when it is handed over from one owner to another.

By means of this Talmudic discussion, Hochstein raises a question: How, if so, is the acquisition of a woman different from the acquisition of property? The answer is that a woman alone may be acquired through intercourse. Furthermore, unlike property, a woman may acquire herself in the event that her husband dies (as opposed to other acquisitions that will belong to his heirs).

This answer raises a new question: Why should the husband die?

With this question, Hochstein hints that this way of effecting marriage is problematic for the husband because it is liable to endanger his life. If the husband relates to his wife as his acquisition, in much the same way as he acquires other forms of property, and if he treats her this way throughout their married lives, then ultimately the "death of the husband" will ensue. The death of the husband is a metaphor for the destruction of their marriage because this type of relationship will lead the wife to desire a divorce. And it may not be just a metaphor, but may in fact pose a real threat to the husband's life.

Hochstein proposes an alternative model as the basis for the connection between the members of a couple. This model comes from the description of the first couple in the Garden of Eden: *Hence a man leaves his father and mother and clings to his wife, so that they become one flesh* (Gen 2:24). The husband must *cling* to his wife in a manner that suggests reciprocity rather than ownership. In such a bond, the husband will find strength, according to Ecclesiastes's charge to *Savor life with a woman you love* (9:9). One who lives a life of love with his wife will merit a long and good marriage.

2

The second part of the midrash describes an imagined dialogue that took place in the beit midrash between the sages and Michal, the daughter of Saul. Michal is mentioned in the Jerusalem Talmud as someone who was stringent about the commandment of putting on tefillin, a commandment generally regarded as binding for men alone (Eruvin 10:1[25d]). Hochstein thus regards her as a disciple of the sages who takes part in the halakhic conversation. Michal is also the only woman in the Bible who is described as loving her husband (1 Sam 18:20), but nonetheless, she did not merit to enjoy a happy marriage.

Hochstein opens with a question that the Talmud raises at b.Kiddushin 2a, presented as if it were posed by Michal bat Shaul: Why does the mishnah open with the verb "acquire" (Kiddushin 1:1) but then go on to use the verb "betroth" (Kiddushin 2:1)?

The answer Michal receives is the original answer provided by the Talmud: the verb "acquire" is used because the mishnah raises the possibility that the woman is "acquired through money" much like the acquisition of property, as in the verses *fields shall be acquired with money* (Jer 32:44) and *the field that Abraham acquired* (Gen 25:10). These verses refer to the acquisition of a field specifically because a field is a common image for a woman. The sages regarded marriage as similar to the acquisition of property. Later the mishnah goes on to use a different term to describe marriage, namely, betrothal, which connotes the designation or consecration of an individual for a particular purpose. Consecration is about limiting an object or an activity to a special purpose only—most commonly for use in the Temple. The sages sought to describe the connection between the members of a couple as an act of consecration on the part of the husband, who limits and designates the woman for himself alone and forbids her to all other men in the world.

This response leads Michal to ask about the way in which the rabbis chose to define the marital relationship: "He made her forbidden as consecrated property" (b.Kiddushin 2b). She tries to ascertain: Who exactly has made her forbidden to all other men?

The sages respond, in accordance with the Talmudic passage, that it is the husband who acquires the wife and makes her his own.

Michal challenges them by invoking a biblical verse: *Hence a man leaves his father and mother and clings to his wife, so that they become one flesh* (Gen 2:24). When the Bible first describes the connection between man and wife, it uses the phrase "*clings to his wife,*" which suggests that it is specifically the husband who designates and consecrates himself to his wife alone, and not vice versa. This has halakhic ramifications because it implies that the husband is the one who forbids himself to all other people, and not the woman who becomes forbidden, as the Talmud had previously taught.

This question has personal significance for Michal, whose father brought her back to his home while she was still married to David on account of political circumstances and then married her off to Paltiel ben Layish. The Bible describes that when she was returned to David, her husband, Paltiel, followed her weeping (2 Sam 3:16).

The sages are silent and do not respond to Michal, presumably because they can think of no satisfactory response to her challenge.

Hochstein's goal in this section of the midrash is to point out that the Bible itself contains various terms to describe the marital bond between man and woman. She seeks to arrive at conclusions that diverge from the patriarchal model that the rabbis derived.

3

The third part of the midrash describes an additional imagined dialogue in the beit midrash between the sages and Michal the daughter of Saul. It begins with a quote from a baraita—a Talmudic passage from the time of the Mishnah—which appears in the continuation of the Talmudic discussion on b.Kiddushin 2b. The baraita asks why the Torah uses the term "take" (*Should a man take a woman and possess her?*) to refer to marriage, a phrasing that emphasizes the man's active role, rather than saying, "should a women be taken unto a man," a phrasing that would emphasize the woman's passivity.

Hochstein adds an additional question, which she prefaces with "and some say," a phrase used often in the Talmud to present an additional opinion. She asks: Why does the Torah say *should a man take a woman* and not "should a woman take a man"? That is, why shouldn't the woman be the active partner in the marriage?

The explanation provided by the baraita for the active role of the man alone is that it is the way of the world that a man pursues a woman, and not vice versa. The Talmud offers a parable to illustrate this principle. The parable features a man who lost something and goes looking for it. It is not the lost item that searches for the man, but the man who searches for the item. So too the man searches for the woman, and she is like an item he has lost according to the notion that woman was created from a rib taken from man (Gen 2:22).

Hochstein brings Michal, the daughter of Saul, again to challenge the reasoning underlying this parable, objecting to the analogy between a woman and a lost object. She cites the verses describing the creation of woman: *Then the man said, This one at last is bone of my bones and flesh of my flesh. This one shall be called Woman, for from man was she taken* (Gen 2:23). Here the woman is described as something created, not something lost. The woman is a subject with a name of her own, not an object that is lost.

In the tradition of Talmudic deliberations, the sages reject the explanation offered by Michal, the daughter of Saul. They juxtapose her reading with the Tannaitic source and point out that her explanation does not accord with the language of the mishnah. The mishnah does not describe an egalitarian model; rather, it is the man who betroths the woman, like a man who loses an object. How will Michal resolve this contradiction?

Michal responds by offering a close reading of the language of the mishnah. The rabbis of the mishnah stated that "the man betroths," which, she argues, implies an act of mutual adherence of two independent subjects, and not an active unilateralism. To prove her claim, she quotes a rule cited in the continuation of the Talmudic discussion: "Distinction—is a conjoining of things that are separate from one another." When the Talmud is dealing with concepts that are differentiated from one another, it uses the term "ways." When it is dealing with concepts that are not differentiated, it uses the term "things."

Michal makes this claim in an attempt to point out that when it comes to the discussion of marriage as well, the mishnah used the term "ways"—"a woman is acquired in three ways." According to the Talmudic rule she cited, marriage must be a complex matter with various differentiated aspects, namely, the man and the woman, who are two independent subjects.

The rabbis respond by asking, "What is the distinction when it comes to betrothal?"

Michal responds that "distinction" is the conjoining of things that are separate from each other. To prove her point, she returns to the Talmudic discussion in the continuation of the passage, where the rabbis bring the example of a disagreement about the status of the etrog used on the holiday of Sukkot (see Lev 23:40). Does it resemble a tree or vegetation (Mishnah Bikurim 2:6)? Those who think the etrog resembles only a tree use the term "things," whereas those who think the etrog resembles both the tree and vegetation (namely, that it is a complex, differentiated concept) use the term "ways." Michal explains that as with the etrog, betrothal is a complicated concept that involves sharing and distinction between two separate entities.

Hochstein concludes her midrash by expressing a preference for a relationship between two distinct individuals, two distinct subjects who cling to one another. She proves her point by invoking a verse from Ecclesiastes (4:9–11) about the value of two individuals who can support one another: *Two are better than one, in that they have greater reward from their toil. For if one should fall and there is none to lift him up . . . When two lie together, they are warm; and as for one, how will he be warm?*

YAEL UNTERMAN

One Who Did Not Find a Wife

The Jewish community regularly exerts tremendous pressure to marry and raise a family, and a woman (and, to a lesser extent, a man) who remains single is often treated as an object of pity. The following midrash deals with the suffering of those who strive for many years to get married, in vain. By means of this account of the "one who did not find a wife," we are presented with various methods of attempting to deal with this situation and ultimately with a religious and theological dilemma about God's responsibility for this man's fate. This midrash tells a tragic story. By invoking various ancient rabbinic midrashim dealing with existential situations of injustice and the fate of the righteous who suffer, this midrash focuses on our inability to understand God's ways, without offering any rationale or consolation apart from the compassion of the Shekhinah.

A tale of one who came of age but did not find a wife.

And that man was righteous and good of heart—he honored his father and mother, arose early and gave charity and confessed his sins and repented, for he said, "Perhaps I've sinned in my heart and 'blessed' God in my heart, Heaven forbid." And so he would do all his days.

He found a helpmate who would not confront him, and a confronter who would not help him, and he grew very despondent.

With the passing of many days, he became lonely and weary of life. He spent two Sabbaths by himself, and took no nourishment, until Elijah of blessed memory came and revealed himself to him.

He said to him: My son, why do you weep?

He said: Because I am considered dead, as is written "one who exists without a wife, exists without life."

He said to him: If you desire to marry a woman, *Get thee out of your country, and your birthplace and your father's house* (Gen 12:1) and go up to Jerusalem.

He went up, and it availed him nothing. He prayed forty days and forty nights, and it availed him nothing. He thought hard about his doings, and it availed him nothing.

His spirit became faint.

He *went to seek out God*. He cried out, a great and bitter cry, and said: Master of the Universe, it says *so shall a man leave his father and mother and cling to his wife and they shall be one flesh* (Gen 2:24). The first part I fulfilled, what will be of the second?

God answered him: *Who is this, shrouding good advice in words without understanding . . . Bind up your loins like a man . . .* (Job 38:2–3).

He cried Master of the Universe, You commanded us the mitzvot of procreation, of circumcision, and educating children, and conjugal duties. How can I fulfill them without a wife?

The Holy Blessed One answered: *Will you thwart My justice, condemn Me so you are in the right?* (Job 40:8).

He fell to the ground and said: My King and God, no—*I am Your servant, son of Your maidservant* (Ps 116:16). I beg You *loose my chains*.

The Holy Blessed One said: *It is good for a man to bear a yoke in his youth. That he sit alone, and be silent, for he has taken it upon him* (Lam 3:27–28).

The man said: *I will not die, but live, tell of God's works. I've received God's lashes, but He hasn't handed me over to death* (Ps 118:17–18). He accepted the verdict.

Elijah of blessed memory came and said: Master of the Universe, the whole world is married, from the wood-chopper to the king in the palace; yet from a man like this You withhold a wife and children? Is there no justice and no judge?

God said to him: Silence! Such is My decree.

Elijah was silent.

The Holy Blessed One was silent.

And the Shekhinah wept repeatedly: *My son, My son, would that I could suffer instead of you, My son.*

Commentary

This midrash tells the story of a righteous man who is unable to find a wife. The opening sentences, which recount the man's virtues, are meant to invoke the protagonist of the book of Job, whose virtues are also enumerated in the opening verse: *There was a man in the land of Uz named Job. That man was blameless and upright; he feared God and shunned evil* (1:1). The Bible relates that Job would offer sacrifices every day, saying, *Perhaps my children have sinned and blessed* [a euphemism for "blasphemed"] *God in their thoughts* (1:5). The righteous man in our tale is described in similar terms: he seeks by means of his actions to atone for sins he did not commit. The allusions to the story of Job are meant to call our attention to God's role in and responsibility for this situation and to clarify that this is not a story of a sinner receiving his just desserts, but rather of a righteous individual who suffers unjustly.

In the story of the creation of the world in the book of Genesis, God says, *It is not good for man to be alone. I will make a helpmate to confront him* (2:18). Unterman plays with the phrase "helpmate to confront him," explaining that the righteous man was unable to find a partner who was both considerate and helpful on the one hand, while also challenging him to grow on the other.

With time, loneliness and the inability to find a spouse drive the unfortunate single man to such depression that he grows sick of life. He spends two Sabbaths by himself. On one level, this is because he is too dejected to engage with his religious community as usual and to put on a happy face when he is in such pain. On another level, though, this serves as a spiritual act that may bring about his redemption, a play on the Talmud's claim that were Israel to keep two Sabbaths, they would be redeemed immediately (b.Shabbat 118b). By isolating himself and fasting (not normally condoned on the Sabbath, so this may be interpreted as fasting over two weeks), he merits a revelation from Elijah the prophet—much like Rabbi Eliezer ben Hyrcanus, who fasted out of a desire to study Torah, as recounted in Pirkei d'Rabbi Eliezer. When Elijah asks the protagonist of Unterman's midrash why he is so distressed, he responds that it is because a person with no wife is considered dead (see Kohelet Rabbah 9:9). Elijah suggests that the righteous man leave his parents' home, as did Abraham, and like Rabbi Eliezer ben Hyrcanus, travel to Jerusalem—where he might merit God's help due to the sanctity of the city, but even more so, where on the most practical level, he would encounter the numerous single women who live there. The protagonist heeds Elijah's advice, but to no avail.

His next step is to pray for forty days and forty nights, a significant number for withdrawal into a spiritual state, as we see when Moses ascends Mount Sinai to plead with God on behalf of the Israelites who sinned by worshipping the golden calf (Deut 9:18) or when Elijah fasted after fleeing to the desert—both for forty days and nights. But this too was of no avail.

Subsequently, the righteous man tries the approach of "thinking hard about his doings," namely, examining and critiquing his moral behavior in an effort to repent (see b.Eruvin 13b). This too has no impact and serves only to weaken and undermine his soul, pushing him to the limits of his faith and leading him to confront God directly.

He goes to seek out God like the matriarch Rebecca (see Gen 25:22), and he engages God in an argument, in the tradition of Abraham, Moses, Job, and others. In his prayers, he cries out with a great and bitter cry like Mordechai (see Esth 4:1), reminding God of the description in Genesis of the way of the world: *Hence a man leaves his father and mother and clings to his wife, so that they become one flesh* (2:24). He insists that in following Elijah's instructions and leaving his parents' home to live in Jerusalem, he fulfilled the first half of the verse. Now it is God's responsibility to fulfill the second half and bring him a spouse.

But God dismisses the righteous man, invoking a verse from Job to the effect that the man is lacking in understanding. God demands that he pull himself together "like a man" and regain his composure.

As with Abraham, Moses, and Job, the righteous man does not accept God's initial response; on the contrary, he intensifies his cries and continues to challenge God. How can he in his single state possibly fulfill the various commandments that are dependent on living in partnership with a spouse, such as raising children, circumcising one's sons, and performing conjugal duties? Once again God rejects his claim and responds with a quote from Job: It is not just that the man fails to fulfill these commandments, but he also sins by trying to cast blame and aspersion on God.

This rebuke crushes the righteous man's spirit, and he falls to the ground and begs for heavenly assistance.

God responds with words from Lamentations, asserting that it is fitting for a man to accept his fate and keep silent. The man accepts his tragic fate and resolves to remain silent, finally. His words (taken from Ps 118:17–18) express his devotion to God in spite of his trying circumstances, deprived even of the option of putting an end to his own life so as to find relief from his suffering.

From this point on, the righteous man keeps silent. His silence is deafening.

The story concludes with the return of Elijah the prophet, this time to speak directly to God on behalf of the righteous man and express his own unease with such gross injustice. He challenges God and asks: How can it be that all sorts of people (who presumably are not all righteous) manage to find a spouse, while this man remains alone? "Is there no justice and no judge?" he demands.

Yet God dismisses Elijah too, telling him, "Silence! Such is my decree." This phrase appears in the Talmud (Menachot 29b) as a response to Moses's reaction when he learns of the cruel fate that will someday befall another righteous man, Rabbi Akiva, who would endure fatal and gruesome torture at the hands of the Romans. Essentially God is telling Elijah not to get involved with God's way of managing the world. God's response shuts down all further possible communication, silencing even Elijah.

The impression of heavenly hard-heartedness is mitigated when we are told that alongside the silenced hero of the story and the silenced Elijah who came to his aid, surprisingly God too is silent—as if the necessity of such a harsh decree has caused God to, so to speak, ruminate or feel some regret. We can only wonder what God is "thinking" at this point.

The midrash concludes with the voice of the Shekhinah, the feminine aspect of God, who cries and wails over the fate of the righteous man like a compassionate mother who wishes she could suffer instead of her son. This lament is reminiscent of David's heartrending lament over the death of his beloved son Avshalom (see 2 Sam 19:1).

The story's painful conclusion gives voice to our helplessness in the face of God's inexplicable response to the suffering of the righteous. God's harshness is thrown into relief implicitly and subtly by God's unexpected silence but explicitly and sharply by the empathy and care expressed by the Divine Indwelling Presence.

The primary message of this story is the sense that humanity cannot comprehend why the righteous man is fated to suffer. It is the age-old question of theodicy, namely, why bad things happen to good people. The Shekhinah's subversive response at the end of the story suggests a theological alternative: that there is divine compassion and empathy for those who suffer unjustly. But despite the best of intentions, this feminine aspect of God is powerless to alleviate the suffering of the righteous.

EFRAT GARBER-ARAN

And Eve Knew

Female pleasure and female initiative in sexual intercourse are issues that remain taboo even in our own day. There is a pervasive sense in midrashim written by men that the man is the active player in sexual intercourse while the woman remains passive, and he alone experiences sexual pleasure. In this midrash, a group of wise women use the same exegetical tools as their male counterparts to give voice to women's experience, thereby overturning these misconceptions.

And Adam knew Eve his wife (Gen 4:1).

Some men said: From this we learn that a man knows, and a woman does not.

The wise women answered them—A woman does not know? *Lo the stork in heaven knows her appointed times* (Jer 8:7)—the stork knows and a woman does not?

And of Jephthah's daughter it is written, *and she had not known any man* (Judg 11:39). The negative implies a positive—Jephthah's daughter did not know, but a woman, who is not a sacrifice, knows.

Rather, a man knows, and a woman knows too, but his knowing is not like hers.

And men cannot grasp what they are unable to know.

The men asked the wise women: What is a woman's knowing like?

They answered:

There are she who knows once and she who knows many times. She who knows with a mighty shout and she with a soft, still voice; one who knows "from one day to another," and another who knows "from one observation to another"; she who knows from one place in her, and she who knows from another. And not only this, but there's she who knows like this one time and like that at another, in her girlhood one way, her adolescence another, and on and on this way.

And the wisest among the women added: A woman is a mighty depth, as is written, *the fountains of the mighty depth broke open* (Gen 7:11). And Rabbi Eliezer said, "This opening opens all the way to the mighty depth," and the fountains in her stir with the higher waters and lower waters and her mouth broke open to the mighty depth, from which the world was created.

Commentary

Efrat Garber-Aran's midrash focuses on the verse that describes the first sexual act in the history of humanity: *And Adam knew Eve his wife* (Gen 4:1). The biblical word "knew" is a euphemism for sexual intercourse, but, of course, the verb also means to understand deeply. There is a connection between these two meanings, because sexual intercourse can be a way for a woman and a man to get to know one another. In this midrash, Garber-Aran uses both meanings of the verb "to know," while adding another meaning as well—the individual also gets to know herself or himself during intercourse. The midrash begins with the male view of sexual intercourse: According to the biblical verse, it is the man, and not the woman, who "knows." In other words, the man is the active player in sexual intercourse, and he is the one who experiences deep and satisfying pleasure, whereas the woman does not. This understanding reflects a general male perspective on female sexuality, and it has decisive consequences on the gendered dynamic during intercourse and on women's own expectations.

The wise women who hear this masculine interpretation know, from their own experience, that this understanding is misguided, and they rally to refute it. Applying the same exegetical tools employed by their male counterparts, they cite as proof two verses from the Bible in which the root word *yada'* (know) appears. The first proof is a verse from Jeremiah stating that the stork "knows" the cycle of the seasons when she determines her migration route. Garber-Aran uses the rabbinic technique of *gzera shava*, which draws a parallel between two biblical contexts that employ the same terminology. She understands the term "know" as referring to sexual intercourse, as in Gen 4:1. According to her midrash, the verse from Jeremiah attests that even the stork understands her sexual needs and desires. The midrash plays with the folk association between storks and the delivery of babies. Garber-Aran uses the rabbinic technique of *kal vachomer* (an argument *a fortiori*, where it would not make sense for something to obtain in a simple, marginal case but not in a more difficult, significant case) to argue that it could not possibly be that the stork would have this knowledge, but a flesh-and-blood woman would not.

The second biblical proof that the wise women cite is taken from the story of Jephthah's daughter, who was offered as a sacrifice while still a maiden in order to fulfill her father's vow. (For more on the story of Jephthah's daughter, see page 89.) The wise women quote the Talmudic principle that "the negative formulation implies a positive alternative," meaning that a negative statement also serves to teach its inverse. If, as the Bible teaches, Jephthah's daughter had not yet known a man, then it must be the case that a woman can indeed come to know a man. Thus, sexual relations can be just as much about female initiative and female pleasure.

Garber-Aran concludes her treatment of Jephthah's daughter by asserting that "a woman, who is not a sacrifice, knows." That is, Jephthah's daughter, who was offered as a sacrifice, never knew a man, but a woman who is not offered as a sacrifice can know a man. It is difficult to miss the double entendre in this line. Garber-Aran is trying to convey that a woman who is laid on the bed like a passive sacrifice will not be able to experience sexual pleasure. Only a woman who actively lies with a man of her own initiative can fully enjoy the experience.

The wise women conclude with the assertion that both men and women can experience pleasure during sexual intercourse, but that men and women differ in terms of character. Therefore, men should not express their opinion on matters about which they know nothing. Once again Garber-Aran devises a brilliant play on words, invoking both meanings of "know." This is not just about knowledge but about a kind of sexual experience about which men are ignorant. Although this claim is being made in a specific context, it also serves as a harsh critique of the rabbinic tendency to pontificate and rule halakhically on various aspects of female biology about which they cannot have sufficient knowledge and understanding.

The second part of the midrash depicts a utopia in which the men realize their error and seek to better understand the nature of women's sexual experience. They ask the women, "What is a woman's knowing like?" The response they receive is complex and multifaceted. Women experience pleasure differently from one another and throughout different stages of their lives.

The women conclude by explaining that women's pleasure comes from a divine source. The wisest of these women explains that "a woman is a mighty depth (*tehom*)," and she quotes Rabbi Eliezer's statement in Ecclesiastes Rabbah 3:11 that "this open opening opens all the way to the mighty depth (*tehom*)." The phrase "open opening" is used in rabbinic literature to refer to a woman's sexual organ. The connection between this open opening and the mighty depth (*tehom*) allows the wise woman to interpret the various appearances of this expression "mighty depth" (*tehom*) in the Torah as a reference to female sexuality.

Tehom (mighty depth) is also an Ancient Near Eastern mythical figure representing the mother of all the gods, who preceded and served as the wellspring for all of creation. The wise woman quotes Genesis 7:11, *the fountains of the mighty depth broke open*, which describes the waters that flooded the earth during the time of Noah. The verse continues, *And the floodgates of the sky broke open*, describing how alongside the fountains of the mighty depth that burst forth, the rains also poured down from the heavens and the floodgates of the sky opened. The midrash draws a parallel to the fountains of a woman, which teem from the "upper" and "lower" waters and serve as an image for female sexual arousal. (See Genesis Rabbah 13:13 for a description of the flood as a generative encounter between the upper and lower waters, which were separated at the time of creation.)

The midrash draws an analogy between a woman and her physical body, and the divine experience of creating all of existence. A woman's sexual awakening is thus depicted as worthy and exalted—as something that stood at the foundation of creation and continues to constitute the world's generative force.

SEVEN

Fertility and Parenthood

ETTI ROM

Seven Clean Days

According to rabbinic halakhic norms, a woman is regarded as menstru-
ally impure (*niddah*) and is forbidden to her husband not just on the days
when she is menstruating, as the Torah mandates, but also on seven
additional days known as "seven clean days." Some women, however,
ovulate during their seven clean days, and since they are forbidden from
engaging in sexual relations during this period, they are effectively infer-
tile. The various medical solutions proposed often involve interventions
with harmful side effects. Etti Rom, a gynecologist, proposes a solution
that blends halakhah (traditional Jewish law) and prophecy.

*When a woman has a discharge, her discharge being blood from her body,
she shall remain in her impurity seven days; whoever touches her shall be
unclean until evening* (Lev 15:19).

There was a woman in Israel, Tanya was her name. A saintly and pious
woman. All her days she rendered kindness, gave charity to the poor, shined
her countenance to all, and opened the chambers of her heart to the sorrows
of others. But she had no fruit of her womb. Tanya would weep in her heart
when she lay down and when she arose.

One year, on the Day of Judgment, her grief was overpowering, and she
begged for death.

Acatriel Yah Hashem Tzvaot [a name of God] revealed Himself to her,
behind her tears.

He said: Tanya, My daughter, bless Me!

She said to Him: May it be Your will that Your mercies will overcome
Your anger and Your mercies wash over Your attributes, so that You deal
with Your daughters through the attribute of mercy.

He said to her: What troubles you, My daughter?

She said to Him: Even since Rabbi Zeyra established that the daughters of Israel have taken upon themselves the severity of waiting out their purity for seven clean days after the way of women has ceased for them, I have been denied fruit of the womb. Yet in the Torah of Your mouth You blessed us: *Be fruitful and multiply and fill the earth* (Gen 1:28). And in the order of creation which You have fashioned, You have established only one time in every moon in which fruit of the womb may come to be. And I, who in the way of women sees nine days, and my man is permitted to me only after another week has passed, precisely at that time my man is forbidden to me.

His mercies washed over His attributes and He said to her: *When a woman has a discharge . . . she shall remain in her impurity seven days* (Lev 16:19) and your husband is permitted to you with the passing of the way of women.

And the knot in her womb was untied, and she came to her husband, became pregnant, and gave birth.

And He nodded at them with His head.

Commentary

The Bible distinguishes between two different kinds of impurity in a woman's body that require immersion in living waters before resuming sexual relations: the impurity of a niddah, which concludes at the end of her monthly menstruation (*When a woman has a discharge, her discharge being blood from her body, she shall remain in her impurity seven days; whoever touches her shall be unclean until evening* [Lev 15:19]); and the impurity of a zava, who bleeds pathologically outside the confines of her monthly period or for more than seven days (*When a woman has a discharge of blood for many days, not at the time of her impurity . . . she shall be unclean, as though at the time of her impurity, as long as her discharge lasts . . . When she becomes clean of her discharge, she shall count off seven clean days, and after that she shall be clean* [Lev 15:25–28]).

These extra seven days are known as the "seven clean days." In the Talmud (b.Niddah 66a) Rabbi Zeyra reports that the daughters of Israel took upon themselves the stringency of observing an additional "seven clean days" each time they menstruated as well. In the Talmud there is a dispute about whether this stringency is a custom or a law. Effectively, however, it was accepted as a halakhic norm, and thus women are forbidden to sleep with their husbands for twelve to fourteen days each month, namely, for the five to seven days of their monthly period and for another seven clean days. Women who ovulate during one of their "seven clean days" are prevented from conceiving, and they are considered to suffer from "halakhic infertility." For generations, halakhic decisors have tried to permit women to immerse in the ritual bath before their seven clean days have elapsed, and today there are those who propose medical solutions involving hormonal treatments to delay ovulation. Such treatments are not always successful.

The midrash opens with a description of a woman named Tanya: "There was a woman in Israel, Tanya was her name. A saintly and pious woman." This description is reminiscent of the opening verse of the book of Job: *There was a man in the land of Uz named Job. That man was blameless and upright; he feared God and shunned evil* (Job 1:1). The similarity between the two passages suggests that Tanya, like Job, was God-fearing and free of sin. Her suffering was unfair and undeserved, as was the case with Job.

The climax of the midrash takes place on the Day of Judgment, when Tanya is overcome by pain and she wishes to die. Just then she experiences the revelation of Acatriel Yah Hashem Tzvaot, who asks her to bless him.

Etti Rom bases this revelation on a Talmudic story (b.Berakhot 7a) about Rabbi Yishmael ben Elisha, the high priest. The Talmud relates that one year on the Day of Judgment (Yom Kippur), when Rabbi Yishmael ben Elisha entered the Holy of Holies to light the incense, Acatriel Yah Hashem Tzvaot (a name of God) revealed himself to him and requested that he bless Him. Rabbi Yishmael blessed him, saying: "May it be Your will that Your mercies will overcome Your anger and Your mercies wash over Your attributes, so that You deal with Your sons through the attribute of mercy and You go beyond the boundary of judgment." In response, God nods His head.

Like Rabbi Yishmael, Tanya too merits experiencing a revelation on Yom Kippur, and God asks her too for a blessing. Tanya blesses God, but she changes the wording of the blessing so that she asks God to "deal with Your daughters through the attribute of mercy." In response, God asks her, "What troubles you, My daughter?" Tanya responds that she has been unable to conceive on account of halakhic infertility. She always ovulates during the days when she is forbidden to engage in sexual relations with her husband, and so she cannot fulfill the commandment to be fruitful and multiply.

As Tanya requested in her blessing, God's mercies indeed overcome

God's anger, and her prayer is answered. God quotes to her the verse from His Torah that teaches, *When a woman has a discharge . . . she shall remain in her impurity seven days* (Lev 15:19). According to this verse, a woman is impure only during the days of her period, and not beyond. God thus permits her to resume relations with her husband after the conclusion of her period. The midrash has a happy ending: Tanya acts in accordance with God's instructions, she conceives, and gives birth, and God nods approvingly.

The midrash of the "seven clean days" gives voice to Etti Rom's frustration with a halakhic system that does not adequately respond to women who suffer from infertility on account of Rabbi Zeyra's stringency. There is a sense that the development of Halakhah in the study houses was far removed from God's original intentions. By returning to the realm of prophecy, Rom encourages us to have the courage to listen to the divine voice and challenge the halakhic system. Nonetheless, God's solution is presented in halakhic language, as it is rooted in a close reading of a biblical verse. It is as if God is taking part in the conversation among the sages of the study house, giving voice to a position that Etti Rom wishes that contemporary halakhic decisors would embrace as well.

NEHAMA WEINGARTEN-MINTZ

He Supports the Fallen

The deep pain of women who suffer from miscarriage is contrasted with the technical formalistic way in which the rabbis treat this issue in their halakhic discussions. The midrash concludes by offering a source of comfort to the grieving woman.

And to the woman he said, O I will increase your grief, with grief you will bear children . . . and to Adam he said . . . a curse on the land on account of you, with grief you will eat from it all your days . . . until your return to the land, for from there you were taken (Gen 3:16–19).

What is the grief that has no end? This is the grief of the woman who miscarries before her time.

For the grief of pregnancy and the grief of birth and the grief of the land have a beginning and an end, and great joy comes after.

And the grief of a woman for her babe, who was snug and enfolded end to end, and never saw the light—that has no time, and no end, and no healing.

And our Rabbis said, on the death of a stillborn, a fallen babe (*nefel*), a father's heart does not grieve, and you don't rend garments for him, or mourn for him, nor weep. And what's more, the babe was to them like a fish or insect or locust, or crawling thing, or even a sandal.

From now on say, *The earth shook from the sound of their falling, in the sea of reeds the voice was heard* (Jer 49:21). The earth should shake for each and every fallen babe that returns to her, and their voices should be heard, from sea to sea.

And from whence can the grieving soul find relief? Nothing is left to us but to turn our eyes to our Father in heaven, who supports the fallen and heals the sick as is written, *Who heals the broken-hearted, and binds up their grief* (Ps 147:3), and know *His anger is but a moment, and He desires life, in the evening, one goes to bed weeping, and in the morning, joy* (Ps 30:6).

Commentary

This midrash opens with the question, "What is the grief that has no end?" That is, what kind of grief is measureless, timeless, infinite, and incurable? The reference to things that are measureless is from the mishnah in Peah (1:1), which describes commandments that can be performed an unlimited number of times, like acts of loving-kindness. The use of this terminology is dissonant and hints at what is to come. The response offered by the midrash is that the grief of a woman who miscarries is measureless and infinite, and knows no end.

Nehama Weingarten-Mintz compares the grief of the woman who miscarries to other experiences of grief. The word for grief, *etzev*, is mentioned in Genesis (3:15–19) in the context of the divine punishments meted out to Adam and Eve. God tells Eve that He will multiply her toil (*itzavon*) in child rearing, and she shall bear children in grief (*etzev*). Adam, too, is told that the earth will be cursed on his account, and he will eat bread by dint of his toil (*itzavon*). According to Weingarten-Mintz, the grief of pregnancy and childbirth, and the grief of the land by means of which Adam and Eve were punished, are forms of grief that are finite and measured. Pregnancy and childbirth, for all that they are difficult and painful, end with the joy of new life. And the grief and toil of working the land, which is accompanied by constant worry and uncertainty, ultimately end in the joy of reaping the harvest and eating the bread that has grown from it.

The grief of miscarriage is far more painful. Weingarten-Mintz describes the way in which a woman develops an attachment to her child, who is snug and secreted away inside her (a description she takes from Leviticus Rabbah 14:8). The fetus, nestled and protected in her womb, has not yet been exposed to the light of the world (see Job 3:16). The grief of the woman who miscarries is infinite and measureless because it is grief for the loss of tremendous potential. In the absence of the happy conclusion of childbirth, it is a grief that can never be assuaged.

In contrast to the sense of loss and hurt of the mother who experiences a miscarriage, Weingarten-Mintz cites the halakhic sources on pregnancy loss. She references those halakhic decisions concerned with the question of mourning for a stillborn baby. She also cites the various images the rabbis invoke to describe a stillbirth, all of which reflect a coldness and a lack of empathy and refer only to the external appearance of the miscarried fetus.

The halakhic ruling in the case of a stillbirth, which is practiced to this day, is that one does not rip one's garments or mourn for the traditional seven days (see Shulchan Arukh, Yoreh Deah, Laws of Mourning 374:8; Responsa Yabia Omer, [Rav Ovadia Yosef, late twentieth century, Israel], vol. 8, Yoreh Deah 38). These halakhic rulings are concerned with the case of an infant who dies within thirty days of birth, though they apply to a stillborn as well. The rabbis note, in a discussion of an unrelated matter, that when a baby dies within thirty days, "a father's heart does not grieve" (b.Niddah 23b). According to Weingarten-Mintz, this attitude stands in stark contrast to the emotional experience of the mother, who carried the baby in her womb. In spite of the halakhic ruling that we do not mourn such a birth, the woman continues to mourn in her heart. The seven days designated for mourning become, for her, a measureless and infinite grief.

There is also a tremendous disparity between the woman's relationship to the loss of potential life secreted inside her and the mishnah's cold, clinical description of the appearance of the stillbirth, which they describe as a fish, an insect, a locust, a crawling thing, or even a sandal (Mishnah Bekhorot 8:1). For the woman, the fetus contains infinite potential and untold secrets; for the sages, the fetus is a bodily secretion consisting of nothing more than what meets the eye.

In the next part of the midrash, Weingarten-Mintz insists that the earth should shake from every pregnancy loss and from the pain and hurt of the grieving mother. She cites a verse from Jeremiah (49:21) that describes the fall of Edom: *The earth shook from the sound of their falling* (*niflam*). She argues that this description should also apply to the loss of a stillborn baby, which is referred to in rabbinic literature by the term *nefel*, which literally means "fallen one." This kind of loss ought to shake the earth. In the continuation of the verse, Jeremiah describes the suffering of the collapsing kingdom of Edom: *In the Sea of Reeds the voice was heard.* The pain of the woman who miscarries should also resound from sea to sea.

The midrash concludes by asking how it is possible to overcome grief and find consolation. According to Weingarten-Mintz, the answer lies in turning to God, whom she refers to as "our Father in heaven." God is referred to as a father in the hope that this parental role will enable God to understand the pain of pregnancy loss. God supports the fallen—God supports those who experience loss, and perhaps God even gathers up and protects the miscarried fetuses. Likewise, God heals the broken-hearted, and God has the power to transform the individual's experience from tears to joy.

EFRAT GARBER-ARAN

The Blessing for Breastfeeding

Rabbinic literature refers to "blessings on pleasures," a general term for the category of blessings that express our awareness of—and our gratitude for—the daily pleasures related to our senses. These blessings were formulated by the ancient sages, and they appear in Tractate Berakhot of the Mishnah and Tosefta. They relate to the enjoyment of various foods, scents, and unusual sights. In this midrash, Efrat Garber-Aran seeks to fill in a gap in the blessings on pleasures by formulating a blessing for breastfeeding, an activity that is a source of pleasure for both the infant and the mother.

The sages, men and women, differed on from what age does one recite a blessing on eating.

One man said—when one has attained the age of mitzvot.

One man said—when one has attained the age of schooling.

And one woman said—when one first emerges into the air of the world.

For the one who said when one first emerges into the air of the world, what blessing should the baby say on its mother's milk?

Up to one year, "Blessed are You, Lord our God, King of the Universe, Who has provided me with all I need" (*Sh'a'sa li kol tzorki*). For all one's needs are in a mother's milk: food and drink, closeness and warmth. Once the child is a year old and its mother's milk is yet within her, she should say, "Blessed is He Who is good, and does good" (*Barukh ha'tov v'hameitiv*).

The sages asked: And how will the infant bless if it has neither language nor insight?

They answered: Let the mother bless, for she has an "extra measure of insight within her."

And if she blesses for her child should she not bless for herself?

She ruled, the mother will bless for her child and for herself!

And what shall she bless for herself? "Blessed are You, Lord our God, King of the Universe, Who has made me a woman" (Sh'a'sani isha).

Commentary

Efrat Garber-Aran's blessing on breastfeeding deals with a halakhic question that was never previously discussed in the halakhic literature: What blessing does an infant recite when suckling its mother's milk? The infant derives pleasure from breastfeeding—in terms of the nutrition, the hydration, the warmth, and the closeness—and thus it seems fitting to recite a "blessing on pleasures."

The structure of the discussion is modeled on a Talmudic deliberation. It opens with a question concerning the age at which a child is required to bless over food, and it presents the various responses in the form of a classical Talmudic debate. The first two opinions are familiar from earlier sources in other contexts, but the third introduces a novelty.

The first opinion is that children are obligated to bless over food from the age when they become obligated in the commandments: girls from age twelve and boys from age thirteen (as per Mishnah Avot 5:21). The second opinion is that the obligation sets in a few years earlier, "when one has attained the age of schooling," that is, the age when children are able to understand and fulfill the commandments. According to this opinion, children must be taught and trained to bless even before they reach the age when they become obligated in the commandments (see b.Sukkah 42a). The third opinion, which has no precedent in rabbinic literature, is attributed to one of the women sages in the beit midrash. She teaches that the obligation to recite the blessing sets in from the moment the infant first benefits from his or her food, that is, effectively from birth.

The Talmudic discourse continues to unfold in this characteristic manner. Focusing on this third opinion, the midrash asks: If so, what blessing is the newborn infant supposed to recite before breastfeeding? The midrash responds that until one year of age, the infant should recite, "Blessed are You, Lord our God, King of the Universe, Who has provided me with all I need." The wording of this blessing is derived from one of the traditional morning benedictions. Breastfeeding is understood to satisfy all of the infant's needs, in the sense that it supplies all the baby's nutritional content while also serving as a source of closeness and warmth.

After a year of age, if the baby is still enjoying its mother's milk, the baby must bless, "Blessed is He Who is good and does good." The assumption is that at this age, milk is no longer the child's sole source of nutrition. The wording of the blessing derives from one of the "blessings on pleasures" recited upon experiencing goodness, and it expresses our gratitude and our awareness that nothing good in life can be taken for granted.

As is common in the Talmud's halakhic discourse, the sages then raise an additional challenge to this position and to the two blessings that were just proposed: How can an infant recite a blessing if it lacks the cognitive ability to speak? An infant lacks understanding and insight, let alone speech, and so how can the infant be obligated in this commandment? The woman sage responds cleverly that the mother blesses on behalf of the infant, since she has "extra measure of insight within her." This phrase, which appears in b.Niddah 45b, is often used apologetically to dissuade women who seek the same halakhic status and the same access to Torah as their male counterparts; such women are told that on account of their "extra measure of insight," they do not need the same level of learning and obligation as men. But in this midrash, the additional insight granted to women serves to compensate for the infant who lacks insight.

The sages continue to raise objections. Speaking of the mother, doesn't she also have to recite her own blessing for breastfeeding? The woman sage responds that, yes, she must recite a blessing on behalf of both the infant, invoking the blessing proposed above, and herself, invoking the blessing, "Blessed are You, Lord our God, King of the Universe, who has made me a woman." This blessing is the opposite of the blessing traditionally recited by men as part of the daily morning benedictions: "Blessed are You, Lord our God, King of the Universe, who has not made me a woman." As such, the suggestion that the breastfeeding woman recite this blessing serves as a defiant coda to the Talmudic deliberation. The experience of breastfeeding is unique to women, and they should bless and thank God for it and, more generally, for being a woman.

NAAMA SHAKED

All the Mitzvot for the Son and the Daughter

In Tractate Kiddushin of the Babylonian Talmud, the rabbis defined the responsibilities of parenthood. Since the Talmudic conversations took place only among men, they led to conclusions perhaps very different from those that women would have reached.

In the following two midrashim, Naama Shaked expands the Talmudic discussion about parenthood and illuminates different facets of parental obligation and experience. She shows that the Talmud's gendered parental roles are by no means inherent. Shaked adds her own voice to the Talmudic deliberations, deepening the discussion and offering new insights and strategies that can help today's parents bear the burdens of their responsibilities.

Women are exempt from the mitzvot that a father must do for his son.

All the mitzvot that a father must to do for his son—men are obligated, and women are exempt. We have already heard this, as our early sages have taught: a father must circumcise his son, and redeem him, and teach him Torah, and take him a wife, and teach him a trade. And some say: Even to teach him how to swim (b.Kiddushin 29:1).

And though they may be exempt—they do it, for so we read regarding Zipporah and Eve and Batsheva and Hagar and Rebecca and Yocheved.

To circumcise him? This we learn from Zipporah, as is written *and Zipporah took a flint and cut her son's foreskin* (Exod 4:25).

To redeem him? This we learn from Eve, as is written *I've acquired a manchild from God* (Gen 4:1).

To teach him Torah? This we learn from Batsheva, as is written *The words of King Lemuel, the burden of his mother's reproof* (Prov 31:1) and it is written *do not abandon your mother's Torah* (lit. teaching) (Prov 1:8).

To take him a wife? This we learn from Hagar, as is written *And his mother took him a wife from the Land of Egypt* (Gen 21:21).

To teach him a trade? This we learn from Rebecca, as is written *Go, pray, to the flock and bring me from there two choice kids* (Gen 27:9).

To teach him how to swim? This we learn from Yocheved, as is written *and she placed her son in the basket and set it in the reeds on the bank of the Nile* (Exod 2:3).

Commentary

The mishnah in Tractate Kiddushin (1:7) teaches that the commandments that fathers are obligated to fulfill for the sake of their sons apply only to fathers; the mothers are exempt.

These commandments are:

1. Circumcising a son on the eighth day of his life.
2. Redeeming the firstborn son according to the biblical notion that first-borns belong to God. The Bible stipulates that a son who is the first child born to his mother, and who is not a priest or Levite, must be re-deemed for five sela coins on his thirtieth day so as to exempt him from having to serve in the Temple.
3. Teaching him Torah or hiring a teacher to do so.
4. Marrying him off by helping him finance the wedding.
5. Teaching him a trade so that he can support himself.
6. And, according to some opinions, teaching him to swim.

Naama Shaked examines each mitzvah in turn and demonstrates how the biblical matriarchs observed these commandments and took upon themselves these religious responsibilities, sometimes to a greater extent than their husbands.

The commandment of circumcising one's son was performed by Moses's wife, Zipporah, on their journey from Midian to Egypt, when she took a flintstone to his foreskin and thus saved Moses's life (Exod 4:24–26). The commandment to redeem the firstborn son was seemingly performed by Eve, who redeemed her son Cain, as per her statement, "I have gained (*kaniti*) a male child with the help of God" (Gen 4:1). The biblical verb *kaniti* generally means "I created." But Shaked interprets Eve's declaration as invoking a different sense of the verb *kaniti*, namely, "I acquired." She testifies that she has acquired her son from God, as we do today in the ceremony of redeeming the firstborn (*pidyon ha-ben*).

The commandment to teach one's child Torah is performed by Batsheva, the mother of King Solomon. Shaked brings two proofs from the book of Proverbs, which is traditionally attributed to Solomon. First, she cites the verse in which Batsheva rebukes her son Solomon for his behavior and warns him that foreign women and wine will cause him to violate law and justice (based on Prov 31:1–9, where Lemuel is identified as Solomon). Second, she understands the verse in Proverbs that reads, "Hear, my son, the teachings of your father, and do not forsake the Torah of your mother" (1:8) as referring to Solomon's attribution of all the Torah he learned to his mother, Batsheva.

The commandment to marry off one's son is performed by Hagar, who arranged a marriage between her son Yishmael, born to her and to Abraham, and a woman from Egypt, her own land of origin.

The commandment to teach one's son a trade was performed by Rebecca, who taught her son Jacob how to cook and which dish to prepare for his father in order to receive his blessing. She showed him how to select two choice kids from the flock and how to prepare Isaac's favorite delicacies.

The commandment to teach one's son to survive in the water was performed by Yocheved, mother of Moses, who placed her son securely in the Nile in a basket of reeds covered in bitumen and pitch. In so doing she kept her son alive, saving him from the fate that Pharaoh had decreed upon all Israelite males.

In this midrash, Shaked highlights the key role that women play in performing the various mitzvot enumerated in the Talmud as parental responsibilities. In two of the cases she lists, that of Zipporah and that of Yocheved, the mothers save their sons' lives. And so even if women are halakhically exempt from performing these commandments, it is sometimes critical that they take on these obligations in order to ensure the Jews' continued survival.

———

And to take him a wife.

To take him a wife—from where do we learn this? As is written: *Take wives and have sons and daughters and take wives for your sons and your daughters give to men* (Jer 29:6). Granted, when it comes to his son, it's in his power.

But his daughter? It depends on others wanting to take her! This is what Jeremiah was trying to say to them: Her father should give her something for her dowry, and dress and bedeck her so that men will jump to take her (b.Kiddushin 30b).

To find him a wife or find her a husband—Is my daughter in my hands? Is my son?

Rather I would say to teach him to take a wife—and above all, to teach him to take up, to take and to give, to take hold, to receive and bestow, to take on responsibility, to take on grace, to be a living person who takes themselves up.

And how to teach him? All that's in my hands is to take him up, to bear him:

> To take up—as is written *God has taken you up as a man takes up, bears his son* (Deut 1:31), to hold, protect, meet his and her needs.
>
> To take up—as is written *to take him to your bosom, as the nursemaid takes up the suckling child* (Num 11:12)—to take to the bosom, to hug, to kiss, to crown with warmth and love.
>
> To take up—to hold fast, to take, to accept him or her just as they are, as is written *God heard the lad's voice just where he was. Rise, take up your lad, and hold him fast with your hand* (Gen 21:17–18).
>
> To take up—to forgive, to wrap oneself in patience and tolerance as is written *and I will bear with and I will save* (Isa 46:4).
>
> To take up—to bear, to raise up, to raise her as one and only, to raise her up till she becomes a woman. That the home be a bed for growth, as is written *a good field . . . to make a branch, and bear fruit* (Ezek 17:8), and it says *One is my dove, my pure one, one and only for her mother, dazzling to she who bore her* (Song 6:9).

Commentary

The Babylonian Talmud establishes that it is incumbent upon a father to marry off his children, drawing on a verse from the book of Jeremiah: *Take wives and have sons and daughters and take wives for your sons and your daughters give to men* (29:6). The Talmud asks: Whereas a father can provide financially for his son's wedding, he cannot do the same for his daughter because according to Jewish law it is the man who actively takes a spouse for himself and not vice versa. And so how can a man be obligated to marry off his daughter? Whether she marries depends not on her but on her potential partner. The Talmud responds that the father can actively help his daughter to wed by furnishing her with a dowry and dressing her well, so that men will be eager to marry her.

Naama Shaked offers a fresh look at the Talmud's question about marrying off a daughter. She asks about the meaning of this commandment today, with regard to marrying off both sons and daughters. How can parents marry off their children in a world in which they no longer have the authority to intervene in their children's lives?

She suggests that we understand this commandment in a new light. Rather than focusing on how a father might provide financially and materially for his children, she considers the kinds of relationships that parents can model for their children and the behaviors they can strive to inculcate so that their children too will be able to forge deep and lasting partnerships. She conditions the ability to form a marital relationship on the ability to communicate with people and to know oneself.

As Shaked's midrash notes, one of the terms used in Hebrew for "to wed" literally means "to take up" (Lase't). Shaked considers the various connotations of this term as they relate to the various characteristics that a child should learn to embody in preparation for married life. That is, a child must learn to take up, to take and to give, to take hold, to receive and bestow, to take on responsibility, to take on grace, to be a living person who lifts himself or herself up. Shaked explains that the only way for a parent to teach all these behaviors to a child is by way of personal example, once again invoking the various connotations of the word "to wed": to hold and protect, to crown with warmth, to hold fast, to bear with, to raise up.

Here too, she offers different biblical examples of the use of this verb to refer to ways of supportively bearing another: the way in which God protectively carries and nourishes the people of Israel; the way in which a nursemaid takes up a suckling child and crowns that child with warmth and love; the way in which Hagar is commanded to carry her son Ishmael, accepting him as he is; the way in which God carries His people with patience and tolerance; and the way in which a branch bears the fruit, raising it as if it were one and only. Shaked argues that if parents can model these behaviors for their children, they will succeed in transforming the home into fertile ground in which children may take root, blossom, and bear fruit.

HILA (HALEVY) UNNA

Daughters of the Place

A scholarly discussion took place in the imaginary beit midrash of Beruriah regarding the feasibility of advancing the status of women within
the religious system. The midrash deals with the difficulty of recruiting
support for this project and with anxieties about the influence it will have
on the next generation. Hila Unna includes women from various historical
periods in the imagined conversation, allowing for a more panoramic
perspective. The midrash is entitled "Daughters of the Place." The title
touches on the various meanings of the Hebrew word for place, *makom*,
which refers to a physical and geographical place but is also a term for
God, the Omnipresent. The midrash explores women's search for closeness to God. The women ask whether they have indeed arrived at the
place they have desired and sought from a religious and an ideological
perspective.

And He has brought us to this place, and has given us this land (Deut 27:9).

They asked in Beruriah's beit midrash, What is *this place*?

Esther told them, the one that Mordechai spoke of to me, *relief and rescue will come to the Jews from some other place* (Esth 4:14).

They further asked, and who will bring us to *The Place*, i.e., The Holy Blessed One?

Esther answered, every single one of you, *for just for a time like this you have reached rulership* (Esth 4:14). Each one of you *do not think you can run away* (4:14).

They went on and asked, and when?

She answered, *be ready for the third day, for on the third day God will come down before the eyes of all the people* (Exod 19:11). Just like I gathered up my courage and dressed in sacred garb, as is written *and so it was on the third day that Esther dressed in royal garb* (Esth 5:1).

So, you *Pave the path, clear the way, get rid of the obstacles out of the way of My people* (Isa 57:14). For the third generation, your daughters' daughters will reach The Place.

Their minds were yet uneasy, and they discussed their daughters among themselves: Perhaps building up the road will be vexing and bad for them? Maybe opening the way will rob their time and energies for nothing?

Maybe clearing the obstacles will bring up new hardships?

And all the while Esther was weeping and pleading *How can I bear to see the evil that will happen to my people?* (Esth 8:6).

Until Beruriah said to them, here as elsewhere, read the end of the passage to uncover its beginning: *And one who trusts in Me will inherit the land, and take hold of My holy mountain . . . clear the obstacles out of the way of My people . . . to bring to life the spirit of the downtrodden and bring to life the spirit of the crushed . . . Peace, peace, to far and near, says God* (Isa 56:13–15, 19).

And the way is very hard, and the way is very long.

But the women who seek shelter in God, to inherit the land, to steep the world in sanctity, and to get to The Place—it is up to them to rouse and wake up others.

To bring to life the spirit of the downtrodden and the hearts of the crushed women, to see those far and those cast away and bring them near and bring them to reconciliation.

And that is why Scripture repeated *peace, peace*—peace unto you, peace unto your daughters, in your days and in theirs.

On that day they added a prayer in the beit midrash:

Happy the woman who reveres God, who walks in His ways.
When you eat of the toil of your hands, you're happy, it is good for you . . .
May God bless you . . .
And may you see your daughters' daughters.
Daughters in understanding,
Daughters in deep reflection,
Daughters in the work of building,
So that there will come *peace upon Israel* (after Ps 128).

Commentary

The midrash begins with a question that was raised in Beruriah's beit midrash (see page xxiii).

The discussion begins with a conversation about the verse *And He has brought us to this place* (Deut 26:9), which describes how the people of Israel arrived and settled in their land after many years of wandering in the desert. The midrash uses the word "place" not in the geographical sense but as a reference to God. The arrival at this desired destination is essentially becoming closer to God.

The question that the women ask takes on new meaning when spoken in their voices: Can women become a stronger force within the patriarchal religious world? The discussion in the study house transcends historical boundaries, allowing for a conversation among women who were not contemporaneous: the figure of Queen Esther from the biblical period, Beruriah from Talmudic times, and the first generation of feminists in modern Israel.

When the latter ask who will bring them to the desired destination, Esther responds that each of them has to take responsibility for her spiritual destiny and to strengthen herself religiously. She empowers the women by speaking of her own experience as a young queen. She interprets the words from the book of Esther *for just for a time like this you have reached rulership* as signifying that by the merit of her bravery, her readiness, and her empathy for her nation's plight, she succeeded in arriving at the "rulership," namely The Holy Blessed One.

When the women ask when is it the right time to take action, Esther responds by invoking an array of biblical verses. She points to other occasions in the biblical account in which the third day had crucial significance. Just as God revealed the Torah at Mount Sinai on the third day, so too Esther mustered the strength on the third day to approach King Ahasuerus for the fateful encounter that ultimately saved her people. These examples link the concern for the fate of the people with the quest for closeness to God. In other words, the activism Esther displays in taking responsibility for the women of the nation is identified as a religious act that saved the nation and brought the Jewish people closer to God.

Esther concludes with a quote from the book of Isaiah (57:14), reading it as a call to Jewish women to remove the barriers that prevent the advance-ment of the Jewish people. Just as Mordechai demanded that she rally to the aid of her people, Esther demands that her fellow women in the beit midrash must advance the religious status of all Jewish women, even if their actions will not bear fruit for three generations—which is presumably how Unna has experienced the pace of historical change.

The women express their concerns and anxieties regarding the influence of religious feminism on their daughters. Will the next generation continue to advance the cause of religious feminism, or will they rebel against it? Does the movement stand any chance of succeeding? What new difficulties will it raise? Esther is not afraid, and she persists in pleading with the women scholars to take action: *How can I bear to see the evil that will happen to my people?* (Esth 8:6). This verse is traditionally chanted in synagogue to the mournful tune of Lamentations. Esther pleads and warns that if the women do not cooperate, they will all be met with ruin and destruction.

At this critical stage, the head of the beit midrash, Beruriah, interjects. She bolsters Esther's statements by invoking a verse from Isaiah that teaches that anyone who wishes to find shelter in God's holy mountain must remove the obstacles blocking the path of the people and bring life to those who are downtrodden and crushed, namely, as Beruriah sees it, the women who are oppressed.

Beruriah invokes the Talmudic phrase "read the end of the passage to uncover its beginning," a hermeneutical technique in which the end of a passage is read as shedding light on what preceded it. The verse in Isaiah 57:14 concludes with *Peace, peace to far and near, says God*—meaning that in the end, all will be well and all will be at peace with one another. This conclusion sheds light on the beginning—it is the crushed and downtrod-den women who are promised peace. Beruriah joins Esther in exhorting the students in the beit midrash—the religious feminists—to continue to advance the status of women in social and religious settings. She explains that the desire to be brought to The Place—to God—can be attained only if we strengthen the women in the community. Even though this process involves clearing a new path and confronting obstacles, the verse promises that ultimately it will lead to peace. The repetition of the word "peace" is meant to apply to both the religious feminists and their daughters in future generations.

The midrash concludes with a prayer that the students in the beit midrash composed on the day of this discussion. It is a paraphrase of Psalm 128. The psalm describes the ideal man as reverent towards God, walking in God's ways, and meriting to see his descendants following in his footsteps. The women rewrite these lines in the feminine as a way of saying that women too can reach this ideal place of adhering to God and revering Him. In the context of the midrash the conclusion of the psalm takes on a new meaning. Women who revere God, who are not afraid to clear new paths, will merit to have daughters and granddaughters who walk in their footsteps.

Their prayer concludes with a play on the phrase "daughters to your daughters" (*banot l'vnotayich*), which sounds like the words for understanding (*tvuna*), reflection (*hitbonenut*), and building (*binyan*). Future generations of daughters will be blessed with understanding, the ability to reflect with religious sensitivity, and the power to build up and change reality. And thus peace will come to the entire people of Israel.

EIGHT

Rape
and
Incest

TIRZA BARMATZ-STEIN

And Now Be Silent

Responses of parents, siblings, and others to incest and rape have a deep impact on the victims. The midrash focuses on the rape of King David's daughter Tamar by Amnon, her half-brother, and expands on the ending of the biblical story in 2 Samuel 13:1–22 to suggest another perspective.

And Tamar put ashes on her head, and she tore the striped cloak that was upon her, and she placed her hand on her head and walked back and forth and wailed. And Avshalom her brother said to her: Has Amnon your brother been with you? And now my sister be quiet, for he is your brother. Don't set your heart on this. And Tamar sat desolate in the house of her brother Avshalom (2 Sam 13:19–20).

And Tamar went out from Amnon's house and went home to her mother, who was Ma'akhah bat Talmai the king of Geshur.

And she told her all that Amnon, son of Ahinoam the woman of Jezreel, had done to her.

And Ma'akhah was silent, and went to speak with Abigail, for she was *a woman with a good mind* (1 Sam 25:3).

And told her all that Tamar had said.

And they were silent.

And each one said in her heart, and what can we do? Amnon after all is the eldest of David's sons.

And each said to the other:

Nothing happened. These were just imaginings. Tamar was probably trying to make her beauty known *and ravish him with her heart-shaped dumplings* (1 Sam 13:6).

And what does she have to do with Amnon's house? She knows that an Israelite maiden isn't to go by herself to visit her father's sons! Rather, it's known that she descends from Yehudah's daughter-in-law Tamar, who *wrapped herself in a veil and sat at Opening Eyes on the road to Timnah* (Gen 38:44) like a whore.

And Ma'akhah returned to her home and didn't speak to her daughter, for good or ill.

And Tamar saw her mother's face, and sensed what was in her heart, and left her home.

And Tamar put ashes on her head, and the striped cloak that was upon her she tore, and she placed her hand on her head and walked back and forth and wailed.

And her brother Avshalom found her and gathered her into his house. *And he said to her . . . And now my sister be quiet.*

Commentary

This midrash offers an expansion of the biblical story in 2 Samuel about the rape of Tamar. The midrash fills in the missing details in the biblical story and describes what happens between Amnon's banishment of Tamar and the moment when her brother Avshalom discovered her wailing in the street and brought her home.

Barmatz-Stein relates that immediately after she was raped and banished by Amnon, Tamar went to the home of her mother, Ma'akhah, where she sought refuge and assistance. But her mother, who did not know how to react to the situation, abandoned her daughter and sought counsel with Abigail, another of David's wives who was known for her wisdom (1 Sam 25:3). Ma'akhah and Abigail, who were well aware of the tremendous stature accorded to Amnon in David's home, denied the rape and claimed that effectively nothing had happened. Instead they blamed the victim by implying that the heart-shaped dumplings Tamar prepared for Amnon (2 Sam 13:6) were her attempt to ravish and seduce him.

Ma'akhah and Abigail imply that Tamar's "licentious" behavior can be traced to that of her biblical forebear. According to the genealogy at the end of the book of Ruth (4:18–22), Tamar was a descendent of another Tamar—the daughter-in-law of Yehudah, who dressed up like a prostitute after Yehudah prevented her from marrying his son Shelah and treated her improperly (Gen 38). Yehudah slept with her, mistaking her for a prostitute, and she became pregnant with his children—including Peretz, an ancestor of King David. One Tamar is thus blamed for inheriting the behavioral traits of the other.

The midrash goes on to relate that when Ma'akhah returned home, she refused to speak to her daughter. Tamar understood that her mother would not support her and in fact even blamed her for the tragedy. After exhibiting tremendous courage in relating to her mother what had happened, Tamar experienced her mother's rejection as a shattering blow that drove her into the streets, where she walked about crazed and wailing, as the Bible relates. The midrash concludes by describing how Tamar's brother Avshalom—who shared the same mother—gathered her into his house, saying, "And now, my sister, be quiet." His words can be understood in two ways: either he was continuing to suppress her voice, as did Ma'akhah and Abigail before him, or he was silencing her temporarily as a way of protecting her before he exacted revenge. As the Bible goes on to relate, Avshalom was ultimately responsible for Amnon's death, as recounted in 2 Samuel 13:28–33.

This midrash describes and interrogates a difficult social reality. Sometimes those who are closest to the victims of rape and abuse ignore or even deny the reality of the experience and blame the victim instead of the perpetrator. For the victim, this adds insult to injury, making it even more difficult to overcome their trauma and heal.

OSHRAT SHOHAM

The Father's Scream
Concealment and Revelation

In the story of Noah and his sons after the flood, Noah gets drunk and
his nakedness is revealed in his tent. Shoham depicts Noah as sexually
violating his grandson Canaan, the son of Ham. She constructs a detailed
account of the reactions of the various other family members to this revelation, as well as Noah's response to the exposure of his actions. What is
the appropriate response of parents and other family members, and how
does the offender react when he discovers that others have learned of his
transgression?

*And the sons of Noah who left the ark were Shem and Ham and Yafet,
and Ham was the father of Canaan* (Gen 9:18).
   *And Ham the father of Canaan saw his father's nakedness and told
his two brothers outside* (Gen 9:22).

Why did Scripture repeat "the father of Canaan"?
   Noah had said, "When I leave [the ark] I will raise a little son to serve me."
   Noah took Ham's young son Canaan and made use of him, and being
made use of is none other than sexual abuse.
   And he [Noah] exposed himself inside the tent (Gen 9:21). Ham, Canaan's
father, passed by, and discovered his father using his son. What did he do?
   And he told his two brothers outside (Gen 9:21). There he screamed the
scream of his son and cried out in his brothers' faces. He said, "Look what
our father has done to my little boy."
   *And Shem and Yafet took a cloak and put it over both their shoulders and
walked backward and covered their father's nakedness, their faces turned backward so they did not see their father's nakedness* (Gen 9:23).
   What did they "cover"? They covered their father's deed, hid it away,
sought to hush him up, and cover up what their brother had revealed.

Ham got angry with his father and harmed him. "Rav and Shmuel [each had an opinion on this]. One said he castrated him, and one said he sodomized him."

"He castrated him"—so that he not do this again. "He sodomized him"—to punish him for what he did, measure for measure.

Noah awoke from his wine *and he knew what his little son had done to him* (Gen 9:24).

Who was "his little son"? Some say this meant Yafet, who covered him; some say this meant Ham, who uncovered him; and some say Canaan, for it's the way of the incestuous to cast off their own guilt and lay it on their victims.

And he said, *Cursed be Canaan, the lowliest of slaves he will be to his brothers* (Gen 9:25). Noah said to Ham: You have kept me from doing something in the dark and revealed what I did to your seed, therefore your seed will be ugly and dark—he will carry the stain of incest forever.

Commentary

Oshrat Shoham's midrash is woven around the biblical account of Noah after the Flood. The Bible relates that Noah planted a vineyard, drank the wine, and became drunk (Gen 9). His son Ham discovered his father naked in his tent and relayed his discovery to his brothers, Shem and Yafet, who covered up their father without looking at his nakedness. When Noah emerged from his drunken stupor, he was furious about what Ham had done to him. He cursed his grandson Canaan, the son of Ham, and blessed Shem and Yafet.

The rabbis try to explain why Noah was naked in his tent, and why he cursed his grandson Canaan. According to the midrash, when Noah was in the ark, he decided that he wanted to have an additional son who would serve and assist him on a daily basis. "He said: 'When I emerge, I will raise a little son to serve me'" (Genesis Rabbah 36:7). Noah was naked in his tent, according to the rabbinic midrash, because he had just had relations with his wife in the hope of impregnating her. Ham discovered his father naked in his tent, and thus his son was cursed. This was a case of measure for measure: Since Ham prevented his father from having another son, his own son Canaan was cursed by Noah.

Oshrat Shoham constructs another narrative to account for what happened in Noah's tent under cover of darkness. She bases her account on a line from the midrash: "I will raise a little son to serve me." The word used for "to serve me" (*l'shamsheni*) also has a sexual connotation in rabbinic Hebrew, in which "the service of the bed" (*tashmish hamitah*) is a euphemism for sexual relations. Shoham derives from this terminology that Noah was interested in having an additional son so as to take advantage of him sexually. When deprived of such a son, he used Canaan instead for this purpose. According to Shoham, the words *And he [Noah] exposed himself inside the tent* (Gen 9:21) is a reference to Ham's revelation of Noah's sexual abuse of his grandson Canaan. Ham does not remain silent. He screams. This is the father's scream referenced in the title of this midrash. The Torah relates, *And he told his two brothers outside* (Gen 9:21). Shoham reads this verse as implying that Ham revealed to his brothers what their father had done, giving voice to his own agitation and seeking assistance. But Shem and Yafet preferred to cover up what happened: *And Shem and Yafet took a cloak . . . and covered their father's nakedness* (Gen 9:23).

Ham, who received no support or assistance from his brothers, was full of anger and resolved to harm his father. Shoham bases this part of her midrash on a traditional midrash recorded in the Talmud (Sanhedrin 70a), which describes how Ham violated his father sexually. The Talmud relates, "Rav and Shmuel disagreed. One said that Ham castrated Noah, and one said that Ham sodomized him."

Shoham invokes these rabbinic statements to imply that Ham acted so as to prevent his father from committing the same sin, perhaps as a way of exacting revenge.

Noah emerges from his drunken stupor, the Bible relates, *And he knew what his little son had done to him.* Shoham suggests three interpretations. According to the simple reading of the biblical text, she explains that the "little son" may be a reference to Yafet, who covered Noah. Alternatively, this may be a reference to Ham, who exposed Noah's actions. Finally, the "little son" may refer to Canaan, in which case Noah punished his victim instead of taking responsibility for his actions, as is so often the case with perpetrators of sexual crimes.

Shoham uses quotations from Genesis Rabbah 36:7 to give voice to Noah's curse of Canaan. But whereas in the midrash, Noah's grievance was that Ham prevented him from sleeping with his wife, Shoham turns these words on their head, implying that Noah was upset that Ham prevented him from clandestinely abusing his grandson Canaan and exposed the matter publicly. Noah therefore cursed Ham's descendants, decreeing that Canaan would have to bear the stain of guilt and shame forever.

This midrash offers an unsparing exploration of the difficult fallout from an incestuous relationship, including the attempt of family members to conceal what happened. Even after the abuse is exposed, the victim continues to bear his guilt, like a stain inflicted on him for generations. In her midrash, Shoham traces this phenomenon back to the dawn of humanity in the generation of Noah, highlighting the terrible ramifications of concealing rather than confronting such horrors.

OSHRAT SHOHAM

The Mother's Scream
Uncovering and Expulsion

The banishment of Ishmael in this midrash was precipitated by a mother's discovery of the incestuous relationship between her children. Oshrat Shoham proposes that Ishmael was banished from Abraham and Sarah's home on account of his incestuous relationship with his sister and on account of the fear that he would commit incest with Isaac as well. Her midrash gives voice to the moral imperative for parents to assume responsibility and take immediate action upon discovering that their children are engaged in such behavior.

And Sarah saw the son of Hagar the Egyptian who had borne a son to Abraham laughing. And she said to Abraham, Drive out this slave girl and her son, for this slave girl's son will not inherit with my son Isaac (Gen 21:9–10).

And Sarah saw the son of Hagar the Egyptian . . . laughing. Rabbi Akiva expounded *laughing* is none other than incest.

And with whom was he laughing?

With Bakol [in all], as is written: *his hand will be in all [bakol]* (Gen 16:12).

And who was Bakol? They said: Abraham's daughter she was, as is written: *And God blessed Abraham in all [Bakol]* (Gen 24:1).

Sarah saw that Isaac was laughing with his sister Bakol, screamed and called out: *Drive out this slave girl and her son,* lest he laugh with my son, with Isaac, too.

That is why it is written, *And the matter seemed very evil in Abraham's eyes because of his son* (Gen 21:11).

What is the significance of *very evil*? As with David, who heard about his son Amnon and his daughter Tamar, as is written: *and he was very angry* (2 Sam 13:21).

But David kept silent, while Abraham banished Ishmael.

Commentary

Genesis 21 describes the sequence of events leading to the banishment of Ishmael and Hagar from Abraham's home. Sarah caught sight of Ishmael "laughing," and in response she demanded that Abraham banish him. The meaning of the term "laughing" is unclear, and the sages suggested various explanations. Oshrat Shoham chooses the explanation of Rabbi Akiva, who interprets "laughing" as illicit sexual relations (Genesis Rabbah 53:11). Shoham asks with whom Ishmael engaged in such relations, and her answer is that Ishmael was committing incest with his sister whose name was Bakol.

The word "bakol" appears in the verse, *And God blessed Abraham in all* [*bakol*] (Gen 24:1). According to a rabbinic midrash, God blessed Abraham with a daughter whose name was Bakol (Tosefta Kiddushin 5:20). But as Shoham notes, the word "bakol" also appears in the Bible's description of Ishmael: *He will be a wild donkey of a man; his hand will be in all* [*bakol*] (Gen 16:12). Based on the Bible's use of the same term in both contexts, Shoham proposes that Ishmael's hand was on his sister Bakol, that is, he committed incest with her.

Sarah responds forthwith. She screams at Abraham to banish Ishmael and his mother far from their home. She refuses to stay silent and expresses her fear that Ishmael will sexually violate her son Isaac as well.

When Abraham hears Sarah's words, the matter does not find favor in his eyes: *And the matter seemed very evil in Abraham's eyes because of his son* (Gen 21:11). Abraham is displeased to learn what Sarah wants him to do to Ishmael. He does not wish to banish his son, but he listens to her and does it anyway. By contrast, according to Shoham's midrash, it is Ishmael's behavior that displeases Abraham, and he shares Sarah's concern for what Ishmael might do to Isaac. And so he agrees to banish him.

A similar response appears in the story of King David's discovery of the incestuous relationship between his son Amnon and his daughter Tamar. Although the matter was evil in his eyes, he did not respond. By contrast, Abraham intervened and banished the offender.

This verse contains a harsh critique of parents who become aware of an incestuous relationship between their children but elect to remain silent. The behavior of Sarah and Abraham, the matriarch and patriarch of the Jewish people, is portrayed as a challenge to that model and a call to action.

OSHRAT SHOHAM

The Woman's Scream
Cover-Up and Tikkun

Focusing on incest between a parent and an adopted child, Oshrat Shoham depicts the relationship between Mordechai and his adopted cousin,
Esther, in the Scroll of Esther as sexually abusive, with Esther as the mute
victim of Mordechai's desire. Even after Esther marries King Ahasuerus,
Mordechai continues to sleep with her, and those around them elect to
keep silent. But then something changes, and Esther summons the courage to break the silence. She screams, confronts Mordechai directly, and
exposes his actions, thereby changing her fate.

*And he became guardian to Hadassah, which is to say, Esther, his uncle's
daughter, for she had no father and mother; and the young woman was
attractive and good-looking, and when her father and mother died, Mordechai took her in as a daughter* (Esth 2:7).

*And when her father and mother died, Mordechai took her in as a daugh-
ter*—a tanna said in the name of Rabbi Meir: Don't say "as a daughter"
but "as a home" (i.e., a wife), as is written (in the parable with which the
prophet Nathan rebuked King David for taking Uriah's wife Batsheva,
comparing her to a pauper's lamb): *and the poor man had only one little
ewe lamb that he had bought. He tended her, and sustained and she grew
up together with him and his children, she used to share his morsel of bread,
drink from his cup, and nestle in his bosom; and she was like a daughter to
him* (2 Sam 12:3).

Because she (the ewe lamb, i.e. Batsheva) nestled in his bosom she was
like a daughter? Rather, as a home (i.e., a wife). So, here too (Esther in
Mordechai's bosom), as a home (i.e., a wife) (b.Megillah 13a).

Mordechai took little Esther as a daughter to him, from his bread she would eat, from his cup she would drink, and she grew up with him.

When she grew older and beautiful, bearing favor and grace, Mordechai took her to lie in his lap. Because she lay in his lap she became *as a daughter to him*? Rather, as a home (i.e., a wife).

Esther would hide (*masteret*) her words and was silent. She bore her fate in silence. And where could she turn?

After Esther was taken to Hegai the Keeper of Women, Mordechai didn't let go of her, as is written: *And every single day Mordechai would go walking in front of the women's court to learn how Esther was doing and what would be done with her* (Esth 2:11). And even after Ahasuerus took her as his queen, she would get up from his lap and immerse (in the mikvah) and go and sit in Mordechai's lap, as is written: *And what Mordechai ordered Esther did, as she had done when she was in guardianship with him.* (Esth 2:21).

Everyone started to speak ill of her. They asked the sages: Isn't Esther committing one of the sins over which one must die rather than transgress, and what's more, in public?

The sages answered them, Esther was like the soil of the earth, she does not do, but is done to.

Esther heard this and kept silent. For such was her life, soil of the earth, things are done to her and she does not do, she only keeps silent, and weeps.

When Mordechai came forward and said to her, *For if you keep silent now* (Esth 4:14), she screamed at him: I've kept silent all my life, and you tell me *if you keep silent*! I wept, and grieved in secret, and you, who've had just a taste of sorrow, started screaming out loud, as is written: *he gave a great and bitter scream* (Esth 4:1).... Me too. I'm not going to be silent anymore. I won't cover up, or go on hiding, *lo astir ve-lo esater*.

As Mordechai was going on to say *and you and your father's house will perish* (Esth 4:14), she said: But you took me in as your daughter, you are my father's house! You say your fate depends on mine? Then and there she rose up and took hold of the power of speech as is written: *And Esther said, in answer to Mordechai* (Esth 4:15); she took hold of the power of request, and demand, as is written: *my petition and request* (Esth 5:7).

At the end, she sent word to the sages: By your lives, you said Esther is soil of the earth for she does not do, and in the end, it is written: *And Esther's order established these days of Purim!* (Esth 9:32).

Commentary

The Scroll of Esther relates that Mordechai and Esther were cousins, and after her parents died, *Mordechai took her in as a daughter* (Esth 2:7) and he became her adoptive father. The sages understood the word "took" and the description of the closeness between the two to imply that they were a couple. According to the sages, Mordechai "took" Esther not just as a daughter (*bat*) but also as a house (*bayit*), which in rabbinic Hebrew refers also to a wife (b.Megillah 13a). The Babylonian Talmud bases this claim on a similar expression used in a parable in the book of 2 Samuel (12:3): *But the poor man had only one little ewe lamb that he had bought. He tended her and she grew up together with him and his children: she used to share his morsel of bread, drink from his cup, and nestle in his bosom; she was like a daughter to him.* This parable refers to the connection between Uriah and his wife, Batsheva, and so the term "daughter" (*bat*) as it appears in the Scroll of Esther is also read as referring to house (*bayit*), meaning a wife.

Oshrat Shoham takes the story in the Scroll of Esther and the Babylonian Talmud's description to another place entirely. She depicts the relationship between Mordechai and Esther as an abusive one, in which an adoptive father forces his daughter to engage in sexual relations with him. Shoham invokes the biblical verse about the little ewe lamb to describe what befell Esther. She ate from Mordechai's bread and drank from his cup, but when she reached maturity, Mordechai began to take advantage of her sexually and she *nestle[d] in his bosom*. Esther could not protest because there was no one in her life to whom she could turn, and so she bore her fate silently. Shoham reads Esther's name as deriving from the Hebrew word for "concealment" (*hastara*), since she concealed her distress and kept silent.

One might have thought that the move from Mordechai's home to Ahasuerus's palace would provide Esther with relief. But according to Shoham, even after Esther was taken to the women's palace, Mordechai did not leave her alone. He continued to *go walking in front of the women's court to learn how Esther was doing and what would be done to her* (Esth 2:11). After her marriage to Ahasuerus, Mordechai continued to lie with her whenever she was not with the king.

The rabbis sought to judge Esther favorably, based on the verse. *But Es-*

*ther still did not reveal her kindred or her people, as Mordechai had instructed
her, and what Mordechai ordered, Esther did, as she had done when she was in
guardianship with him* (Esth 2:21). They concluded that even though Esther
was married to a non-Jewish king, she continued to "obey Mordechai's bidding." According to the rabbinic understanding, she internalized the values
she had learned at home and observed the laws of menstrual purity even
while sleeping with a foreign king. According to one Talmudic opinion,
even after Esther married Ahasuerus, she remained married to Mordechai
as well, and she would "stand up from the bosom of Ahasuerus, immerse
herself, and sit down in the bosom of Mordechai" (Megillah 13a).

Oshrat Shoham turns the biblical verses and the Talmudic passage on
their heads. She explains that even though Esther was Ahasuerus's wife,
she was forced to obey Mordechai's bidding, that is, to keep sleeping with
him against her will. The Babylonian Talmud's description of how Esther
would get up from one man's bosom and sit down in the other's becomes,
in Shoham's midrash, a disturbing description of the plight of a sexual slave.

The Jewish community around Esther does not just fail to come to her
aid; they go so far as to slander her. Surprisingly, Shoham does not just
criticize the Jewish community of Esther's time, but also the rabbis of the
Talmud, for treating Esther so unjustly. She quotes from the Talmudic discussion (b.Sanhedrin 74b) in which the sages question whether Esther, in
sleeping with a gentile, was guilty of one of the most grievous sins in Jewish
tradition—those sins for which a person must die rather than transgress.
Moreover, is she guilty of committing such a sin in public?

In Shoham's midrash, the sages are depicted as criticizing Esther not just
for marrying Ahasuerus but also for sleeping with two men simultaneously.
The Babylonian Talmud responds that "Esther was like soil of the earth."
Shoham's reading is informed by the commentary of Rashi, who explains
this metaphor as signifying that "she did not act; an act was done to her." In
other words, Esther lay during sexual intercourse as passive as the ground,
and the men who slept with her were solely responsible.

Shoham regards the Talmudic treatment of Esther as an instance of unjustly blaming the victim. Instead of sympathizing with the tragedy of her
distress, they implicate her in a grievous sin.

Esther hears what everyone says about her—not just the people around
her who slander her but also the sages of the Talmud and Rashi, who de-

scribe her as "soil of the earth." She weeps and keeps silent, thus internalizing society's image of her as passive.

The next part of the midrash describes a turning point. Mordechai suddenly finds himself in a threatening situation, since Haman has issued a decree *to destroy, massacre, and exterminate all the Jews, young and old, children and women, in a single day* (Esth 3:13). Mordechai entreats Esther to plead with Ahasuerus to repeal the decree, and she responds by pointing out that doing so will endanger her own life. Mordechai asks Esther to take action and not to remain silent (Esth 4:14). His request provokes Esther, who has remained silent for so many years. At long last Esther's voice is heard when she refuses to remain silent any longer and to conceal what she has endured. Mordechai threatens her that if she reveals that he has abused her, *you and your father's house will perish* (Esth 4:14). Esther responds that he has sealed his own fate because he is her father's house! Over the course of their argument, Esther becomes increasingly confident, both in speaking up to Mordechai and in insisting on what she rightfully deserves.

At the climax of the midrash, Esther achieves her victory over the Talmudic sages. She proves that they cannot treat her however they want and call her "soil of the earth," because she is an individual with agency. Shoham emphasizes the force of Esther's words by quoting the concluding line of the ninth chapter of the Scroll of Esther: *And Esther's order established these days of Purim!* (Esth 9:32). Esther's story was indeed recorded in the Megillah as she commanded and is read publicly every year. History has proven that her words have enduring force.

NINE

Inequality in Jewish Law and in the Rabbinic Court

RIVKAH LUBITCH

The Assembly of God

This midrash and the following two, "Rachel, A Mother of Mamzerim" and "Moses Visits Beruriah's Beit Midrash," reflect Rivkah Lubitch's deep concern for the religious and legal issue of mamzerim: "illegitimate off-spring" according to Jewish law.

According to Deuteronomy 23:3, mamzerim and their descendants (for all generations to come) are forbidden to marry Jews. The Torah does not explain what constitutes a mamzer, but the rabbis identified them as children born of those sexual liaisons forbidden by the Torah. These include, for instance, a woman who marries a man who was married to her sister in the past (as long as this sister is still alive); a man who marries his aunt; a parent who sleeps with his or her child; and children born to a married Jewish woman and a man who is not her husband. By Jewish law, mamzerim may marry only other mamzerim, maidservants, or converts. These midrashim deal with the phenomenon of mamzerut as it exists to this day.

Throughout Jewish history, sages and rabbis in various communities employed a range of halakhic strategies to try to minimize the number of individuals who fell into this category. In the modern State of Israel, where there is no separation of religion and state, all legal marriages must be religious—in accordance with the laws of each individual's religious tradition. The result is that bastards are not allowed to wed unless they marry one another or a convert. The Chief Rabbinate, which oversees all marriages in the state, maintains a computerized list of the names of many of those who are considered bastards, all of whose descendants are considered illegitimate—meaning that according to Jewish law, they are forbidden to marry most of their fellow Jews.

Rivkah Lubitch, the author of these midrashim, is an Orthodox woman who served for many years as a rabbinical court advocate in the rabbinical court system, where she represented the mothers of bastard children in these courts. The midrashim she has written shed light on the painful, unjust reality confronting bastards in Israel. Lubitch illuminates the extent of the suffering that bastards endure and points toward possible fundamental halakhic solutions to this problem. She also shows that several of our forefathers fell into this category, thereby helping to remove some of the stigma associated with these individuals.

In the beit midrash of Beruriah, they "stuck a sword" and said—halakhah: a mamzer will come into the assembly of God.

And what of the verse, *No mamzer will come into the assembly of God* (Deut 23:3)?

They read closely and learned: In a place where there is an assembly of God—a mamzer will not come. In a place with no assembly of God—a mamzer will come.

They were asked: And where is an assembly of God? And they did not answer, until one of the learned scholars of the beit midrash arose and said, I have received from my mother's house that in the assembly of God, ascetics are they, pious are they, righteous are they, and learned are they, and doers of loving-kindness too, are they. And they dwell beyond the river Sambatyon. My revered grandmother went from ocean to ocean and compassed all the winds of heaven, and never found the assembly of God.

They reckoned and concluded in the beit midrash: An assembly of God, never was, nor was it ever created, but rather it is a parable.

And why was it written? Study and search it, and receive your reward.

Commentary

The book of Deuteronomy states *No Mamzer will come into the assembly of God* (23:3). A mamzer, most commonly translated as a bastard, refers to someone born out of wedlock or through some other forbidden liaison. According to Jewish law, all future descendants of a mamzer are not permitted to "come into the assembly of God," that is, to marry Jews. Lubitch's midrash questions this absolute prohibition by means of exegesis on the phrase "the assembly of God," using techniques from legal rabbinic exegesis known as midrash halakhah.

The midrash begins with a description of a pivotal, dramatic moment that took place in the beit midrash of Beruriah, a fictional study house headed by Rabbi Meir's wife Beruriah, which appears in many of Lubitch's midrashim (see pages 9, 47, and 106). The women sages ruled decisively and resolutely that bastards are permitted to come into the assembly of God, that is, to marry Jews. The Talmudic phrase "stuck a sword," which is used to describe their manner of ruling, appears in several Talmudic stories, such as the account of a particularly fierce dispute between the house of Shammai and the house of Hillel, in which the sages stuck a sword in the study house so that no one would be permitted to leave until they decided the law (b.Shabbat 17a).

Lubitch then provides an account of the Talmudic deliberations that took place in the beit midrash, presumably just prior to this ruling. The sages ask the obvious question: How can it be possible to suspend the biblical prohibition that a mamzer may not enter the assembly of God? May a mamzer marry any Jew? The radical ruling that yes, they may in fact do so, is derived by means of exegesis on a biblical verse, a common midrashic technique. The Torah states, *No mamzer will come into the assembly of God.* And so, these learned women reason, only in a place where there is an *assembly of God* is there a prohibition against marrying mamzerim. In a place where there is no *assembly of God*, there is in fact no such prohibition and a mamzer may marry any member of the community.

The women in the beit midrash are then posed with a challenge: Where does such an assembly of God exist? One of the women sages responds that she has a tradition to this effect from her mother's house, which is a paraphrase of the rabbinic phrase, "I have received from my father's house" (see, for instance, b.Rosh Hashanah 25a). She is referring to an oral tradition passed from teacher to student throughout the generations, and here it is transmitted from a learned mother to her learned daughter. Often a legal ruling is arrived at by means of an oral tradition, which is considered even more binding than a ruling derived from biblical exegesis.

The woman sage explains that, according to the tradition she inherited from her mother's house, the phrase "assembly of God" refers to people who are ascetic, pious, righteous, learned, and engaged in acts of loving-kindness. The phrase "assembly of God" is understood as a reference to those who are in a close circle with God, comprising people of the highest moral standards chosen by God. Such an ideal community does not actually exist in the real world, and so she adds that they dwell on the other side of the Sambatyon River—a magical river that appears in rabbinic legends and can never be crossed, and beyond which live the ten lost tribes (see, for instance, Genesis Rabbah 11:5).

The discussion in the beit midrash concludes, "they reckoned and concluded," referring to a vote in which the majority rules. The women sages decide that the assembly of God "never was, nor was it ever created," that is, it is a description of a fictional reality that does not actually exist. Therefore, they rule, a mamzer may enter the community and marry any Jew. The phrase "never was, nor was it ever created" is taken from halakhic debates regarding extreme situations and circumstances of tremendous moral difficulty, which the sages presented as merely theoretical—such as the killing of the rebellious son (b.Sanhedrin 71a) and the story of Job (b.Bava Batra 15a).

The use of legal rabbinic exegesis, oral tradition, and the terminology of halakhic debates has other implications as well. It serves as a challenge to the rabbinical courts to act boldly and creatively when it comes to the problem of the mamzer. It requires that the courts follow in the footsteps of the sages, so that Jewish law will not become fixed and ossified, and so that it will be possible to come up with creative solutions to the most painful problems of our day.

RIVKAH LUBITCH

Rachel, a Mother of Mamzerim

Rivkah Lubitch continues to explore the pain and injustice caused by the laws of mamzerut. This midrash gives voice to the anguish of a mamzer's parents.

At that moment Rachel leaped up before The Holy Blessed One and said: Before You wrote in Your Torah, *And a woman and her sister you will not take to become rivals to lay bare her nakedness in her sister's lifetime* (Lev 18:18), I married Jacob and became my sister's rival. Before You wrote in Your Torah, *No mamzer will enter God's community* (Deut 23:3), I bore two sons for Jacob, Joseph and Benjamin.

Rachel—a mother of mamzerim was she. Thus it is written, *Rachel weeps for her sons, refuses to be comforted for her sons, for they are no more* (Jer 31:14). *Her sons . . . her sons*—twice, those who are in exile and her own children who are mamzerim. *Refuses to be comforted*, those are the mamzerim, of whom it is said, *they have none to comfort them* (Eccl 4:1). *For they are no more*—Rachel saw that in the future the mamzerim would be forbidden to enter the community of God, as if they were no more.

The Holy Blessed One said to her, *Still your voice from weeping, and your eyes from tears* (Jer 31:15). *Your voice from weeping* for the sons who are in exile, *and your eyes from tears*, for the mamzerim, of whose tears it is written, *and lo the tears of the oppressed and there is none to comfort them* (Eccl 4:1). *For there is recompense for your deeds, says the Lord, and they will return from hostile land* (Jer 31:15). These are the sons who return from exile. *And there is hope for their end, and the sons will return to their borders* (Jer 31:15), these are the mamzerim who in future days will return to enter the community of God.

Jeremiah's mind was put at ease, as he had been fearful for the mamzerut of his son Ben Sira, born from his daughter when she was impregnated in the bathtub by his own seed, and he prophesied, *In those days it will no longer be said that the fathers ate sour grapes and the children's teeth are set on edge.*

For each shall die by his own sin, every man who eats sour grapes his own teeth shall be set on edge (Jer 31:28–29).

And that is the secret of the matter between Jacob and Rachel. For Rachel said to Jacob, *Bring me sons, and if not, I die* (Gen 30:1). You think that if you come to me you will be punished with excision and your children will be mamzerim, yet I think that if you don't come to me and I don't have children—that will be my death.

Commentary

This bold and provocative midrash portrays our foremother Rachel, one of the matriarchs of the Jewish people, as a mother of bastards. As is well known, Jacob married two sisters, Leah and Rachel, while both were still alive—which constitutes a forbidden sexual liaison according to the Torah's laws (Lev 18:18). Although the Torah had not yet been given on Sinai, the rabbis maintained that the forefathers observed all the Torah's commandments. And thus according to the Torah's laws, Rachel's two sons were bastards. In this midrash Lubitch deals with the distress of the parents of bastards, who are concerned about their children's fate. Jeremiah the prophet, too, is portrayed as the father of a bastard in search of some form of consolation.

The midrash imagines a dialogue between our foremother Rachel and God, based on verses from Jeremiah: *Thus said the Lord: A voice is heard in Ramah. Rachel weeps for her sons, refuses to be comforted for her sons, for they are no more. Thus said the Lord: Still your voice from weeping, and your eyes from tears. For there is recompense for your deeds, says the Lord, and they will return from hostile land. And there is hope for their end, and the sons will return to their borders* (31:14–16).

In these verses, Rachel is depicted as weeping over her sons, the people of Israel, who were exiled to Babylonia in the sixth century BCE. God hears her weeping, reveals Himself to her, and promises her that her sons will return home.

The opening image in the midrash, "At that moment Rachel leaped up before The Holy Blessed One and said," is a quote from a rabbinic midrash (Lamentations Rabbah 24) that invokes the language of the book of Jeremiah to describe the moment that Rachel stands up to plead for mercy for her children, the people of Israel, who have been exiled for the first time.

Lubitch understands the repetition of the term "her sons" in Jeremiah's prophecy as describing the distress and weeping of Rachel not just for the exiled children of Israel, but for her own biological children as well. Her distress arises from her own personal circumstances: she is the mother of two bastards, Joseph and Benjamin, since she gave birth to them after her sister Leah married Jacob and bore him six sons and a daughter. This is one of the forbidden sexual liaisons enumerated in the book of Leviticus, and thus her sons Joseph and Benjamin are technically bastards.

Rachel, in her lamentation, refuses to be comforted for her sons because *they are no more*, since they can never marry into the people of Israel. Her distress over her sons' exclusion from the Jewish people broadens to encompass the foremother's distress over the situation of all bastards more generally.

Lubitch uses a well-known midrashic technique that juxtaposes the same term used in different biblical contexts. She quotes a verse from Ecclesiastes (4:1) that also refers to *the tears of the oppressed* and contains the phrase *they have none to comfort them*, echoing the verse from Jeremiah. According to a midrashic tradition (see Leviticus Rabbah 22:8), Lubitch is suggesting that the tears of the oppressed are also the tears shed by bastards, who must pay for the sins of their mothers or fathers though they themselves are blameless. The rabbinic court invokes the power of the Torah to drive them away, and only God offers consolation.

The words of consolation that God offers to Rachel in Jeremiah's prophecy repeat themselves in a parallel structure: *Still your voice from weeping, and your eyes from tears.* Lubitch interprets this parallelism as referring once to Rachel's own bastard children and once to the children of Israel. Just as the children of Israel will return from hostile lands, so too all bastards will one day be embraced and accepted into the congregation of Israel.

The continuation of the midrash features the prophet Jeremiah. According to Lubitch, the dialogue between Rachel and God assuaged Jeremiah because he too experienced a similar distress on account of his son, Ben Sira, who was also a bastard. According to a medieval tradition, Jeremiah's daughter was impregnated by her father when she washed herself in a bathhouse immediately after her father had bathed there. Her father, when he bathed there, had had a seminal emission and his seed had remained in the water and penetrated her body (*The Alphabet of Ben Sira: Otzar Hamidrashim*, Eisenstein, 1928, 43).

After Jeremiah hears God's response to Rachel's weeping, he offers the prophecy that appears later in the chapter: *In those days, they shall no longer say, Parents have eaten sour grapes and children's teeth are set on edge. But every one shall die for his own sins: whosoever eats sour grapes, his teeth shall be set on edge* (31:28–29). Jeremiah's words of consolation promise that in a brighter, more just future, children will not be punished for their parents' sins. Parents will bear the punishment themselves, and their children will not be called bastards.

The midrash concludes with the claim that Rachel was barren not because she suffered from a biological condition, but because her husband, Jacob, avoided sleeping with her because he knew that any children born of their union would be bastards and he himself would be excised from the people. Rachel understands that this would be the case, yet she preferred to give birth to bastard children because she felt that not having children would be tantamount to death. And so she demanded that Jacob sleep with her nonetheless.

This conclusion brings the midrash full circle. Rachel preferred to give birth to bastard children rather than have no children at all. This midrash calls our attention to a painful reality: women are faced with a harsh dilemma when their husbands deny them a divorce while they themselves go on to remarry and have a new family. These women cannot remarry and face the risk of losing out on their fertile years. In the midrash, Jacob understands his wife's distress and agrees to her request. God's comforting assurance that Rachel's lost sons will be restored to their mother's embrace legitimizes the sense of injustice inherent in the laws of mamzerut and serves to embolden those who fight for change.

RIVKAH LUBITCH

Moses Visits Beruriah's Beit Midrash

In this last midrash in Rivkah Lubitch's trilogy on mamzerut, we learn, along with Moses, the astonishing fact that he and his siblings are techni- cally mamzerim. That this is true of the "First Family" of the Exodus and Sinai, so to speak, opens a new conversation about the sheer loss to the community of mamzerim and the stigma they are forced to bear.

When Moses ascended to heaven, he sat and wrote the Torah as dictated by God. He came to the verse *Do not uncover the nakedness of your father's sister, she is your father's near kinswoman* (Lev 18:12), and he said, isn't my mother my father's aunt? After all, Amram, my father, is the son of Kehat and the grandson of Levi, as is written: *And these are those numbered of the Levi (tribe), by their families ... of Kehat, the family of the Kehati ... and Kehat begat Amram* (Num 26:57–58). And Yocheved, my mother, is the daughter of Levi, as is written: *And the name of Amram's wife was Yocheved, daughter of Levi, whose mother bore her for Levi in Egypt and she bore to Amram, Aaron and Moses, and Miriam their sister* (Num 26:59). In other words, Yocheved and Kehat (my grandfather) were siblings, and Yocheved was thus forbidden to the sons of Kehat. Moses felt faint.

He came to the verse, *No mamzer will enter the assembly of God, even to the tenth generation will not enter into the assembly of God* (Deut 23:3). He said, The Holy Blessed One has not explained what a mamzer is. He heard some say a mamzer is one born of sexual relations forbidden by the Torah, aside from sex during menstruation. He said: Could I and my siblings, Aaron and Miriam, be mamzerim? He grew weak. He went and wept for thirty-nine days until he imagined he heard a voice saying "Silence! That is what I intended." He wanted to die.

He turned around and sat in the beit midrash of Beruriah. He heard a woman ask: Why is the law of mamzer not practiced today? And they answered her: Because we do not receive testimony on a mamzer, because it has already been decided that the entire community are presumed to be mamzerim, and are permitted to one another. Moses's mind was eased.

Commentary

This story is about Moses's first encounter with the Torah while transcribing it as it was dictated to him by God in the heavens. In the process of writing, Moses stumbled upon a verse that deeply unsettled him; in the list of forbidden sexual relations, he learned about the prohibition on a man marrying his aunt. Moses knew that his mother, Yocheved, the daughter of Levi, was the aunt of his father, Amram, who was the grandson of Levi (as in Exodus 6:20: *Amram took his father's sister Yocheved as a wife, and she bore him Amram and Moses*). Moses concludes that his parents engaged in a forbidden sexual relationship, and upon realizing this, he feels faint.

Moses then learns an additional divine command that further unsettles him: the prohibition on marrying bastards and their descendants for all eternity. The Bible does not clarify what constitutes a bastard, and Moses ponders the matter. He "hears" the rabbinic explanation that a bastard is one born of those sexual relations forbidden by the Torah aside from sex during menstruation, and he understands that he and his siblings and all their descendants fall into this category. He grows so frightened that he grows weak and weeps for thirty-nine days.

This story is in dialogue with the well-known Talmudic tale about Moses's ascent to receive the Torah on Mount Sinai, where he found God tying crowns onto the letters (see b.Menahot 29b). God affords Moses the ability to travel forward in time and visit the study house of Rabbi Akiva, the sage for whose sake God is tying the crowns. Moses discovers that he does not understand a word of the learning taking place in the study house, and he grows faint. He is assuaged only when he hears Rabbi Akiva assert, "It is a law given to Moses on Mount Sinai." Lubitch uses the story in the Babylonian Talmud to consider the disparities between the written Torah and the way it is interpreted throughout the generations. The connection to the Talmudic story anchors the halakhic solution she proposes in this midrash in the traditions of the Oral Torah.

The climax of Lubitch's story is Moses's personal crisis, when he hears God's voice saying, "Silence! That is what I intended." This line is a quote from the continuation of the Talmudic story about Moses's visit to Rabbi Akiva's study house. When Moses is apprised of the tragic fate of Rabbi Akiva, who is tortured to death by the Romans, he questions God, who responds, "Silence! That is what I intended." God's response gives voice to the human inability to understand God's ways. Moses will never understand why he was fated to be born a bastard. At this point, Moses wishes to die. Lubitch thus depicts the experience of being a bastard as a catastrophe.

The second half of the midrash offers a comforting solution. As in the Talmudic story, Moses "turns around" and travels forward in time, though this time he visits Beruriah's study house—the fictional beit midrash of women headed by Beruriah, the wife of the tanna, the mishnaic sage, Rabbi Meir. Moses hears the discussion taking place there, which is about the laws of mamzerut. One of the students asks why these laws are not practiced today. According to Lubitch, she receives two answers, which reflect two optional halakhic strategies for contending with this phenomenon. First, it is impossible to receive testimony on bastards because the rabbinic courts refuse to hear testimony from individuals who suspect that others are bastards. Without such testimony, it is impossible to incriminate anyone suspected of having this status or to prevent them from marrying Jews. Second, the halakhah maintains that the entire Jewish community is presumed to be bastards, and thus all are permitted to marry one another. Throughout the generations, the rabbis made other such general statements, or legal presumptions, applicable to the entire Jewish community—for instance, that all members of the entire Jewish community are presumed to be trustworthy as witnesses unless proven otherwise (hezkat kashrut). Similarly, the entire Jewish community is presumed to have been rendered impure by contact with the dead, such that most of the purity and impurity laws no longer apply. Moses is convinced that in the future, there will be no significance to the status of being a bastard. This glimpse of the future that he catches sight of in the beit midrash of Beruriah comforts him and sets his mind at ease.

RIVKAH LUBITCH

The Refused Woman

A woman wishes to get divorced, but her husband refuses to grant her a *get* (bill of divorce); a familiar and all-too-painful phenomenon. The legal process of divorce as it is presented in rabbinic sources is contingent on the husband's active role. During the divorce ceremony, the husband has to give his wife a *get* in the presence of two witnesses. Only then is she considered divorced and permitted to marry someone else. If the husband is unwilling to give her this document, the woman is still considered legally wed. This is true even in cases where the couple is no longer living together, or the husband is living with someone else, or the husband has simply disappeared. A *get* is considered valid if and only if it is given by the husband voluntarily, that is, not under duress.

This unilateral process continues to result in much unjust suffering for women. The sages throughout the generations have suggested various halakhic strategies to deal with this problem. In the State of Israel, where marriage and divorce may legally take place only in a religious framework (administered by the Chief Rabbinate or its representatives), women who are denied a *get* by their husbands then appeal to the rabbinical courts for assistance and a way out of the impossible situation in which they find themselves. But many rabbinical court judges refuse to avail themselves of the various halakhic solutions that have been proposed over the centuries.

The midrash of the refused woman is modeled on the well-known Talmudic story of the oven of Akhnai (b.Bava Metzia 59b). The Talmudic story is brought as an example of "verbal wronging" on the part of the sages in the beit midrash. Rabbi Eliezer's demand that the other sages in the beit midrash accept his ruling regarding matters of purity and impurity is harshly rejected. In this modern midrash, the violent dynamic takes place in the rabbinical court and involves a woman who is refused a *get* and the rabbinical judges who control her destiny. The woman employs legal terminology and is clearly comfortable in the world of Halakhah. She proposes various halakhic tools to the sages that can release her from the bonds of her marriage. The sages reject one suggestion after another, thereby allowing the husband to persist in his harmful behavior.

On that day one of the women who had been refused a *get* answered them all the answers in the world, and they would not accept them.

She said to the sages: Give me my *get*, and I will leave.

They said to her: The man divorces, and he divorces only by his own will.

She said to them: Compel him to divorce, since after all "they may strike him until he says 'I want to divorce.'"

They said to her: We cannot compel him, lest this be considered a *get* under duress, and it will end up with a married woman "going out into the marketplace," and her children will be mamzerim (illegitimate).

At that moment the carob tree was uprooted a hundred cubits. The sages saw, but didn't take note.

She said to them: If so, I'm a living widow.

They said: It has already been said "It is better to dwell as two than to dwell as a widow."

She said to them: But my husband has done this and that to me, and he's repulsive to me, and I'm not some captive to be bedded by someone I despise.

They said to her: Who are we, so much lesser than our teachers, to be so rash. We must heed the opinion of Rabbeinu Asher, the Ra'Sh.

At that moment, the stream turned backward, and they paid it no mind.

She said to them: Annul my marriage, since he's done something improper to me.

They said to her: We have no authority.

She said to them: Abrogate my wedding transaction as "fraudulent conveyance"—If had I known he would do these things to me, I would not have consented to marry him.

They said to her: We cannot.

At that moment, the walls of the study hall leaned inward and began to fall, went on leaning and falling.

She said to them: A rabbinic court is the father of orphans, and am I not orphaned, forlorn?

They said to her: That is not an argument, and we do not hear your claims at all. Maybe he asked something of you, and you refused him?

She said: Yes, he piled conditions on to my *get*, and I couldn't keep up with them.

A divine voice emerged and called out: What are you doing to this woman, whose husband is repulsive to her? She does not have to give him a thing to obtain her *get*.

The sages said: *It is not in heaven* and we pay no heed to a divine voice.

At that moment, The Holy Blessed One wept, and said: My sons have defeated Me, My sons have defeated Me.

Commentary

In the Talmudic story in b.Bava Metzia 59b, Rabbi Eliezer ben Hyrcanus attempts to persuade the other sages in the beit midrash that his halakhic opinion regarding the purity of certain vessels is correct. But the sages reject each of his claims. In the course of their debate, Rabbi Eliezer causes various miracles and wonders to take place—involving a carob tree, a stream of water, the walls of the beit midrash, and ultimately a divine voice that speaks out in his defense. But all to no avail. The sages of the beit midrash reject these strategies as inadmissible in a halakhic debate, insisting that *it is not in heaven* (Deut 30:12). The purpose of the story is to provide the grounds for the authority of the sages to rule in halakhic matters. Halakhic decision-making is presented as a human affair that is dependent on the deliberations of the sages and the ruling of the majority, and not on any absolute truth or on divine intervention. The Talmudic story concludes with God in heaven smiling and attesting that His sons have defeated Him. But the real tragedy of the story comes later. The sages of the beit midrash excommunicate Rabbi Eliezer, an emotional blow with devastating and tragic consequences.

Like Rabbi Eliezer, the woman in this modern midrash stands alone and lonely before the group of rabbinical judges who reject the halakhic solutions she proposes in an attempt to alleviate her situation. As with the Talmudic story, here too there are miraculous interventions that attest to the justness of the woman's claims: the carob tree is uprooted, the stream turns backward, the walls of the beit midrash lean inward and begin to fall, and ultimately the divine voice also speaks out in the woman's defense.

But to no avail. The comparison between the woman and Rabbi Eliezer serves to present the woman as a learned sage in her own right. The group of rabbinical judges are portrayed as determined to fortify their position as halakhic decisors and to display their legal prowess publicly, even at the cost of harming the woman on the other side.

God's response in this midrash is notably different from the conclusion of the Talmudic story. In the Babylonian Talmud God supports the decision of the sages and smiles down upon them. By contrast, in the midrash of the refused woman, God identifies with the woman's suffering. God laments the sages' cruelty to the woman and their use of halakhic tools toward unjust ends.

The discussion unfolds with three sections identical in structure and a fourth that breaks the template and leads to the story's tragic conclusion.

The midrash opens with the woman's request for a *get*. The rabbinical judges refuse her, explaining that only the husband can divorce his wife and the entire process is contingent upon his volition (b.Gittin 49b). The woman asks the court to force the husband to give her a *get* and to beat him until he says he wants to divorce her (b.Bava Batra 48a). The rabbinical judges respond that the *get* is valid only if it is given voluntarily by the husband, and not under duress. They raise the concern that if a woman thinks she can remarry after receiving a bill of divorce under duress, her children will be considered illegitimate. At that moment a miracle takes place that proves the woman right: the carob tree is uprooted and replanted a hundred cubits away. But the sages pay no heed.

In her second attempt, the woman claims that she is like a "living widow" (2 Sam 20:3). She lives alone like a widow but is trapped by her halakhic status as a married woman. The rabbinical judges respond by invoking the Talmudic claim that women prefer to be married than to live alone (b.Ketubot 75a).

The woman employs an additional strategy, claiming that her husband treated her in a way that made him seem repulsive to her—a halakhic status whereby, according to the sages, a woman is no longer obligated to engage in conjugal relations with her husband. The woman invokes the language used by Maimonides in his canonical code of law, the Mishneh Torah. According to Maimonides, after a woman makes this claim, the court must force the husband to give her a *get* (Laws of Personal Status 14:8).

The rabbinical judges respond that many of the greatest medieval sages debated Maimonides' ruling, and the Ra'sh (Rabbi Asher ben Yehiel, 1250–1327) ruled that it was preferable not to grant a divorce on these grounds (Responsa of the Ra'sh, 33:8). At that moment, another miracle occurs, which proves the justness of the woman's claim: the stream of water flows backward. But the rabbinical judges still do not pay heed.

In the next round, the woman requests that the court annul her marriage in accordance with the Talmud's assertion that the court has the authority to annul a marriage under certain circumstances, thus rendering it invalid (b.Yevamot 110a). The rabbinical judges deny her request without explaining why—they merely insist that they do not have the authority to accede to it. The woman employs an additional halakhic strategy and asks the judges to abrogate her wedding transaction since it was fraudulent, based on the rule that a transaction can be abrogated if it was based on an erroneous or a misleading claim during the preceding deliberations (Mishnah Kiddushin 2:3). The rabbinical judges once again reject her request without explanation and merely assert, "we cannot." At that moment another miracle occurs to vindicate the woman: the walls of the beit midrash lean in and begin to fall, threatening to bury the inhabitants.

The final round begins with the woman's claim that she is like a forlorn orphan, weakened and isolated by her social status. The court is the legal body responsible for the care, support, and education of orphans. And so the judges are responsible for providing for her.

The judges respond with a flat-out rejection. They claim that a woman who has been refused a *get* is not an orphan, and therefore they have no obligation to care for her. From that point on, they explain, they will not hear any further claims from her. They even cast blame on her, suggesting that perhaps she refused to accede to her husband's request for money or property, in which case she is at fault for her husband's refusal to divorce her. (For more on the grounds for divorce, see the Responsa of Rabbi Samuel ben Moses de Medina, Even Ha'Ezer 41.)

The woman confirms that indeed her husband piled conditions onto her *get* that she could not meet. At that point, yet another miracle occurs to vindicate the woman: a divine voice emerges from the heavens to rebuke the rabbinical judges. The woman's first claim was sufficient halakhic grounds to release her from her marriage. The giving of a *get* need not have anything to do with any financial disagreements between the couple.

The rabbinical judges respond that "it is not in heaven and we pay no heed to a divine voice." Like Rabbi Yehoshua's rejection of Rabbi Eliezer in the Talmudic story, the sages assert that the authority to rule in matters of Halakhah has been entrusted to human beings and the divine voice has no role in the court's legal proceedings.

The story concludes with an image of God weeping and lamenting the reality in the rabbinical court, where the judges have seized control of the Halakhah and interpreted it contrary to the divine will.

This midrash was first published in 2004. In 2017, Lubitch published a book in Hebrew, whose title in English was *From One End of the Earth to Another: The Path of Suffering of Women in the Rabbinical Courts*. The book described the various attempts to assist women who have been denied a *get* in their struggles against their husbands in the rabbinical court system, which becomes a struggle against the institution of the rabbinate itself.

RIVKAH LUBITCH

Jamila the Objector

The twenty-fifth chapter of the book of Deuteronomy teaches the commandment to perpetuate the name and lineage of a man who dies without a son, so that he may live on after his death. The widow and her brother-in-law are obligated to *establish a name in Israel* (Deut 25:7) for the deceased by giving birth to a son who will bear the name not of his biological father but of the widow's late husband. Until the widow performs this obligation, she is not permitted to marry anyone else. If none of her brothers-in-law is interested in performing "levirate marriage"—or "yibum," as it is called in Hebrew—with her, a ceremony known as "halitzah" is performed, which severs the tie of mutual obligation between the widow and her brother-in-law. In our own day, this ceremony is performed in a rabbinical court. The widow takes off the brother's shoe, spits in his face, and declares his refusal to perform levirate marriage with her. At the end of the ceremony, she is "liberated" and permitted to marry someone else.

In the State of Israel, in which there is no separation between religion and state and all marriage and divorce proceedings are under religious jurisdiction, the law dictates that levirate marriage is forbidden and halitzah is obligatory. If the brother refuses to perform halitzah with the widow—for instance, in a case where he seeks to extort her—the rabbinical court has the authority to impose various sanctions on him. But in other places in the world, the rabbinical courts act as they see fit.

The following midrash deals with an actual case that took place in Morocco in 1940. A widow's late husband's brother refused to perform halitzah and insisted on performing levirate marriage with her. She refused to marry him, opting instead to pay a difficult price both socially and economically. The case is briefly documented in Elimelech Westreich's "Family Law Facing the Challenge of Modernity: The Polemic on Yibum among the Sages of Morocco" in *Dinei Yisrael* 26 (2009–2010). The midrash recounts this incident and affirms a woman's right to refuse to perform levirate marriage, or to have sexual relations, against her wishes.

When brothers dwell together and one of them dies and leaves no son, the
wife of the deceased shall not be married to a stranger, outside the family.
Her husband's brother shall unite with her: he shall take her as his wife and
perform the levir's duty. The first son that she bears shall be accounted to
the dead brother, that his name may not be blotted out in Israel. But if the
man does not want to marry his brother's widow, his brother's widow shall
appear before the elders in the gate and declare, "My husband's brother
refuses to establish a name in Israel for his brother; he will not perform the
duty of a levir." The elders of his town shall then summon him and talk to
him. If he insists, saying, "I do not want to marry her," his brother's widow
shall go up to him in the presence of the elders, pull the sandal off his foot,
spit in his face, and make this declaration: Thus shall be done to the man
who will not build up his brother's house! And he shall go in Israel by the
name of "the family of the unsandaled one" (Deut 25:5–10).

In Morocco, there was once a great woman named Jamila who rebelled
against levirate marriage.

A true story. Jamila and her husband, David, lived in peace and tranquility
forty-seven years, and they had no children. When David died, Yamin, his
older brother, arose and wished to perform levirate marriage with the wife of
the deceased. The rabbinical court told Jamila to enter into levirate marriage
with Yamin and uphold the name of the deceased. She told them, I do not
want to. I want to perform halitzah and be done with it. They told her, It is
accepted by us in this bet din that levirate marriage takes precedence over
the halitzah ceremony. She said, I shared my bed with David for many years.
I do not want to share it with his brother Yamin. The judges said to her, Your
will is null and void relative to the commandment of levirate marriage. She
said to them, What do you want with me? I'm sixty years old and not fit
to give birth. They said, How many old and barren women were visited at
this age and fit to uphold a name. What's more, they said, the command is
obligatory even on those who aren't fit for it.

The judges saw she was steadfast in her refusal, and they rebuked her
time and again to make her fulfill the commandment, until she said, I will
fulfill the commandment—but with Yaakov, the youngest of the brothers.
The judges wondered, What is the difference between Yaakov and Yamin?
She said, This is my will, and the will has no reason. The judges returned

to Yamin, the eldest, and said, We will let him decide. Yamin said, "Let the law pierce the mountain," and I will uphold the name of my dead brother David. In his heart, Yamin said, If I do levirate marriage with her, I will inherit my brother David's estate.

Jamila stood her ground and declared, I will not enter into levirate marriage with Yamin. They said to her, My daughter (another version has it, You fool), you will be left without support from the estate, and with no dowry, only whatever cash you have on hand. She said to them, I know, but I cannot have relations with someone I loathe.

In the end, Jamila was steadfast in her refusal and lived the rest of her days with neither son nor daughter, without support from the estate and with no dowry, aside from whatever cash she had on hand. And this goes to teach how great is the strength of a woman who refuses to have relations with someone she loathes.

In the beit midrash of women they said: Jamila was a great woman. Not only did she uphold her own dignity, but the dignity of all daughters of Israel who refuse to have relations with people they loathe. Moreover, they said, Not only did she uphold the dignity of daughters of Israel who refuse to have relations with people they loathe, but also the dignity of the Torah. And people said, Jamila the Great, she had no children, but she made for herself a very great name.

Commentary

Over the course of the history of Jewish law, it was decided that Jewish identity depends on matrilineal rather than patrilineal descent. Nonetheless, the biblical patriarchal tradition continues to reverberate in various laws that remain in effect in our own day, like the laws of levirate marriage and halitzah.

The commandment to perform levirate marriage proved problematic at various points throughout history, as is already evident in biblical stories, such as Judah and Tamar in Genesis 38 and the book of Ruth. Rabbinic sources have been known to deal with a case in which the brother is interested in performing levirate marriage and the woman is not. In such a situation, she can request that the rabbinical court authorize her not to marry her late husband's brother. But in medieval times, the question of whether the court could force the brother to perform halitzah was a matter of dispute.

The midrash elaborates on the true story of Jamila, a woman who was left widowed and childless after forty-seven years of marriage to David. Yamin, David's older brother, is interested in performing levirate marriage, but Jamila prefers to perform halitzah and thus sever the tie with him. The presiding judges explain to her that in their court, they act based on a certain Sephardic halakhic tradition, according to which levirate marriage takes precedence over halitzah.

Lubitch focuses primarily on the dialogue between Jamila and the rabbinical judges. Jamila offers various justifications for her refusal to marry Yamin. Firstly, she does not wish to have sexual relations with Yamin. The rabbinical judges respond that her will does not hold weight when it comes up against the force of Halakhah, traditional Jewish law. Secondly, she is already too old to get pregnant again. The judges respond that the commandment is incumbent on her regardless of age or situation.

Jamila partially cracks under the judges' pressure and agrees to perform levirate marriage, but only with her husband's younger brother, Yaakov. But the judges cater to the will of the older brother Yamin, who refuses to agree to this plan. Lubitch incidentally reveals that the reason Yamin refused to allow Yaakov to marry Jamila in his stead is because he is after his brother's money. This is a reason that he, and the court, do not mention. This revelation allows us to observe the situation from without, highlighting the gap between the halakhic rationale (which is concerned with perpetuating the name of the dead) and Yamin's ulterior motives, which are subsumed under the framework of Halakhah.

The judges threaten Jamila that if she persists in her refusal to perform levirate marriage, then according to that same Sephardic halakhic tradition, she will be treated like a wife who refuses to engage in sexual relations with her husband. That is, the court will declare that she is a "rebellious wife." Being deemed a "rebellious wife" has severe halakhic repercussions. The woman's economic rights are impaired, and with time, she loses the right to the money owed to her in her marriage contract (*ketuba*) and sometimes also to the property she brought with her into the marriage.

The judges explain to her that she will be left "without support from the estate, and with no dowry"—only with whatever cash she has already. According to Jewish law, daughters do not inherit. When a man passes away, neither his daughters nor his wife benefit from the inheritance, which is passed on only to the sons. Those sons give support payments to their mother from then on. In our case, Jamila does not have any children, and her husband will be inherited by the brother who weds her in levirate marriage. If she refuses to wed Yamin, the judges tell her that she will not receive the support payments that he is supposed to pay her. And like a rebellious wife, she will not receive her ketuba money, but will be granted only the money or property that she brought with her into the marriage.

Jamila's response, "I cannot have relations with someone I loathe," invokes the language of Maimonides in the Laws of Personal Status, chapter 14, Halakhah 8, in which he deals with the laws governing divorcing a rebellious wife. Maimonides rules that if a woman explains her refusal to sleep with her husband on the grounds that she is "not like a captive woman who can sleep with someone she loathes," then the court must require her husband to give her a divorce document, but he is exempt from paying her ketuba money (and other payments). By placing this language in Jamila's mouth, Lubitch closes off the possibility of all further dialogue in the court. On the one hand, Jamila is reminding the justices that a woman has the right to opt not to sleep with someone against her wishes and the court may not pressure her to do so. On the other hand, this language also reflects Jamila's awareness of the high economic price that she will pay as a consequence of this decision.

The midrash concludes with a series of declarations regarding Jamila's contributions to Judaism and her heroism in standing her ground and refusing to sleep with a man against her wishes. She is credited with elevating the status of women and upholding the dignity of those who might otherwise tragically concede to wed a brother-in-law they do not love. She is also credited with upholding the status and dignity of the Torah, which does not force women to marry against their wishes.

The final line of the midrash notes rather ironically that ultimately Jamila, in refusing to wed her brother-in-law and perpetuate the name of her dead husband, merited a great name for herself. She stood up for herself in spite of the steep price she had to pay, thereby serving as a role model for other women of how to assert their rights in a halakhic court. In so doing, she acquired a measure of dignity and an enduring legacy that the patriarchal system sought—but failed—to seize for itself.

RIVKAH LUBITCH

Vows

These midrashim seek to come to terms with the patriarchal assumptions underlying the inequity between the value and capabilities of men and women in the biblical passage about vows. They propose an alternative subversive reading of the biblical text that suggests that the Torah's inequitable ruling is not principled and essential, but is reflective of its cultural context and irrelevant to our own times.

The midrashim about vows are presented as a product of the learning that took place in Beruriah's beit midrash, an imaginary study house (see page 89). The students in the study house encounter a textual difficulty and uncover a satisfying solution.

Speak to the Children of Israel and tell them—If a man should set aside a votive offering to God your estimated value of a person, your valuation of a male age twenty to sixty will be fifty shekels of sanctuary shekalim; and your valuation of a female will be thirty. And if it be for someone age five to twenty, your valuation will be twenty shekels for the male and for the female, ten. And if it be for from a month old to five years, your valuation will be five silver shekels for a male, and for a female, three shekels of silver. And if it be for someone sixty years and up, for a male, your valuation will be fifteen, and for a female, ten shekels (Lev 27:2–7).

The women learning in the beit midrash of Beruriah came to the passage *if a man should set aside a votive offering to God,* and were grieved at heart.

They said, could it be that a female's value is less than that of a male?

The women sages answered them:

You thought that the Torah is assessing the value of males and females, the elderly and babes!? Yet all humans were created equal and all stand equally before the Creator. Rather, these words are per human reckoning, which is why the verse specified, *Speak to the Children of Israel and tell them—If a* man should set aside a votive offering to God **your estimated** value of a person. **Your** valuation—the value from your point of view and what you think.

The Torah got to the bottom of what males and females think, and knew that all thought that males are worth more than females. If a male made a vow by his own value, he intended more, and if a woman vowed by her own value, she intended less.

And in a place where all know that male and female are equal—if one makes a vow by their own value, be it male or female, one must give the same.

———

Should a man take a vow or make an oath to the Lord, to take upon him-self a binding pledge, he shall not profane his word. According to all that issues from his mouth he shall do. And should a woman take a vow to the Lord and make a binding pledge in her father's house in her youth, and her father hear her vow and her binding pledge that she took upon herself, and her father remain silent to her, all her vows shall stand and every binding pledge that she took upon herself shall stand. But should her father restrain her when he hears all her vows and her binding pledges that she took upon herself, it shall not stand, and the Lord will forgive her, for her father re-strained her. But should she indeed become a man's with her vows upon her or her lips' utterance that she made binding upon herself, and her husband hear of it at the time he hears and remain silent to her, her vows shall stand, and her binding pledges that she took upon herself shall stand. And if at the time her husband hears, he restrains her and annuls her vow that is upon her and her lips' utterance that she took upon herself as a binding pledge, the Lord will forgive her (Num 30:3–10).

The learning women came to the passage *Should a man take a vow, etc.*, and once again were sad at heart.

They said, could it be that a woman's word is worth less than a man's?

For a man must keep his vows, while a woman, her husband and her father annul her vows.

The women sages answered them:

Could you really have thought that a woman's word is inferior to a man's? Rather, the Torah got to the bottom of what people who make pledges are thinking and knew that a male would take a vow with a mind that it be kept, and a woman would take a vow with a mind that her father or husband would consent, and if they would not, they have the right to annul it.

And in a place where all know that a woman doesn't need her husband's or her father's consent and her word is graven in stone, her husband and father can't annul her vow, and this is what the wisest of men meant when he said *when you make a vow to God, don't delay in fulfilling it, for there is no pleasure in fools. What you vow, fulfill. Better not to vow at all, than to vow and not fulfill* (Eccl 5:3–4).

Commentary

The first midrash deals with vows, and specifically with the amounts of money that people would customarily pledge to dedicate to the Temple. The sum of money was determined by the assessed value of the individual making the pledge. These sums of money were used for the continual up-keep of the Temple and its rituals. The Bible stipulates the various sums that individuals were to dedicate, depending on gender and age.

The students in Beruriah's beit midrash are distressed: Are these verses meant to conclude that women are valued less than men? The women sages in the beit midrash respond that upon close reading, it becomes evident that the commandment is to pledge the value of a human being. The Hebrew term for "value" is in second person, so that it literally reads "your value." The women sages interpret this term as referring to a person's assessment of himself or herself. In the past, women were regarded as lesser in value than men, and so women vowed to contribute less and the Torah's law reflects this practice. But in today's egalitarian world, the value pledged by men and women ought to be equivalent.

The second midrash deals with vows that are essentially oaths taken in the name of God to abstain from certain activities, according to the book of Numbers 30:3: *Should a man take a vow or make an oath to the Lord, to take upon himself a binding pledge, he shall not profane his word. According to all that issues from his mouth he shall do.* In the continuation of the biblical passage, the Torah distinguishes between a man's ability to vow to abstain from certain activities and that of a woman. Men who make such a vow are indeed obligated to abstain from the activities they specify. Single women are authorized to make such vows, but if a father hears his single daughter make such a vow, he may "restrain" her from fulfilling the vow and she will not be punished for failing to keep it. Once the woman is married, her husband may also restrain her from fulfilling her vow if he hears her utter it, and here too she will not be punished for failing to keep it. Widows and divorcees who made a vow to abstain from certain activities are obligated to keep their vows much like men.

The patriarchal social order that establishes that a father or husband's desire to restrain a woman from keeping her vow carries more weight than the woman's own choice, and in fact invalidates her choice, provokes the scholars in Beruriah's beit midrash anew, and they again turn to their teachers.

They ask: Is a woman's own choice to vow that she will abstain from a particular activity less significant than the will of the man in her life, namely her father or her husband?

As with the first midrash, the response of the women sages in the beit midrash is that the Torah is a product of its historical context and reflects what women felt and accepted upon themselves long ago. The individuals described in the Torah took vows as part of a patriarchal social reality that is no longer relevant today: men vowed out of a sense of their own unequivocal superiority, and women vowed out of a sense of their inferiority and out of an awareness and an acceptance that the will of their husband or father could trump their own choices. But in a reality in which this patriarchal consciousness has been replaced by an egalitarian ethos, everyone's vows are equal in value and everyone's vows are equally binding. Lubitch concludes her midrash by quoting a verse from the book of Ecclesiastes that emphasizes the fundamental importance of vows and harshly critiques those who take vows and then fail to fulfill them. This conclusion serves to clarify that the struggle against patriarchy is not about a resistance to vows as an institution, but rather about a resistance to the manner in which they discriminate between men and women.

TEN

Post-Holocaust Theology

TAMAR BIALA

A Raven and a Dove

When the rains of the Flood ceased, Noah sent a raven and a dove from the ark to check whether the waters had subsided. The raven and dove survived the destruction of their world, and they bore witness to the catastrophe. Written as an allegory, the midrash describes the attitude toward these survivors in a beit midrash of birds and considers society's, as well as God's, responsibility for them.

A question was asked in the beit midrash of the birds of the sky: That raven and that dove that Noah sent out from the window—whatever became of them? After all, of the raven it is written *it went off, going off and returning, until the waters were dried up from upon the earth* (Gen 8:7), but it does not say what became of him. As for the dove, it is written *so she returned to him into the Ark, for there was water upon the face of all the earth* (Gen 8:9), and later it is said *but she returned to him again no more* (Gen 8:12), and it does not say where she went or what became of her.

They sent the high-flying eagle, which can bear another bird on its wings, to fetch them. The eagle flew away for a day, and another, and then returned with the dove, and all her retinue, since from the day she had found a home and until that day she did not stop being fruitful and multiplying, and kept giving birth, and busying herself with pregnancies, and utterly exhausting herself. But he did not return with the raven.

They asked him: That raven, you didn't find him? He said: I found him, flying here and there at the ends of the earth and he refused to come with me. He said, Ever since the day that Noah sent me forth from the ark, I haven't stood still or rested, for the earth is defiled, so how could I come and dwell among you? I won't join all of you, and won't stop my flight until I'm told to by the Shekhinah, of whom it is written that She dwells among the defiled in their defilement.

On hearing this, they decided to go and find the Shekhinah and bring Her the raven, so that he might cease from his flight.

The birds of the sky asked the celestial lights, where is the place of the Shekhinah? And they did not answer.

They asked the beasts of the field and the fish of the sea, and they did not answer.

They asked the trees and the grasses, and even they did not know.

At the time that they were looking at one another and seeking an answer from one another, they heard the Shekhinah calling to them, Here I am among you, for you are preoccupied with learning Torah and I am listening and growing with you.

She revealed Herself to them in the image of a very large stork.

The eagle went and brought the raven, who was advanced in years, his wings dry and gray, limping in flight.

The inhabitants of the beit midrash said to him: Why do you fly back and forth and find no rest?

He said, Where should I stand, and where should I rest my wings? Anywhere I try to stand, the dead eyes of my brothers and sisters stare at me. And anywhere I try to sit, the earth stirs, and groans, and the weeping voice of my brother's blood rises upward from it.

They answered, But the dove found land on which grass grows, and took an olive branch in its mouth, and then went, and blossomed, and sought out a new life, and she is still giving birth even now. And it is written *the waters left firm ground upon the earth* (Gen 8:13) and the earth is waiting for you and those like you, for thousands of years now, to come back.

He answered them, Even if the waters have left firm ground upon the earth, I cannot dwell on it, for it says *the face of the soil was destroyed* (Gen 8:13), and a place that has no face, neither its tears nor its disgrace can be wiped away.

At that moment, the sun began to set, and the sky seemed to them as red as blood.

The inhabitants of the beit midrash cast their eyes upon the dove, and saw that she was tired and weeping. They looked at that raven and saw that he was losing his mind.

They looked upon the Shekhinah and saw that She was spreading Her wings, and they were large, and a warm wind emanated from them.

The Shekhinah arose from Her place and went over to the dove and the raven and sheltered them with Her wings.

The raven ceased his flight. The dove's soul was rested.

And some say that at this moment one could hear the murmuring of the Shekhinah saying to those birds who dwelled in the beit midrash, What do you know about the dove and the raven, you are not doves, or ravens, and it wasn't you who were sent forth from that window, to go and look.

Commentary

In this midrash Tamar Biala imagines a study house of birds in which there is a discussion about the fate of the raven and the dove from the story of the flood. What became of them? The birds decide to send the eagle to search for them. The eagle, which is capable of carrying another bird on its wings (in Deuteronomy 32:11, God's deliverance of Israel is analogized to an eagle bearing its young) will be able to transport the birds back to the study house, assuming it can find them.

The eagle returns with the dove, who seems to have integrated back into society. The dove seems to be functioning normally, though ever since the flood, she has not desisted from procreation and is exhausting herself with pregnancy after pregnancy. The dove is keeping herself busy as a defense mechanism so that she never has the time and space to remember the catastrophe and feel the pain.

The eagle then finds the raven consumed by suffering. The raven refuses to return with the eagle to join the other birds. It views the post-diluvian world as "defiled," and it hears the voice of the dead crying out from the earth—much as God heard Abel's blood crying out from the earth (Gen 4:10). The restless, tortured raven, which can find no rest, insists that it will return only if the Divine Presence, the Shekhinah, instructs it to do so—since according to the midrashic tradition (Bamidbar Rabbah 7:8), the Shekhinah dwells among Israel in their defilement.

The birds in the beit midrash are unable to locate the Shekhinah. Ultimately the Shekhinah reveals Herself to them in the figure of a large stork. It turns out that She was among them all along, in keeping with the Mishnah in Avot 3:6, which teaches that the Shekhinah dwells among any ten individuals engaged in the study of Torah.

The raven arrives in the study house on the eagle's wings. It tries to explain itself to the other birds in the study house, but they are unable to comprehend its plight. They point out that the dove has already put her life back together and started anew. After all, they tell the raven, the land has already dried up and the waters have left firm ground upon the earth. But the raven responds with a close midrashic reading of the biblical verse that describes what Noah saw when he removed the cover from the ark: *The face of the soil was destroyed* (Gen 8:13). The soil had been rendered faceless, and when a place has no face, its tears and disgrace can never be wiped away and its shame will endure forever.

The members of the avian beit midrash feel compassion for the raven and the dove, but they do not know how to ease their suffering. Thus, they are catapulted into a torment of their own. The midrash concludes with the Shekhinah spreading Her wings and sheltering the two survivors. This great embrace calms the dove and enables it to desist from its exhausting struggle for survival and to allow herself her final rest. At the same time, the sheltering wings of the Shekhinah put an end to the raven's loneliness and distress and allow it to rest at last. This image recalls the prayer for the souls of the dead, "El Malei Rachamim," in which we ask for the dead to find shelter under the wings of the Shekhinah. The midrash closes with the Shekhinah rebuking the birds of the study house for judging these survivors without having any real sense of what they had endured.

The use of an allegorical midrash that anthropomorphizes birds so as to give voice to the human plight recalls the kabbalistic literary tradition, in which both the Shekhinah and the human soul are depicted as birds (see, for instance, Tikunei Zohar 21).

DINI DEUTSCH FRANKEL

The Shepherd in the Lilies

This midrash collection deals with the connection between God and Knesset Israel, the people of Israel, at a time when they are in a state of distress and catastrophe. Where is God? How does God feel when bearing witness to the suffering of the people of Israel? Why does God not intervene to save them? Dini Deutsch Frankel answers these questions by means of a series of midrashim on verses from the Song of Songs, which the rabbis read as an allegory between The Holy Blessed One (the male lover) and Israel (the female lover). In her midrash Deutsch Frankel presents a piercing post-Holocaust theological reflection.

1

My love is mine and I am his, the shepherd in the lilies (ha-ro'eh ba-shoshanim) (Song 2:16).

And why is He called, *ha-ro'eh ba-shoshanim*? Because He sees evil, *ro'eh ba-ra*, and is like one hemmed in by thorn-hedged lilies, and says: woe to Me from the flowers and woe to Me from the thorns that I created.

Knesset Yisrael said to The Holy Blessed One: *Before day breathes, before the shadows of night are gone, run away, my love! Be like a gazelle, a wild stag on the jagged mountains* (Song 2:17)—Woe is me that from the day that the Temple was destroyed the face is hidden and the knots undone and in their place jaggedness has come.

The Holy Blessed One answered: I turn about on nothing but mountains of fragrant spices, as is written: *Before day breathes, before the shadows of night are gone, I will hurry to the mountain of myrrh, the hill of frankincense* (Song 4:6)—There I hear the voice of bitterness and fiery cleansing in you, and see therein your beauty, as is written: *You are all beautiful my love, and there is no blemish in you* (Song 4:7).

The nations of the world said to Knesset Yisrael: *Where has your lover gone, O beautiful one?* (Song 6:1).

She answered them: *My love has gone down to his garden, to the beds of spices, to graze and gather lilies* (Song 6:2)—wherever He goes, He is with me, sees my afflictions and sorrow.

The nations of the world were astonished: And can't He protest against it, *limchot*?

Knesset Yisrael answered: Wiping away *mocheh* (tears), is what He does.

2

I'm my beloved's and my beloved is mine, the shepherd in the lilies (Song 6:3).

The one who sees evil and is like one hemmed in by thorn-hedged lilies, who says, Woe is me, *My own vineyard, I didn't guard* (Song 1:6).

Knesset Yisrael said to The Holy Blessed One: What is that which is written, *And just as God rejoiced in being good to you and multiplying you, so He will rejoice to make you perish and to destroy you* (Deut 28:63). He said: Never was, and never will be.

She said to Him: I sat on their graves, and I saw their crematoria.

He said: From the day that the world was given choice, I am preoccupied with nothing but looking with anticipation (*tzipiyah*), as is written: *God's eyes look with anticipation over the evil ones and the good ones, tzafot ra'im ve-tovim* (Prov 15:3), and it is said: "He who looks with anticipation at the evildoer and desires his righteousness," and likewise He looks out for the righteous man and desires his good.

She said to Him: Our portion is better than that, for we have the power to do good deeds and acts of kindness.

3

My dove is in the cleft of the rock, in the hollow of the cliff, show me your gaze, let me hear your voice, for your voice is sweet, and your look is lovely (Song 2:14).

This is what the sacred community of Israel said to The Holy Blessed One, that there is none who is so hidden like a dove in the rock, but The Holy

Blessed One, who hides His face from Israel from the day the Temple was destroyed, and Israel calls to Him and say show us Your look, let us hear Your voice. And He answers them: Look deeply into the world I created, and you will see My gaze, search the Torah that I gave, and you will hear My voice.

4

Till day's breeze blows and shadows fly, turn round like a deer, my love, or a gazelle, on cloven mountains (Song 2:17).
   Fly, my love, like a deer, or gazelle, on mountains of spices (Song 8:14).

Twice it is said, be my love like a deer or gazelle on the mountains: in a shadowy time, night drawing close, on mountains of spices—there my love goes round (*sovev*); in the light of day on mountains of cloves—there my love runs away?

   Rather this comes to teach that in a time of sorrow people need God to go around (*mistovev*) among them. Do not say "turn around" (*sov*) but rather "grandfather" (*sav*), go around like a grandfather does, comforting his grandchildren. But at times of ease, they do not search for Him, and if one does not choose God and cleave to God, God runs away.

Commentary

1

The first midrash begins with a question: Why is The Holy Blessed One referred to in the Song of Songs as *the shepherd in the lilies (ha-ro'eh ba-shoshanim)*? Throughout rabbinic literature the shepherd is understood as a metaphor for The Holy Blessed One, and the lilies as a metaphor for the people of Israel. By interpreting "the shepherd" (*ha-ro'eh*) in two unexpected ways, Deutsch Frankel uses this phrase to depict a devastating, painful rift in the relationship between The Holy Blessed One and the people of Israel. First, she reads this word as written not with an 'ayin (*ha-ro'eh*: the shepherd), but with an aleph (*ha-ro-eh*: the one who sees). Second, she links the root of the word not to shepherding but to evil (*ro'a'*). These two new interpretations suggest that God sees Israel and is aware of its evil lot.

When God dwells among the people, it is as if God is pricked by the thorns and is suffering alongside Israel.

Deutsch Frankel remains vague about the cause of Israel's suffering. Are these their own thorns, or are they the thorns of the other nations that afflict them? Deutsch Frankel's parable suggests that the lilies symbolize the suffering of humanity in its entirety, and in this specific case, God is lamenting not just the suffering of Israel but also the suffering of all His human creatures.

Deutsch Frankel goes on to discuss the rift created between God and Israel following the destruction of the Temple. The feminine lover in Song of Songs 2:17 bewails the male lover who turned his back on her and made his way to the *jagged mountains*. She evokes the image of cracked, broken mountains to describe the fissure between Israel and God following the destruction of the Temple, which led to the present situation of divine hiddenness in which the knots of relationship and reciprocal obligation have become undone.

The male lover responds to her by invoking a similar verse from Song of Songs 4:6 in which he repeats her initial words but concludes differently: *I will hurry to the mountain of myrrh, the hill of frankincense.* He explains that throughout the period of exile, He was not turning his back on her but was rather setting His steps toward Israel, which is symbolized by *the mountain of myrrh, the hill of frankincense*. Deutsch Frankel understands the word "myrrh" (*mor*) as relating to the Hebrew word *mar*, meaning bitterness, and "frankincense" (*levona*) as relating to *libun*, clarification (literally "fiery cleansing"). Throughout the exile, God assures the people of Israel that He senses their bitterness and recognizes their efforts to understand their fate, and He sees the beauty in their struggle, despite their pain.

The nations of the world sense the distance between the lovers, and they torment the people of Israel by asking, *Where has your lover gone, O beautiful one?* How could your God disappear and abandon you? The female lover responds by invoking Song of Songs 6:2: *My lover has gone down to his garden, to the beds of spices, to graze and gather lilies.* The beds of spices are the fragrant mountains mentioned earlier, which represent the people of Israel. There God can be found amid His people. The words *to graze and to gather lilies* hearken back to the beginning of the midrash, in which the male lover is described as the *shepherd in the lilies*. The people of Israel's response to the nations of the world is that God is with them even in times of distress and exile. God is in the thorny hedges, witnessing their distress and suffering alongside them (as per Sifrei Zuta 10, "I am still with them in distress").

This response is followed by the most direct and pointed question of all, attributed to the nations of the world: "And can't He protest against it?" How is it that God, the omnipotent Creator, can look on at the suffering and distress of Israel and not put an end to it or at least protest against it? The female lover, playing on the different meanings of the word *limchot* (to object) answers that God is indeed *mocheh* (wiping away). God does not object but rather wipes away Israel's tears (see Isa 25:8).

2

The second midrash takes this theme one step further, directly tackling the question of God's role in the atrocities of the Holocaust. The midrash begins with the recurrent motif of God as the "shepherd in the lilies," observing the suffering of Israel. But this time the verse is invoked as a lamentation spoken by God: "Woe is me, *My own vineyard, I didn't guard*" (Song 1:6). God laments His failure to fulfill his role of guardian of the people of Israel's seeds and saplings.

The people of Israel challenge God, invoking a verse from Deuteronomy (28:63) stating that God will rejoice in the suffering that He will inflict on the people of Israel as punishment and that He will even rejoice in destroying them and making them perish. God responds unequivocally that such a reality never was and never will be. This response recalls the Babylonian Talmud's discussion of the use of the death penalty to punish those who committed specific transgressions—a punishment that some of the sages regarded as immoral (Sanhedrin 71a). Several sages explain that this punishment is merely theoretical, while others insist that it is a real punishment that was actually inflicted, and they "sat on his grave" and "saw the ashes" of those who were taken to be executed.

In Deutsch Frankel's midrash, the people of Israel defiantly object that this is not a merely theoretical situation, because they themselves bore witness to the atrocity. They saw the burning and sat on the graves of their fellow Jews. The testimonies of survivors about the crematoria and the mass graves serve to refute God's claim.

In response, God tries to explain His way of running the world. He quotes from Proverbs to explain that He gave humanity free choice, and from that point on He examines the good and bad deeds of His creatures but does not interfere. However, God does not observe impartially—His looking (*tzfia*) is bound up in anticipation (*tzipiyah*). He hopes and anticipates that the evildoers will mend their ways; to paraphrase one of the liturgical poems recited on the High Holidays: "He who looks with anticipation at the evildoer and desires his righteousness."

The people of Israel respond defiantly, "Our portion is better than that." They note that their situation is better than God's. God cannot intervene in the world and in human decision-making, whereas the people of Israel can influence the way people behave "for we have the power to do good deeds and acts of kindness."

3

This midrash deals with the rift between God and the people of Israel in the wake of the destruction of the Temple. It is based on a verse from the Song of Songs (2:14) in which the male lover tries to seduce the female lover by comparing her to a dove hidden in the cranny of the rock and encourages her to reveal her presence. In rabbinic tradition, this is a reference to God's courtship of the people of Israel. But in this midrash, Deutsch Frankel reverses the roles and attributes these words to the people of Israel, who analogize God to a dove.

According to this reading, the people of Israel feel that God has been hidden from them ever since the destruction of the Temple, and they plead with Him to reveal Himself to them. God responds that by looking directly at the world, they will discover God's gaze, and by expounding His Torah, they will hear His voice. This clear-eyed, pragmatic theology gives pride of place to the role of hermeneutics in the relationship between God and humanity.

4

The fourth midrash returns to the classical rabbinic allegory in which the male lover is God and the female lover is the people of Israel. Deutsch

Frankel points out that twice the male lover is described by the female lover as a deer or a gazelle wandering in mountains. But these analogies point to a surprising inconsistency.

How could it be that at the end of the day, when it grows dark, the lover is on the jagged mountains (Song 2:17), in a place of harshness and danger, whereas in the daytime, he is found on the pleasant, safe mountains of spices (Song 8:14)? Deutsch Frankel reconciles these two verses by expounding on the different verbs that describe the deer in each of these locations. At night he wanders around (*sovev*), and in the daytime he flees (*bo're'ach*). The word for God's wandering around (*sovev*) comes from the same root as "grandfather" (*sav*)—because it is in time of danger and harshness that people need God to wander in their midst and support them like a kindly grandfather. But in daytime, when people do not need God's reassurance, God flees (*bo're'ach*) because they do not choose (*bocharim*) God and connect (*chovrim*) to him.

Deutsch Frankel concludes her midrash by coming theologically full circle. She emphasizes how important it is for humanity to feel God's presence, especially in a difficult, frightening, and painful period. At the same time, she notes the human tendency to forget God and ignore His presence when all is well. The closeness between God and humanity depends on both working to ensure that the bond endures.

ELEVEN

Holidays

RUTH GAN KAGAN

Sukkot *Prayer for Rain*
(Tefillat HaGeshem)

On the holiday of Shmini Atzeret, which immediately follows Sukkot, we begin praying for rain with a special prayer that is recited prior to the Musaf service or during the reader's repetition of the Musaf Amidah. It is customary among the various Jewish communities to add liturgical poems to this prayer. In Ashkenazi communities, one of the more common liturgical additions is "Remember the Father," by an anonymous poet.

The poem consists of six stanzas written in alphabetical acrostic, in which the prayer community beseeches God to grant rain by the merit of the forefathers of the nation: Abraham, Isaac, Jacob, Moses, Aaron, and the twelve tribes. Each stanza focuses on one of these figures and explores his special connection to water. And each stanza concludes with a refrain that calls for rain by the merit of the biblical figure mentioned in that stanza: "For his sake do not withhold water; for his righteousness's sake grant abundant water."

Ruth Gan Kagan's midrash is a prayer for rain that essentially expands the traditional poem by adding five stanzas that present seven biblical women: Sarah, Rebecca, Rachel, Leah, Miriam, Deborah, and Yael. Kagan writes:

"I don't remember when I first began to hear the voices of the matriarchs inside me. But it seems to me that Miriam was the first—Miriam whose whole life, and even her name, were bound up in water. If it was by Miriam's merit that we were given water in the desert, how could we not mention her when we pray for the grace of water? Over the course of a few years, I became increasingly aware that the merit of our matriarchs, too, stands before us each year when we pray for rain, and it was only the words that were lacking.

"I had never written a liturgical poem or even any sort of poem at all. Four years ago, on the eve of Shmini Atzeret, I sat praying in the garden and the words of additional stanzas for the prayer for rain seemed to cry out for release. The stanzas about the matriarchs and the other women were written to match those of the original liturgical poem. Like the original stanzas, they do not explicitly name their subjects, and each line contains hints from the Bible and midrash that link each figure to water—whether it is actual water, or water as metaphor (though the additional verses are not arranged alphabetically). As with the original stanzas, these verses are tinged with sadness and suffering but also promise and hope. They can be sung to the melody of the original liturgical poem.

"From the day I wrote it, this liturgical poem took on a life of its own. Several synagogues have incorporated it into their prayer for rain, either by interspersing the original stanzas with my own, or by reading these stanzas as a unit on their own, preceded by the words, 'Our God and God of our mothers.'

"I pray that by the merit of the patriarchs and matriarchs, we will merit a year of rain of blessing."

Our God, God of our Matriarchs
Remember the mother, anointed in Holy Spirit like water.
Whose laughter rolled like streams of water,
Whose woman's way You resumed, blood flowing like water,
The babes of kingdoms she suckled, milk as abundant as water,
For her sake do not hold back water!

Remember the one who went out in the evening to draw well water,
Kindness flowed from her jar like water,
When she heard the servant ask for a little water,
She hurried, drawing until all camels finished drinking water,
For her righteousness grant abundant water!

Remember the shepherdess who came with her flock to the well of water,
Wailing and bitter crying, she weeps for her children like water.
Whose sister's eyes were tender from tears of water,
Her womb You opened like a river of water,
For their sake do not withhold water.

Remember one who stood by the reeds, watching by the Nile's water,
She breathed life into newborns, saving them from deathdark water,
Who, with her drum and circle-dance, sang at the Sea of water,
By her merit, You bore them the gift—a rolling well of water,
For her righteousness grant abundant water!

Remember she who sat under a palm tree, in the hills of Ephraim,
In her song, the earth quaked, also the clouds dripped water,
The stars in their orbits waged war from skies bearing water,
And she, most blessed of women, who gave milk instead of water.
For their sake do not withhold water!

Commentary

FIRST STANZA

Remember the mother, anointed in Holy Spirit like water.
   We ask God to shower us in blessed rain by the merit of the matriarch Sarah, also known as Iscah, who was enveloped (*sachta*) in prophecy like water (b.Megillah 14a).

Whose laughter rolled like streams of water,
   By the merit of Sarah, whose laughter rolled like water and could be heard even outside her tent when the angels came to foretell the birth of Isaac (Gen 18:12).

Whose woman's way You resumed, blood flowing like water,
   By the merit of Sarah, who merited at age ninety for her menstrual blood to resume its flow like water, and who went on to become pregnant and give birth to Isaac (Gen 18:11–12). According to the midrash recorded in b.Bava Metzia 87a, Sarah had already begun menstruating when the angels visited.

The babes of kingdoms she suckled, milk as abundant as water (Gen 21:7).
   By the merit of Sarah, who was blessed with abundant milk that flowed like water following the birth of Isaac (b.Bava Metzia 87a). Her breasts opened like fountains, and she was able to nurse not just her own son, but also those of many other women, and thus everyone believed that she was indeed Isaac's true mother.

SECOND STANZA

Remember the one who went out in the evening to draw well water,

We ask God to shower us in blessed rain by the merit of the matriarch Rebecca, who went out to draw water in the evening, and encountered the servant of Abraham who had come to Haran to search for a wife for Isaac (Gen 24:11).

Kindness flowed from her jar like water,

By the merit of Rebecca, who always acted with loving-kindness and thus the water rose to meet her when she came to the well (Genesis Rabbah 60:5).

When she heard the servant ask for a little water,

By the merit of Rebecca, who listened to the thirsty servant and heeded his request for water (Gen 24:17).

until all camels finished drinking water,

By the merit of Rebecca, who gave water not just to Abraham's servant but also to his ten camels, until they had all drunk their fill. It was thus that the servant understood that Rebecca was the wife destined for Isaac (Gen 24:19).

THIRD STANZA

Remember the shepherdess who came with her flock to the well of water,

We ask God to shower us in blessed rain by the merit of the matriarch Rachel, who encountered Jacob in Haran next to the well when she came to give water to her cattle.

Wailing and bitter crying, she weeps for her children like water.

Many years after her death, when the Israelites were exiled to Babylonia, Rachel wept for her sons, and her eyes poured forth with tears like water, and her voice could be heard in the heavens. By the merit of her weeping, God promised that the children of Israel would be returned to the borders of their land (see Jer 31:14 and Lam Rabbah Petichta 24).

Whose sister's eyes were tender from tears of water,

We ask God to shower us in rain by the merit of the matriarch Leah, who shed tears like water and thus had soft eyes (Gen 29:17). She cried because she was informed that she, Laban's firstborn, was destined to marry Esau, Isaac's firstborn, and she did not want to fall into the hands of that evil man. Her tears and prayers served to avert the decree, and she merited to marry Jacob instead (Genesis Rabbah 70:16).

Her womb You opened like a river of water,
By the merit of Leah, who was barren until God opened her womb and then she bore the lion's share of Jacob's household—six of the tribes of Israel and Dina (Gen 29:31 and Psikta d'Rav Kahana, *Roni Akara* 20:1).

FOURTH STANZA

Remember one who stood by the reeds, watching by the Nile's water (Exod 2:4),
We ask God to shower us in blessed rain by the merit of Miriam, who stood from afar and watched over Moses when he was placed in an ark made of reeds in the Nile (Exod 2:4).

She breathed life into newborns, saving them from deathdark water,
By the merit of Miriam, who is identified with the midwife Puah (Exod 1:25), who would blow the breath of life into newborns at birth (*mephi'ah*), enabling them to release the amniotic fluid and draw their first breaths, thereby saving them from death (Exod Rabbah 1:13).

Who, with her drum and circle-dance, sang at the Sea of water,
By the merit of Miriam, who, following the miracle of the splitting of the sea, took her drum in her hand and sang songs of praise, and all the women followed her with drums and circle-dancing and joined in her song (Exod 15:20).

By her merit, You bore them the gift—a rolling well of water,
By the merit of Miriam, throughout whose lifetime a well accompanied the Israelites in their journey through the desert and throughout their encampments, providing water for each tribe (see Tosefta Sotah 11:1).

FIFTH STANZA

Remember she who sat under a palm tree, in the hills of Ephraim,
We ask God to shower us in blessed rain by the merit of Deborah the

prophet, who judged Israel while sitting under a palm tree in the hills of Ephraim, where all the people of Israel would come before her for judgment (Judg 4:4-5).

In her song, the earth quaked, also the clouds dripped water, the stars in their orbits waged war from skies bearing water,

By the merit of Deborah, whose song chronicled how the military victory of the Israelites against Yavin king of Hatzor was aided by God in heaven, and described the power of nature and water (Judg 5:4, 20).

Most blessed of women, who gave milk instead of water.

And by the merit of Yael, whom Deborah praised in her song for offering the enemy general Sisera milk instead of water, thereby putting him to sleep so that she might kill him, leading to the Israelites' military victory (Judg 5:24).

EINAT RAMON

Pesach *The Four Daughters*

> The traditional midrash about the four sons in the Passover Haggadah
> appears in various sources including the Jerusalem Talmud (Pesachim
> 10:4). It deals with the commandment incumbent on the father to tell his
> sons the story of the exodus from Egypt, repeated in four different places
> in the Torah, suggesting ways of fulfilling this obligation with each of four
> very different sons. The four types of sons in the Haggadah are described
> as wise, wicked, simple, and unable to ask a question. Einat Ramon's
> contemporary midrash, by contrast, portrays four types of daughters: one
> who is wise-hearted, one who is a rebel, one who is sincere, and one who
> cannot ask questions. Ramon portrays each type by comparing her to a
> biblical woman: Miriam, Tamar the daughter-in-law of Judah, Ruth, and
> the unnamed beautiful captive woman of Deuteronomy, respectively.
> Each of these women poses a challenge to the Jewish community, and
> the midrash instructs us in how we might respond to her voice, include
> her in the tradition, and learn from her.

The Torah addressed itself to four daughters:
One wise-hearted, one a rebel, one sincere, and one who cannot ask.

Wise-hearted, this is Miriam—what does she say?
"Father, your decree is harsher than Pharaoh's ... Evil Pharaoh, perhaps
his decree endures, perhaps not, but you are righteous and yours certainly
will endure." Her father went and followed his daughter's counsel.
So we will follow after her, with dance and tambourines, and spread her
prophecy among the nations.
A rebel, this is Tamar—what does she say?
Examine these, please (Gen 38:25), the ways of enslavement and oppression in the rule of one person over another. Though she rebelled against

authority, it is written *she is more in the right* (Gen 38:26) than he, and we have no freedom until we repent of our ways.

Sincere, this is Ruth—what does she say?

Where you will go, there I will go, and where you sleep, I will sleep, your people shall be my people, and your God shall be my God (Ruth 1:16).

So we will strengthen her in her holding fast to those she loved, and say to her *May God render the woman entering your home as unto Rachel and Leah who together built the House of Israel* (Ruth: 4:11).

And the one who cannot ask, this is the beautiful female captive taken in war.

Only her silent weeping is heard, as is written *and she will weep for her father and mother* (Deut 21:13).

We will begin for her. We will be her voice and she will be our judge. We will return her to her mother's house and the home where she was born, and we will *proclaim freedom in the land, for all who live on it* (Lev 25:10).

Commentary

This midrash begins with the four daughters, who correspond to the four sons in the traditional midrash. The first daughter is characterized as wise-hearted, a phrase from the Bible's description of the women in the desert who wove tapestries for the tabernacle (Exod 35:35). She is distinguished by her highly developed emotional and moral intelligence. Einat Ramon identifies her with Moses's sister Miriam, whose wisdom is reflected in her words to her father, Amram: "Father, your decree is harsher than Pharaoh's." According to the aggadic tradition preserved in the Babylonian Talmud (Sotah 12a), Amram divorced his wife after he learned of Pharaoh's decree to kill all male babies, lest he become the father to the victim of such an atrocity. The Israelites observed the behavior of the righteous Amram and were quick to follow suit. Miriam understood the potentially dangerous consequences of his act: that no more Israelite children would be born. She stood up to her father and rebuked him, insisting that his decree was harsher than Pharaoh's, who put an end only to the male children. Amram accepted his daughter's advice and remarried his wife, Yocheved, and subsequently all the Israelites remarried their wives as well. Amram's second marriage resulted in the birth of Moses, who led the Israelites out of Egypt.

Einat Ramon illuminates Miriam's wisdom, showing how she is able to seek out and sustain life even from the darkest depths of human experience. She insists that Miriam's prophetic abilities be recognized among the nations, and she calls on us to follow in her footsteps with drums and dancing just as Miriam led the Israelite women after the splitting of the sea.

The second daughter, the rebel, is identified with Tamar, the daughter-in-law of Judah. Tamar refused to accept her father-in-law's unjust treatment in refusing to wed her to his third son in levirate marriage, instead leaving her to return to her father's home (see Gen 38). Tamar dressed up as a prostitute and became pregnant with the child of Judah himself. In lieu of payment she asked for his signet, cord, and staff as surety. When she was taken out to be burned at Judah's command, she said to him, *Examine these, please* (Gen 38:25), demanding that he recognize that he was the father of her child and remove the decree of death he placed on her when he learned of her pregnancy. In response, Judah said *she is more in the right than I* (Gen. 38:26).

Einat Ramon quotes Tamar's words to Judah, *Examine these, please*, but she expands their meaning. Ramon turns to the broader community and asks them to recognize the injustice, the tyranny, and the power dynamics that victimize the weaker members of society. Even if Tamar rebelled against authority and acted in ways that were not socially acceptable, her behavior was nonetheless appropriate and justified. According to Ramon, the freedom we aspire to on Passover involves a repair of social injustices.

The third daughter, the sincere one, is identified with Ruth, the Moabite daughter-in-law of Naomi in the book of Ruth. The term "sincere" does not imply ignorance but rather faithfulness and perfection. Ruth loves Naomi and treats her with loving-kindness. She says to her, *Where you will go, there I will go, and where you sleep, I will sleep, your people are my people, and your God is my God* (Ruth 1:16), insisting on accompanying her and sharing in her fate. Ramon quotes the words spoken by the elders who bless Boaz when he decides to marry Ruth: *May God render the woman entering your home as unto Rachel and Leah who together built the House of Israel* (Ruth 4:11). In so doing, she calls out to the community to appreciate Ruth's love and loyalty for Naomi and to accept her as part of the Jewish people and as part of the matriarchal line.

The last daughter, who cannot ask, is identified with the beautiful woman who is taken captive in war. According to biblical law, if a man sees a beautiful woman during wartime and desires her, he may marry her (Deut 21:10–14), which is preferable to raping and abandoning her. But even such marriage can be devastating to a woman who is taken against her will and forcibly removed from her familiar cultural surroundings in order to satisfy a man's sexual desires.

The beautiful captive woman is identified with the daughter who does not know how to ask on account of her inability to express herself and make her voice heard. Ramon explains how only her silent weeping can be heard, and she demands that the community become a mouthpiece for her and help her by returning her to her home.

Ramon's midrash fills a lacuna in the Haggadah by giving women a voice. In contrast to the midrash of the four sons, the attitude to each of the four daughters is accepting and inclusive. Ramon tries to understand each of the four daughters against the backdrop of the difficult situation in which each of them finds herself, even when they can't express themselves. These women represent the weakest members of society (those barred from marriage, converts, strangers, prostitutes), whose femininity only serves to weaken them further. Ramon insists that at a time when we celebrate our freedom and feast around the Seder table, we can experience true freedom only if we attune ourselves to all those who are oppressed and understand the needs of each of these groups of women to be liberated.

ZIVA OFEK AND YAEL ORYAN

Shavu'ot *The Love of Ruth and Naomi*

The book of Ruth depicts the special bond between Naomi and her daughter-in-law. The authors of this midrash suggest that the two women were in a lesbian relationship and focus on the unique emotional bond between them, their sense of mutual responsibility, and the nature of their relationship with Boaz. They discuss the status of the son born to Ruth and Boaz, who was raised as a child of both Ruth and Naomi. And they consider how Naomi and Ruth's relationship was regarded by the other women in their midst.

And Ruth clung to her (Ruth 1:14).

Ruth clung to Naomi to love her.

Boaz said to Ruth, *Haven't you heard, my daughter—don't go gleaning in another field, don't go from here, cling to my young women* (2:8). And didn't Ruth say to Naomi, *And he told me, cling to the young men of mine* (2:21).

And not only that, but when she was at Boaz's feet at the threshing floor, *And he said, Bring me the shawl you have on . . . and he measured out six shares of barley and laid them on it* (3:15)—Ruth said *he gave me these six shares of barley, because, he said, don't come empty-handed to your mother-in-law* (3:17). That Naomi not say in her heart that Ruth clung to Boaz's young women or she abandoned her and was repelled by her. And in the end, she became pregnant by Boaz. As is *written strong as death love is, fierce as Sheol* [the land of the dead] *is jealousy* (Song 8:6).

This is what the sages meant by "Great is peace, for even Scripture spoke falsehood to bestow peace."

And wherever you will find clinging, you will find life: *And he clung to his wife and they were one flesh* (Gen. 2:24); *and you who are clinging to God, you live, all of you, today* (Deut 4:4); and later on it says *and he will be for you one who restores life* (Ruth 4:15).

———

And the neighboring women named him, to say a son has been born to Naomi, and they named him Oved, he's the father of Jesse, who was the father of David (Ruth 4:17).

And from where did the neighbors get the idea to name him for Naomi and not for Machlon, after all, isn't it written *if brothers dwell together and one dies and has no son . . . and the firstborn male to be born will establish the name of his deceased brother* (Deut 25:6)? Rather, they saw the love of Ruth for Naomi like the love of Elkanah for Hannah and called out *for your daughter-in-law who loved you bore him, and she is better for you than seven sons* (Ruth 4:15).

And this is what the sages meant *they were the creators* (1 Chron 4:23) — this means Boaz and Ruth. Precisely, *the creators* and not the ones who gave birth, for on the night that he came to her, he died. And Scripture says *a son is born to Naomi*—the son is born to none other than the one for whose name he is called and who rears him and gives him life, and they reasoned from the sons of Aaron, who are called the posterity of Moses—*and these are the posterity of Moses and Aaron* (Num 3:1), and only Aaron's sons are mentioned, and they are called "Moses' posterity," because he taught them Torah.

And why does Scripture repeat: *And the neighboring women named him . . . and they named him Oved . . .* (Ruth 4:17)?

To teach you that it was not the elders of the town who gave him a name, but precisely, it was the neighboring women. For whenever the elders would be sitting at the gate and attuning their ears to what people were saying, the women would be walking about and paying attention to what they were doing. And when the elders testified that Boaz had acquired the legacy of Elimelekh from Naomi and acquired from her Ruth her daughter-in-law to be his wife, the neighboring women already knew that Ruth was coming and going from Naomi's house, and not empty-handed. And when the elders blessed Boaz that he should establish a house in Israel, and that his house shall be like the house of Peretz in its time, the neighboring women already knew the boy's name from the visage unique to him, and they knew from the ways of Ruth and Naomi that this boy would grow in Naomi's lap, and support her in her old age, and that is why *and the neighboring women named . . . and the neighboring women named him.*

Commentary

At various points in the book of Ruth, we are told of the exceptional bond between Ruth and Naomi. For instance, in describing Ruth's decision to leave her home in the fields of Moab and accompany Naomi to Bethlehem, the Bible relates that "Ruth clung to her" (Ruth 1:14). The verb "clung" appears in the Bible in the description of the bond between the first man and woman: *And he clung to his wife and they were one flesh* (Gen 2:24). The authors of this midrash deduce that Ruth's clinging to Naomi was also one of romantic partnership.

The verb "clung" appears in the book of Ruth in two additional contexts and is explained as having the same connotations. Boaz advises Ruth, *cling to my young women* (Ruth 2:8). But when she relays his words to Naomi, she instead says, *And he told me, cling to the young men of mine* (2:21). Ofek and Oryan propose that we regard this shift in language as a sign of Ruth's empathy and consideration for Naomi. Ruth did not want Naomi to grow jealous and to worry that when she went out to the fields to gather barley with the other women, she would be cultivating romantic relationships with them.

We witness a similar display of empathy when Ruth describes to Naomi the moment when Boaz gave her the barley at the end of the night that she spent with him on the threshing floor. According to the story, the barley was Boaz's gift to Ruth and an expression of his commitment to her. But Ruth reports to Naomi that Boaz said that the barley was his gift for Naomi.

These subtle but sensitive displays of empathy befit the complex connection between the members of a couple, whose love for one another is not without an element of jealousy. Ofek and Oryan quote the sages' claim that even the Torah changed Sarah's words so as not to hurt Abraham's feelings, and thus to ensure that there would be peace between husband and wife (as per Genesis Rabbah 48:18).

The first part of Ofek and Oryan's midrash concludes by noting the special qualities that characterized the relationship between Ruth and Naomi. The verb "cling" is used in the Bible to describe very strong bonds that lead to an affirmation of life and vitality. It appears in the description of the bond between Adam and Eve that led to the birth of the rest of humanity; and in the description of the connection between the people of Israel and their God; and in God's promise that the nation that clings to Him will merit life.

And so we can conclude that the clinging between Ruth and Naomi was also strengthening and affirming, and revived Naomi, as the book of Ruth states: *And he will be for you the one who restores life* (Ruth 4:15).

The second half of the midrash deals with the name the neighboring women give to the son born to Boaz and Ruth. In naming the child, the neighbors signify that Naomi is the child's mother. This is surprising, especially given the fact that the purpose of levirate marriage is to ensure that the name of the dead lives on; in this case, the dead man is Ruth's first husband Machlon, and yet his name is not given to the child. According to this midrash, the neighboring women are consciously trying to give Naomi the status of a parent because they are aware of the love between Ruth and Naomi.

The neighbors compare the relationship between Naomi and Ruth to that between Elkanah and Hannah in the book of Samuel. Like Elkanah, who comforted his wife with the words, *Am I not better for you than ten sons?* (1 Sam 1:8), the neighboring women attest to the love between Ruth and Naomi with the words, *for your daughter-in-law who loved you bore him, and she is better for you than seven sons* (Ruth 4:15).

To further demonstrate their claim that Ruth and Naomi have joint custody of the child, Ofek and Oryan provide several quotations from rabbinic literature about the possibility of attributing parental status to an individual who is not a biological parent.

In the midrashic collection Ruth Rabbah (2:2), the rabbinic sages use the term "creators" to refer to Boaz and Ruth. Ofek and Oryan describe Boaz as one who created his son, but was not alive to raise him. They base this claim on an aggadic tradition according to which Boaz died the night he impregnated Ruth (Ruth Zuta 4:13). If so, the relationship between Ruth and Naomi did not suffer from Ruth's brief marriage to Boaz; on the contrary, that marriage yielded a child whom the two women were able to raise together.

The tosefta stresses that a child is named for the person who raises him. The five children born to King Saul's daughter Merav were raised by Merav's sister Michal and were therefore referred to as her sons. Aaron's sons studied Torah with Moses and were therefore referred to as his progeny. And in the case of Ruth too, Ruth's son was raised by Naomi and was thus referred to as her son (Tosefta Sotah 11:20).

Ofek and Oryan note the repetition of the term "named him" in the biblical verse (Ruth 4:17). The first appearance of the term "named him" refers to the neighboring women's correct reading of the situation, and the second is a reference to their giving a name to the child. Ofek and Oryan show how the men's and women's circles exist entirely apart from another, as if they belong to different cultures. The male "elders," who are the authority figures, are busy with law and justice and specifically with Boaz's acquisition of Elimelech's legacy. At the same time, the women "neighbors" are focused on the actual shape of the family and its emotional dynamics. While the men are validating the legal act of acquisition and blessing Boaz that his patriarchal line should endure, the women are bestowing on the son his place in the matriarchal line and connecting him with his nonbiological mother. In so doing, they are validating and blessing the lesbian relationship between Naomi and Ruth.

This midrash legitimizes lesbian relationships based on a biblical story that could not be more foundational. The product of the relationship between Ruth and Naomi is the esteemed lineage that led to King David and will ultimately lead to the Messiah. Yet the midrash doesn't address the seeming element of incest in Ruth's relationship with Naomi. According to Biblical law, a man may not sleep with his daughter-in-law, but there is no corresponding prohibition on lesbian relationships of any kind. The midrash invites a question as to what extent the halakhic sexual codes that deal with heterosexual relations are relevant to nonheterosexual relationships. Today, as new forms of sexuality gain recognition and legitimacy, should the familiar codes simply be transferred to these new forms, or do these new forms demand new sexual codes?

YAEL UNTERMAN

Shavu'ot *Ruth, Who Interpreted*

Exegesis has the power to open up new existential and normative possibilities in the Jewish world. The midrash pits two women against one another: Ruth, who represents creative interpretation, and Orpah, her sister-in-law, who represents a more conservative fidelity to the text. Each of their fates is considered in light of their approaches to biblical exegesis.

And she left the place where she had been, and her two daughters-in-law were with her, and they went on the way to return to the land of Yehudah (Ruth 1:7).

They walked for three miles until they came to the border of Moab.

Naomi said, *Go, each of you return to your mother's house* (1:8).

Orpah said: O my mother-in-law, did not the Torah say "therefore a woman shall leave her father and mother and cling to her man and they will be one flesh?" My man is gone, and I have left—how should I return?

Naomi said: My daughter, not thus did I teach you! Rather it is written *therefore a **man** shall leave his father and mother and cling to his **wife** and they will be one flesh* (Gen 2:24). So the decision is in your hands!

Then Orpah kissed her mother-in-law (Ruth 1:14). She said, "That is the law (Halakhah) and I accept it" and returned to her mother's house.

Ruth, however, interpreted (*darsha*). She expounded: *A man* includes a woman too! Just as *a man* leaves his family and clings to his woman, so too a woman leaves her family and clings to her man. And when it says *to his woman*, this is intended to include his father-in-law and mother-in-law and all family members.

Hence, *Ruth clung to her* (Ruth 1:14).

Orpah, who did not know how to interpret, merited nothing.

Ruth, because she interpreted, merited the crown of Torah and the covenant of the forefathers, and became the mother of kings.

A different explanation: Ruth said to Naomi, I have no father, no mother, and no man, but only you, and from here on in, I am like a newborn babe.

She *clung to her* (Ruth 1:14).

The Rabbis ruled in accordance with her, that the convert is like a newborn babe.

Commentary

The book of Ruth, which is chanted on the holiday of Shavuot, tells the story of Elimelech's family, who emigrate to Moab on account of a famine. When the book begins, Elimelech's sons are married to two Moabite women, but Elimelech and his two sons soon die on foreign soil. Naomi, the wife of Elimelech, heads back to the land of Judea, accompanied by her two Moabite daughters-in-law, Orpah and Ruth, who wish to join her. Naomi urges her daughters-in-law to return to their mothers' homes, and Orpah complies. But Ruth insists on attaching herself to Naomi, and she returns with her to Bethlehem: *Then Orpah kissed her mother-in-law farewell, but Ruth clung to her* (Ruth 1:14).

Yael Unterman imagines the dialogues between Naomi and each of her daughters-in-law when they made their decisions. These conversations unfold as Torah study and halakhic exegesis.

The first dialogue takes place with Orpah, who does not have the same command of the biblical text and its exegesis. She repeats the words she thinks she has learned from Naomi: "Therefore a woman shall leave her father and mother and cling to her man and they will be one flesh." Orpah deduces from this text that she must accompany Naomi, because she left her own family when she married into Elimelech's family and she cannot return to them again. Naomi corrects her, quoting the verse from Genesis accurately: *Therefore a man shall leave his father and mother and cling to his woman and they will be one flesh* (2:24). Naomi explains to Orpah that the verse is in the masculine form and is directed at men alone. Women, in contrast, may and maybe even should return to their parents' homes. In the wake of this explanation, Orpah announces that she will return to her mother's home.

The second dialogue takes place between Naomi and Ruth. Ruth invokes the same verse from Genesis, and she offers an interpretation as well: "A man includes a woman too." This type of exegesis is common in traditional halakhic midrash composed by the tannaim, rabbis living in the Land of Israel during the first and second centuries. According to this midrashic technique, a verse includes more than it explicitly mentions. The verse mentions only "man," but the Torah intended to include others too, and thus the text must be understood as referring to both men and women alike. Just as a man leaves his parents' home when he gets married and clings to his wife, so too a woman leaves her parents' home when she gets married and clings to her husband, never to return home. Ruth, like Orpah, wishes to remain with Naomi, but she does so by means of creative biblical exegesis.

Ruth goes on to interpret the words *and cling to his woman* using the same midrashic technique: *His woman* comes to include his father-in-law, his mother-in-law, and his other family members. According to her halakhic midrash, the Torah commands married women to cling to their husband's family members as well, and not to return to their parents' homes, even after the husband's death. Thus Ruth deduces that she may refuse to obey Naomi's instructions to return to her parents' home, since she is obligated to cling to the family of her deceased husband. And thus *Ruth clung to her.* Unterman plays with the unusual expression that appears in both Genesis (where a man is instructed to cling to his woman) and Ruth (where Ruth clings to Naomi). When Ruth clings to her mother-in-law, she fulfills, as it were, the commandment of the verse in Genesis. Ruth is depicted in this midrash as a Torah scholar, who has full command over the biblical text and the creativity to use the techniques of rabbinic exegesis.

Orpah, who does not have the same command of the biblical text, headed back to Moab and did not merit clinging to Naomi. Her fate is unknown. Unterman explains that it was on account of Ruth's exegetical skill and the practical conclusions she drew from her exegesis that she merited the crown of Torah (the book of Ruth is named for her), the covenant of the forefathers (since she became part of the Jewish people), and the crown of kingship (since she married Boaz and became the ancestor of King David and, ultimately, of the Messiah).

This midrash imagines another dialogue that took place between Ruth and Naomi. Ruth refused to return home, insisting that her husband died, she has no parents, and Naomi is the only person in her life. She compares herself to a newborn baby who is completely dependent on her mother. The expression *clung to her* reflects her existential state, like a baby completely dependent on the mother to which it clings. Unterman goes on to explain that in light of Ruth's example, the rabbis ruled in the Talmud (b.Yevamot 97b) that the legal status of a convert who has just converted is like that of a child just born. According to Unterman, the rabbis recognized and appreciated Ruth's halakhic intuition and ruled in accordance with her.

ACKNOWLEDGMENTS

The word "dirshuni" in the verse *Thus said the LORD to the House of Israel: Seek Me (dirshuni), and you shall live* (Amos 5:4), is in the plural. God asks the entire community to seek Him out and understand Him. The enterprise of women writing and publishing midrash is the work of an entire community, and there are many to thank.

Thank you with all my heart to the women and men who supported this English edition of *Dirshuni*: philanthropists—friends, students—who were moved by the initiative and for whom completing it mattered. Sue Aeder Auerbach, Lizzie Leiman Kraiem, and another amazing, anonymous donor made it possible for me to work on this book for several years. And thank you to Rabbi Rolando Matalon for bringing me and the anonymous donor together.

A number of people provided much guidance and gave me the confidence to invest so much energy in shaping this English edition: Sylvia Fuks Fried, editorial director of Brandeis University Press and executive director of Brandeis University's Tauber Institute for the Study of European Jewry, with whom I had *havruta* over every midrash for many delightful hours; Lisa Fishbayn Joffe, director of the Hadassah-Brandeis Institute (HBI); Shulamit Reinharz, the institute's founder and former director; and Sylvia Barack Fishman, former co-director, who all grasped the project's meaning and significance and twice awarded me research fellowships. I also thank Debby Olins, Amy Powell, and Nancy Leonard of HBI and the other scholars who worked alongside me there. A very special thank you to Phyllis Hammer, former chair of the institute, who greatly supported me in her serious, quiet way.

I began the work of editing and publishing women's midrashim during the first years of the new millennium, with Nehama Weingarten-Mintz, my coeditor in the first Hebrew volume of *Dirshuni*. She was not able to work with me on this English edition, but her vision accompanied me all the way.

Thanks as always to the contributors to this volume who time and again responded to my varied and sometimes strange requests, sharing with us their Torah, quarried from the very roots of their souls.

Tamar Kadari devoted countless hours to this English volume as well as the Hebrew ones, offering careful scholarly consideration of the different sources and sharing her abundant knowledge. I accepted most of her comments, and every error to be found in this volume is mine.

Professor Moshe Sokolow painstakingly read and made corrections in the manuscript, for which I am most grateful.

Ilana Kurshan agreed to translate the commentaries to the midrashim, and our work quickly became a *havruta*, rich and meaningful for us both.

I thank the adult education groups to whom, in my years in Boston, I taught many of the midrashim in this volume. Their enthusiasm left me with no doubt of this project's significance. In particular, I thank Washington Square Minyan, Minyan Kol Rinah, and Congregation Kehillath Israel in Brookline; Kerem Shalom in Concord; the Beit Midrash of the Israeli American Council in Boston; Temple Reyim and Congregation Shaarei Tefillah in Newton; the rabbinical students of Hebrew College; Yeshivat Maharat; Mechon Hadar; Hartman North America; and the rabbinical students of the Wexner Summer Institute of 2019.

Special thanks to our neighbors on Washington Street in Brookline, my beloved brothers, Steve Goldstein and Steve Greenberg, with whom we talked for hundreds of hours about gender and Judaism over countless Shabbat meals; new ideas every time—unbelievable.

Thanks to Yehudah Mirsky, my beloved, who in all our years together has supported every initiative, idea, and lunacy of mine. Yehudah translated the midrashim in this volume (and others) for classes I taught over the years to English speakers, and gradually women's midrashim became an integral part of his world. Our daughters, Nehara Shulamit and Nofet Shira, were raised on these midrashim as sacred texts, and the naturalness with which they use them is the greatest gift I could ask for.

This book is dedicated to three remarkable women.

Rochelle Isserow, of blessed memory, who in 2005 put her own life in danger to help me when I was the victim of a terror attack on her street in Jerusalem. In the years afterwards, she continued to care for me and my family, and she and her beloved late husband Saul became grandparents to our daughters. She was a Jewish feminist before her time, paid prices for it, but paved the way for us. I will remember her forever.

The other two women are my friends-sisters Lori Kagan and Jody Sampson-Nair. Your devotion over so many years to the Jewish people, and especially to the vulnerable among us, and your faithfulness to the work of feminism, and Jewish feminism in particular, inspire me and give me hope. Your love and support for my family strengthened me greatly, especially in my Boston years, far from home. Thank God you are in my life.

TIRTZA BARMATZ STEIN is a member of Kibbutz Yavneh, and her family has lived in Jerusalem and Hebron for six generations. She studies Torah at the Yaacov Herzog Center. She loves to learn and to cook and is grandmother to thirteen boys and girls.

HAGIT BARTOV received her BA in Talmud and Jewish Thought and MA in Contemporary Jewry at the Hebrew University of Jerusalem. She has worked for many years in the field of Jewish-Israeli culture, running programs, developing materials, teaching, fostering collaborations, and more. She is one of the authors of the 929 Project, an international web project, providing a daily Bible chapter with contemporary commentary. A feminist and mother of Hallel, she lives in Jerusalem.

TAMAR BIALA earned her master's degree in Women's and Jewish studies from the Schechter Institute in Jerusalem. She taught at the Shalom Hartman Institute, trained teachers and Israel Defense Forces army officers. She coedited volume 1 of *Dirshuni* with Nehama Weingarten-Mintz, (2009) and was the sole editor of volume 2 (2018). She teaches in various batei midrash, rabbinical schools, and adult education programs in the United States and Israel. She lives in Jerusalem and is raising her two daughters, Nehara and Nofet, with her husband Yehudah Mirsky.

TAMAR BITTON is the head of Midreshet Be'er, a community-based study program for young women in Yeruham and Ashdod. She loves learning, teaching, writing, creating, and connecting different worlds. She is married to David and is the mother of four.

ADI BLUT heads a branch of the Zahali premilitary academies for religious women, She has an LLM, teaches at the Yaacov Herzog Center, and is an educational group facilitator. She is married to Avi and is the mother of six daughters.

DINI DEUTSCH FRANKEL grew up in Jerusalem and lives in Yeruham. She studies and teaches in the pluralistic batei midrash Atid ba-Midbar and Elul. She began her midrash writing in Elul's Writer's Beit Midrash. She teaches writing workshops in Midreshet Be'er in Yeruham. She teaches life sciences and education at Kaye Teachers College in Be'ersheva. She is married and is the mother of three.

NAAMA ELDAR lives in Hoshaya, teaches Torah, and is a group facilitator in the Galilee. She works in rabbinic literature, Hasidism, Hebrew literature, and the Yemima method.

RABBI RUTH GAN KAGAN is the founder and spiritual leader of Nava Tehila, a Jewish Renewal community in Jerusalem. She teaches Kabbalah and Hasidism in Israel and internationally. She coauthored, with Rabbi Zalman Shachter-Shalomi, *Jewish Renewal: Integrating Heart and World* (in Hebrew, 2006) and creates, together with her community, new music and innovative prayer modality for public prayers.

EFRAT GARBER-ARAN is a high-tech analyst. She earned an MA in Hebrew literature and wrote a thesis about midrashim written by religious women. She is an educational group facilitator, participates in the 929 Project, and is an alumna of the Migdal Oz Women's Beit Midrash.

AVITAL HOCHSTEIN, president of Hadar in Israel, holds a PhD in gender studies and Talmud from Bar-Ilan University and received ordination from Rabbi Daniel Landes. She is the coauthor with the late Chana Safrai of *Women Outside, Women Inside: Women's Place in Midrash* (in Hebrew, 2008).

TAMAR KADARI serves as dean of the Schechter Institute of Jewish Studies in Jerusalem, where she is senior lecturer in Midrash and Aggadah. Her synoptic edition of Midrash Song of Songs Rabbah, based on extensive manuscript research, was launched in 2014 on the Schechter website. She is the author of *Minkhah L'Yehudah: Julius Theodor and the Redaction of the Aggadic Midrashim of the Land of Israel* (2017), focusing on a major figure in the study of rabbinic literature and his influence on the modern study of midrash. Her articles have appeared in leading scholarly journals in Israel and abroad. She is also a sculptor whose work has been exhibited in galleries in Jerusalem and Tel Aviv.

BILHA KRITZER ARIHA holds an MA in arts and society/social change and group facilitation from the Academic College of Society and the Arts. She is a holistic therapist, studied at Beit Midrash Elul, and is a member of the Bavli-Yerushalmi group.

YAEL LEVINE holds a PhD in Talmud from Bar-Ilan University. She has published numerous studies focusing on issues related to women and Judaism. She has also composed many prayers and midrashim.

RIVKAH LUBITCH is a To'enet Rabbanit (advocate in rabbinic courts) and a leader of the struggle on behalf of *agunot* (grass widows), *mesuravot get* (women whose husbands deny them divorce), and *mamzerim* (bastard children). She works at the Center for Women's Justice, lecturing and writing on Judaism and women's issues, and writes midrashim. She is the author of the *Va-Telekh Lidrosh: Midrash Nashi Yotzer* (2003), the first-ever collection of women's midrashim in Hebrew, and more recently *From the End of the World and Beyond: The Long, Hard Road of Women's Suffering in Israeli Rabbinic Courts* (in Hebrew, 2017), and most recently *Laylah be-Veit Ha-Din* ("Night Falls in the Religious Court," 2021).

ZIVA OFEK is an attorney in solo practice and a doctoral candidate in Jewish Thought at Bar-Ilan University. She loves studying and teaching Torah, which is the voice of the heart. She lives with her partner and their two children in Jerusalem.

YAEL ORYAN is one of the founders of Bat Kol, an organization of religious lesbians. She holds an MA in film and television; was a Fellow at Alma, Home for Hebrew Culture in Tel Aviv; and is in the Tehudah Program in Social Leadership at Beit Midrash Kolot in Jerusalem. She works in the Ministry of Health, specializing in technological solutions for the health care system. She lives with her partner and is mother to three children.

ORNA PILZ is a bibliotherapist (MAAT), a writer, and a rabbi. She is a graduate of Hebrew Union College in Jerusalem and holds a master's degree in comparative literature from Tel Aviv University. She is the author of *You and I Together: Making Your Daughter's Bat Mitzvah Meaningful* (in Hebrew, 2013), *Miriam, Tell Me Your Story* (in Hebrew, 2016), and *In the Beginning, She Birthed: Reestablishing the Centrality of Birth* (in Hebrew, 2020).

DANA PULVER is a multidisciplinary creator who looks for new meanings in text, textile, and music. Inspired by a deep feeling that divergent things might share origins, she is passionate about cross-culture, cross-time combinations. Her musical Project of Talmudic ballads explores the encounter of Talmudic stories with European early folk music, and her "Dresstelling" project examines a combination of Jewish and global cultures of textile. Midrash too is an ancient vessel that can hold both tradition and novelty.

EINAT RAMON, born in Jerusalem, is a senior lecturer in Jewish Thought, Women's Studies, and pastoral care at the Schechter Institute for Jewish Studies. She is one of the founders of the field of pastoral care in Israel and the founder of Marpeh, Israel's only academic program for training in pastoral care. She is married and the mother of two.

HAGIT RAPPEL is a member of Kibbutz Sa'ad in the Negev and a lecturer in literature and cultural studies at Ben-Gurion University and Sapir Academic College. Her areas of expertise are literature and popular culture, Talmudic Aggadah, oral histories, and children's literature. Her doctoral thesis explored the oral histories of three generations of members of Kibbutz Yad Mordechai in light of the Holocaust and of the Israeli War of Independence, which exacted a heavy toll on the kibbutz.

ETTI ROM is an obstetrician-gynecologist and a long-time volunteer at a crisis center for victims of sexual assault. She has for many years been a practitioner and therapist in the spirit of Buddhism. She is the mother of four and grandmother of ten.

NAAMA SHAKED, who lives in Jerusalem, works in pottery and agriculture. She is among the founders of the pluralistic Beit Midrash Elul, where she helped establish the Writers' Beit Midrash, which produces creative writing based on Jewish text study and where she facilitates a study group on the thought of Aharon David Gordon. She is the author of the poetry collection *Copper and River* (in Hebrew, 2013). She is a mother and grandmother.

OSHRAT SHOHAM was born, raised, and lives in Jerusalem. Since completing her studies, she has worked in the state attorney's office in Jerusalem District, where she is in charge of investigating and prosecuting sex crimes and the abuse of minors. In 2006 she co-founded Hakhel, an egalitarian prayer community in the Baka neighborhood of Jerusalem, which she has led for over a decade. She is married to Ephraim and is a mother to five sons and a daughter-in-law.

RUTI TIMOR taught for thirty years in the public high school in Shafir in the northern Negev and later at the Yaacov Herzog Center in Kibbutz Ein Tzurim. A retiree, she spends her time reading and writing about her family and about the life of her cleaning person, who came to Israel from Nepal. She was born in Jerusalem eighty-four years ago. She is married to Professor Uri Timor and they have four children, seventeen grandchildren, and four great-grandchildren.

AYALA TZRUYAH (1964–2016) was a member of Kvutzat Yavne, where she was a prominent educator for many years. She held an MA in Talmud from Bar-Ilan University and edited the series Yahadut Kan ve-Akhshav (Judaism Here and Now) at Yediot Books. She coauthored *Ha-Psukim Ha-Yafim ba-Tanakh* ("The Beautiful Verses of the Bible"; in Hebrew, 2013), and wrote a novel, *Korim li Ayah* ("Call Me Ayah"; in Hebrew, 2016). She is survived by her husband and five children.

HILA (HALEVY) UNNA was born and raised on the religious Kibbutz Be'erot Yitzhak and is now a member of the religious Kibbutz Sde Eliyahu. She is a literary editor and deals with the physical and mental pain of a terror attack that she endured. She works for Tikkun Olam in the fields of feminism and peace. She is married to Ron and is a mother of four and grandmother of three.

YAEL UNTERMAN is an international lecturer, bibliodrama facilitator, and author. Her books *Nehama Leibowitz: Teacher and Bible Scholar* (2009) and *The Hidden of Things: Twelve Stories of Love and Longing* (in Hebrew, 2014) were finalists in national book competitions. She has published numerous essays, stories, and reviews; has created and performed a biblical solo show, "After Eden"; and runs bibliodrama workshops for people around the world.

NEHAMA WEINGARTEN-MINTZ is an educator, lecturer, and educational group facilitator on issues of gender, Judaism, and identity. She coedited volume 1 of *Dirshuni: Israeli Women Writing Midrash* (in Hebrew, 2009). She lives at Moshav Nehusha in the Elah Valley, is married to Avi, and is the mother of Naveh, Talia, and Ya'ara.

MIRI WESTREICH is an educator through literature in the AMIT Yeshiva High School of Kfar Ganim and teaches Bible and midrash in Midreshet Lindenbaum in Lod. She is married to Avishalom and is the mother of Tamar, Aryeh, Shmuel, and Ba-Kol.

GILI ZIVAN is a member of Kibbutz Sa'ad in the western Negev. She was director of the Yaacov Herzog Center in Kibbutz Ein Tzurim, where she was a cofounder of the Zahali premilitary program for religious young women and of the Ofek Jewish identity program for students from the former Soviet Union. Her book *Dat le-lo Ashlayah* ("Religion without Illusion"; in Hebrew, 2005) was based on her doctoral dissertation at Bar-Ilan University. She is active in efforts at Arab-Jewish coexistence and volunteers in the Rokmot Project for Ethiopian women in Sderot. She is a mother and grandmother.

INDEX

Aaron, 82, 228

Abigail, 160

Abraham: awakening of, 36–37; family of, 58–60; God and, 126; laughter of, 166; plea from, xvii; sacrifice of Isaac and, 32–34, 35–39, 40–43; story of, 29–31; testing of, 29; travels of, 125

Acatriel Yah Hashem Tzvaot, 135, 137. *See also* God

acquisition, within marriage, 115–22

Adam: creation of, 18; derashah example regarding, xvi; Eve and, 6–8, 229; marriage bond of, 119; punishment of, 7–8, 140; splitting of, 20

Ahasuerus, King, 153, 168, 171

Akhnai, 186

Akiva, Rabbi, 106–109, 110, 127, 166, 184

Amnon, 56, 159–61, 166, 167

Amoraim, xiv

Amram, 183, 184, 224

Apocrypha, xiii

Ariha, Bilha Kritzer, 35–39

Asher, 58

assembly of God, mamzerim within, 175–78

Avimelekh, 31, 40

Avshalom, 160, 161

Azariah, Rabbi, 82

Bakol, 166, 167

Bakshi-Doron, Rabbi Eliyahu, 100

Barmatz-Stein, Tirza, 159–61

barrenness: of Hannah, 108; of Isaac and Rebecca, 44–46; of Rabbi Akiva's wife, 106; of Rachel, 58–60; of Sarah (Abraham's wife), 30, 58–60; of Tanya, 135–38

Bartov, Hagit, 58–60

bastards, 175–78, 179–82, 183–85. *See also* mamzerim

Batsheva, 96–99, 146, 148, 168

Bava Batra, 178, 189

Bava Metzia, 186, 188, 219

Beit Midrashah shel Beruriah (Beruriah's House of Study), xxiii, 106–107, 151–55, 175–78, 183–85. *See also* Beruriah

Beit Midrash Elul, xxiv

Benjamin, 181

Ben Sira (Jeremiah's son), 179, 181

Berakhot, 13, 45, 95, 137, 143

Beruriah, 10, 49, 151–55, 176, 183–85. *See also Beit Midrashah shel Beruriah*

betrayal, 112

betrothal, 120. *See also* marriage

Biala, Tamar, 3–4, 18–21, 40–43, 71–74, 82–86, 110–14, 203–206

Bible/Scripture: female interpretation significance of, xx–xxii; sanctity of, xv; significance of, xiii–xiv. *See also specific books*

Bilhah, 59

Bitton, Tamar, 15–17

Bityah, 66–70

blessings, xxv, 143–45

HBI Series on Jewish Women

LISA FISHBAYN JOFFE, GENERAL EDITOR

RONIT IRSHAI, ASSOCIATE EDITOR

The HBI Series on Jewish Women, created by the Hadassah-Brandeis Institute, publishes a wide range of work at the intersection of Jewish Studies and Women's and Gender Studies by and about Jewish women in diverse contexts, disciplines and time periods.

The HBI Series on Jewish Women is supported by a generous gift from Dr. Laura S. Schor.

For the complete list of books that are available in this series, please see www.brandeisuniversitypress.com/series-list/.